POLITICAL SATIRE
IN THE BIBLE

THE SOCIETY OF BIBLICAL LITERATURE
SEMEIA STUDIES
Vincent L. Wimbush, Editor

Number 32
POLITICAL SATIRE IN THE BIBLE

by
Ze'ev Weisman

12/98

POLITICAL SATIRE
IN THE BIBLE

by
Ze'ev Weisman

Society of Biblical Literature
Semeia Studies

Scholars Press
Atlanta, Georgia

POLITICAL SATIRE
IN THE BIBLE

by
Ze'ev Weisman

Cover photograph:
Foto Marburg/Art Resource NY
1.   S0116304   180.218   B&W Print
Ships carrying tree trunks; various fish and marine animals.
Relief from Khorsabad, period of Sargon II (722–705 BC).
Louvre, Paris, France.

Library of Congress Cataloging in Publication Data

Weisman, Ze'ev.
    Political satire in the Bible / by Ze'ev Weisman
        p.   cm. — (Society of Biblical Literature Semeia studies)
    ISBN 0-7885-0380-4 (pbk. : alk. paper)
    1. Politics in the Bible—Humor. 2. Satire in the Bible.
I. Title. II. Series: Semeia studies.
  BS680.P45W45 1997 1998
  221.6'6—dc21   97-22399
                                                 CIP

Printed in the United States of America
on acid-free paper

TABLE OF CONTENTS

ACKNOWLEDGMENTS

It is a great privilege to have the present work published by the Society of Biblical Literature. I owe a special debt of gratitude to Professor Vincent L. Wimbush, the editor of Semeia Studies, who encouraged me to make my study accessible to the English-reading Bible students. His persistent efforts and important contribution to the editing of the book are gratefully acknowledged.

My work on political satire in the Bible appeared in Hebrew in 1996. The present volume is a revised, concise version of the Hebrew original. Mr. M. Rosovsky has translated the Hebrew monograph into English. His able and studious assistance is much appreciated.

Many thanks are due to Scholars Press, Atlanta, and to its Publications Manager, Mr. Brelsford, for their great care and efficiency in publishing this book.

Finally, I wish to express my gratitude to the personnel of the Research Authority of Haifa University for their part in facilitating the production of the monograph.

Heftzi-bah, 1997   Z. Weisman

INTRODUCTION

The Bible has served as a source for literary works of a satirical nature
that have left their mark on world literature, including Jewish literature.
Poets, storytellers and playwrights have drawn inspiration from it for sharp
social and political criticism of their surroundings; from it they have borrowed motifs and figures for parodies and satirical allegories directed at
personages and regimes in later historical periods and in various cultures.
Some of the finest writers of political satire actually regarded themselves as
the heirs and successors of the biblical prophets of rebuke and of doom.[1]
Biblical influence is especially marked in the political satirical writing that
flourished in England in the 17th and 18th centuries (Marvell, Dryden,
Swift and Pope).[2] Yet this had in fact been preceded by critical satirical writing of a social and even political nature in medieval Europe. In Jewish
literature of the Middle Ages and the "Golden Age," works of a clearly satirical tendency, such as the poetry of Abraham Ibn Ezra and the maqams of
Al-Harisi, took their inspiration directly or indirectly from the Bible. This
tendency grew stronger and more aggressive and politically inclined in the
modern Hebrew literature of the 19th century.[3] More recently we have observed the appearance of political satire written about the Bible, with biblical figures and stories being subjected to satirical interpretation in modern
literary works. This writing takes up certain "delicate episodes" in the Bible,

1 A. Pope, *The Epilogue to the Satires* (1738) Dialogue I, 141–70.

2 V. Carretta, *The Snarling Muse, Verbal and Visual Political Satire from Pope to
Churchill* (Philadelphia, 1983).

3 J. Friedlander, *In the Mystery of Satire* (Bar-Ilan University, 1984), (Hebrew).

not only to explain and illumine the Bible in a secular permissive light, as in Meir Shalev's book *Bible Now*,[4] but also to shoot its arrows at the socio-political manifestation of modern society, as in the "historical" satirical novels of Heller[5] and Heim.[6] The Bible serves their purpose not only as a source and repository but also as an example and model.

The question arises as to whether the Bible may serve as a source of inspiration and a storehouse for political satire in world and Jewish literature without itself including elements and features of this genre. Indeed, some scholars have discerned a satirical note in various places in the Bible. In their different commentaries on particular subjects one may even occasionally find the term "satirical" used to define the quality of certain units. But as a definer and denominator of a specific literary genre the term itself is not in the list of these genres enumerated in the various introductions to the Bible, nor even in the lexica of the series of interpretations of the Bible. True, the term "satire" recently appeared as a title of compositions on biblical subjects,[7] but it has not yet won recognition in literary criticism of the Bible. The few studies thus entitled focus on isolated and sometimes even marginal instances of satire without constructing on this foundation a broader synthesis and without setting it against its political background. The combined term "political satire " has so far not benefited from scrutiny in a biblical studies monograph, although related subjects have been treated in biblical scholarship, for example, "Irony in the Old Testament"[8] and a collection of articles "On Humour and the Comic in the Hebrew Bible."[9] This fact in itself requires explanation. Either political satire does not exist at all in the Bible or this term is not adequate for defining the literary feature in question, and for proving its existence in the Bible.

In the first place, then, the research effort was directed at locating those texts on which the satirical tone is stamped, accompanied by study of the interpretations written about them to ascertain if, accidentally or not, the attribute "satirical" was applied to them there; and if they may be relied on

[4] M. Shalev, *Bible Now* (Jerusalem, 1985), (Hebrew).

[5] J. Heller, *God Knows* (New York, 1984).

[6] S. Heim, *King David's Report* (Jerusalem, 1987), (Hebrew).

[7] C.C. Rondall, "Satire in the Old Testament" (Dissertation, Hebrew Union, Cincinati, 1966); K. Seybold, *Satirische Prophetie,* Studien zum Buch Zefanja (Stuttgart, 1985); T. Jemielity, *Satire and the Hebrew Prophets* (Louisville, 1992).

[8] E.M. Good, *Irony in the Old Testament* (London, 1965).

[9] Y. Radday and A. Brenner (eds.). *On Humour and the Comic in the Hebrew Bible* (Sheffield, 1990).

as proof of the existence of satirical writing in the Bible. At the same time, attention was paid to the study of satire as a literary genre in classical and modern literary history in order to redefine its characteristics and the areas of its use in literary criticism; and hence the reservations resulting from this definition with regard to its applicability in biblical interpretation. Only upon completion of this "cross-examination" did the recognition ripen that there were grounds for a monographic study on political satire in the Bible.

Undoubtedly, the problem of the relevance of the term "political satire" will accompany the reader throughout the book, just as it accompanied the writer. Therefore, an effort has been made to make the detailed and reasoned discussion of each unit containing "satirical elements" or "satirical signs" open and revealing, so that benefit may be derived from it even if the conclusion is that this is not actually "satire," but rather irony or the grotesque; an unequivocal definition of "political satire " is of course in the realm of literary utopia.

Precisely because we are concerned with the "Holy Scriptures," with all that this rubric suggests, it is important to illuminate those issues in the Bible in which political and social criticism find acerbic and sarcastic expression in the mouths of mortal beings.

In the essays that follow a systematic attempt has been made to examine the characteristic elements of political satire as a literary device in the Bible and to ascertain the possibility of drawing the main lines of its development; this has been done by:

a. locating and exposing those core and complex literary units that may be defined as political satire, or at least in which the satirical tone that characterizes them may be pointed out (on the basis of use of the term "satirical" as their literary attribute by ancient and modern biblical exegetes who have dealt with them);

b. interpreting these units by criteria usually applied in literary and historical-philological criticism of the Bible and illustrating them in light of the characteristic principles of satire (especially political), defined in literary theory across its wide and innovative range; and

c. drawing a typological sketch of satire in the Bible, in association with the main types of biblical writings and their milieux.

Exposure of the characteristics of "political satire" in each of the Bible's main divisions (narrative, historiography, prophecy and wisdom literature), and in most of its literary types (epigram, fable, anecdote, elegy and rhetoric) leads to the conclusion that it should be recognized as a widespread literary phenomenon in the Bible. Its special reflection in certain genres, such as "fable," "prophecies of elegy and taunt," and the polemical orations in the historiography, attests to its socio-cultural attachments and its milieux (known in biblical genre research as *Sitz im Leben*). It is therefore reasonable to assume that the roots of satire in the Bible lie in oral utterances whose essence is an immediate encounter between the orator and his or her environment, in which the social, especially political message is voiced in direct speech to the public or to the addressee.

In tracing satirical elements in biblical literature we gradually proceed from the basic components of the biblical composition—appellations, midrashic name derivations, epigrams, proverbs and fables—to the more integrated and amalgamated literary units with respect to structure and form such as etiological stories. Thence to the comprehensive compositions or corpora—prophecy, historiography and wisdom. Thus, the first part of the study consists of three chapters (2, 3, 4) which are entitled according to the generic nomenclature used in form-criticism of the Bible.

The second part focuses on the use of satirical devices in prophetic rhetoric and also consists of three chapters (5, 6, 7) which are named according to their sub-generic forms—oracles against nations, taunt elegies, and "woe" oracles.

The third part of the study deals with the application of satirical polemics in political confrontations, as recorded in biblical historiography. It consists of two chapters (8, 9): one analyzes the witty and tendentious account of the division of Davidic Kingdom; and the other analyzes the political speech of Rabshakeh at the gates of Jerusalem, as well as Isaiah's contrary messages. The last chapter (10) concerns the sophisticated political satire of the Book of Esther which in its nature and tendency is exceptional among the Holy Scriptures.

Although this study makes no claim to be historic and diachronic *per se,* its structure is intended to cast some light on the evolution undergone by the use of political satire in the Bible, and its affinity to the major literary trends that signify the growth of biblical literature.

❧ 1 ☙

METHODOLOGICAL CONSIDERATIONS

At first sight the course of this study seems to have been conceptualized to select from the Bible those compositions, or basic literary units, which seem to be "satirical" and which are applied to political situations, and to analyze them in light of some fairly standard questions: At whom is the satire aimed? What are its literary devices? What characterizes its political and cultural milieu? When and where was it composed? But the work proved far more complicated. To discern the literary units which might be designated as political "satire" one must have a clear definition of the term "satire" and the features that single it out as a genre in literary criticism. However, this in itself is rather ambiguous. There are various definitions of the term that sometimes even contradict each other. For example, some literary critics are doubtful whether or not a generic definition of "satire" can be achieved.[1] Hence, the primary methodological issue arising is the question regarding the relevance of applying to it a literary-generic term whose origin lies in classical Roman literature.

The use of later and even modern terms for the study of ancient literature, and of the Hebrew Bible in particular, is permissible as long as the scholar is aware of the risk involved. These arise from the fact that the borrowed term was initiated and coined in an alien cultural milieu, remote in time and place.

---

[1] H.J. Jensen, *The Satirist's Art* (Bloomington, Indiana, 1972), IX: "Satire's essence is as illusive as the center of Peer Gynt's onion. It is unlike other important kinds of literature because it lacks a definable cathartic effect or at least so far no one has isolated a general effect closely enough for generic definition."

The term "satire" was uprooted from its "cultural homeland" and transferred to different social and cultural environments, where it was transformed and adapted to serve the cultural needs of the adapters. The term
derives from the Latin *satura,* literally "medley," being elliptical for *lanx
satura* "a full dish, a hotch-potch." Later it was modified to denote poetic
or prose compositions (performed in popular festivals in ancient Rome) in
which the prevailing vices or follies are held up to ridicule.[2] Thus, it became a literary term to depict the mode initiated by Lucilius in the second
century BCE. He designed it as a new genre, different from the others that
prevailed in classical literature, such as the elegy, tragedy and comedy.
What particularly distinguished this genre from the others was the sharp
criticism of corruption and ridicule in public life. Many scholars who deal
with the genesis of satire tend to see in Lucilius and his followers Horace
(63–8 BCE) and Juvenal (60–130 CE) the forerunners of satire,[3] which developed later, mainly in the Renaissance, as an influential literary genre.[4]

In modern literary criticism the term "satire" is used to denote both a
specific and particular genre and a mobile generic definer of certain characteristic features shared by different genres, such as poetry and novel, play
and parable, essay and epigram whose common denominator is witty criticism and derision cast at deformities of institutions and wicked individuals. Beyond this common denominator, many attempts have been made to
establish a clear-cut and unequivocal definition of "satire" vis-a-vis other
related generic terms, such as parody, grotesque, humor and irony.

In his book *The Anatomy of Satire*[5] Gilbert Highet proposed eight rules
according to which a satirical composition should be singled out from other
literary compositions. It is not clear whether .all eight are necessary conditions for this identification. Only few of them relate to the substance, and not
enough emphasis is placed on the mood or tone, which several critics con-

---

[2] M. Steiner, "Satire" *Encyclopaedia Hebraica* vol. 25 (Jerusalem, 1974), 702–704
(Hebrew). Cassell's *Encyclopaedia of Literature* (London, 1953), 494–496, D. Alexander, *Political Satire Creation in the Israeli Theater* (diss. Tel Aviv, 1982), 57–62 (Hebrew).

[3] On the beginnings of satire in Rome, see R.C. Elliot, *The Power of Satire: Magic,
Ritual, Art* (Princeton, 1966), 100–129.

[4] Literary compositions in Latin of distinctive satirical character prevailed in Europe
prior to the Renaissance. See: P. Lehmann, *Die Parodie in Mittelalter* (München, 1922); *Paro-
dische Texte* (1923). I am very grateful to Dr. Peter Cramer of Wolfson College, Oxford, for
referring me to these texts. F. Kiley, J.M. Shuttleworth (eds.), *Satire from Aesop to Buchwald*
(New York, 1971). G. Grigson (ed.), *The Oxford Book of Satirical Verse* (Oxford, 1980).

[5] G. Highet, *The Anatomy of Satire* (Princeton, 1962); and see the criticism on his approach in Y. Friedlander, *be-Mistarei ha-Satira* (Ramat-Gan, 1984), 146–147.

sider the most essential feature of satire.[6] In satire tone and mood are no less important than formal means, because on the basis of these alone it is almost impossible to distinguish between satire and other humorous writing.[7] The satirist sharpens and distorts these means in order to convey his message. In this respect Koestler's insights on satire seem to me most commendable:

> The 'satire' is a verbal caricature which distorts characteristic' features of an individual or society by exaggeration and simplification . . . It focuses attention on abuses and deformities in society of which, blunted by habit, we were no longer aware; it makes us suddenly discover the absurdity of the familiar and the familiarity of the absurd.[8]

Hence the principal means of the satirist is wit. Many others in addition to Koestler who have inquired into the unique character of satire regard "wit" as instrumental in molding the mood which is typical of satire and which conveys its special message. Tone is what differentiates satire and tragedy on the one hand, and satire and comedy on the other. By using wit, which is the most sophisticated linguistic device for imparting double entendre and even paradoxical meaning to ordinary words,[9] the satirist stimulates his audience to share his sharp criticism against individuals and social institutions. Wit as a verbal and literary means (with a variety of artistic devices, such as puns, wordplays, etc.) is also employed in other genres, especially comedy. But whereas in comedy it arouses laughter and fun, in satire it evokes disdain and contempt.[10] Indeed, in biblical semantics, wit (שנינה)[11] is coupled with taunt (משל) (cf. Deut 28:37; 1Kgs 9:7 [Jer 24:9]), and both are used as a weapon against the opponents (cf. Ps 64: 4: "They sharpen their tongues like swords and aim venomous words like arrows . . .").

In his stimulating essay on "Wit and its Relation to the Unconscious", Freud alluded to the role that wit plays in what we refer to as political satire:

---

6 E.A. Bloom, Lilian D. Bloom, *Satire's Persuasive Voice* (Cornell University Press, 1979), 110–169.

7 On the differences between them, see M.D. Fletcher, *Contemporary Political Satire* (London, 1987), 1–7. On the relationship between humor and satire, see in R. Paulson (ed.), *Satire: Modern Essays in Criticism* (Englewood Cliffs, 1971), 52–65.

8 A. Koestler, *The Art of Creation* (New York, 1964), 72–73, 92.

9 Fletcher (n. 7), 2–7.

10 See: Alexander (n. 6), 58.

11 שנינה is derived from the term שנן which means to sharpen, like its cognates in Arabic and Syriac; and see *BDB*, 1041.

Society as the third and dispassionate party in the combat, to whose interest
it is to safeguard personal safety, prevents us from expressing our hostile
feeling in action; and hence, as in sexual aggression, there has developed a
new technique of invectives, the aim of which is to enlist this third person
against our enemy. By belittling and humbling our enemy, by scorning and
ridiculing him, we directly obtain the pleasure of his defeat by the laughter
of the third person, the inactive spectator.[12]

Because of the expansion of the usage of "satire" beyond its original
context, and its application to certain elements within literary compositions
which are not *ex generis* pure satire,[13] the way is open to use it in the study
of biblical texts. This is possible provided that equivalent terms to those
which define satire in literary nomenclature are detected in the Bible itself.
My supposition is that the features which characterize satire as a literary
phenomenon did exist in the Bible, hundreds of years before satire was
fashioned as "genre" in the classical world.[14] The tracing of the pre-literary
and pre-generic layers of satire by means of a philological and literary
study may shed some light on the psycho-social origin of satire as a social
and cultural phenomenon.

The semantic field of "satire" in the Hebrew Bible

(Terms and notions equivalent to satire in biblical literature)

The nomenclature related to the characterization of the term "satire" in
encyclopedias and lexicons of literature consists of the terms ridicule,
mockery, taunt, and laughter, which correspond to the semantic Hebrew
equivalents in the Bible—לעג, שנינה, היתול and שחוק.[15] The primary (*lexem*)
term לעג (*l'g*) is used in the Bible not only to depict a kind of attitude to-

12 S. Freud, "Wit and its Relation to the Unconscious" in *Basic Writings* (translated and
edited by A.A. Brill) (New York, 1938), 698.

13 M. Hodgart, *Satire* (London, 1962), 8: "Satire, in my view, is not a well-defined category, but a convenient expression to cover a variety of literary works that have many characteristics in common."

14 Satirical elements in ancient Egyptian Fables are found in Emma Brunner Traut's book
Altägyptische Tiergeschichte und Fabel (Darmstadt, 1984). A satirical note can be discerned in
a letter from Tell el-Rimah, translated into Hebrew by M. Anbar in: *Shnaton, an Annual for Biblical and Ancient Near Eastern Studies V–VI* (ed. M. Weinfeld) (Jerusalem, 1978–9), 221–222.

15 A. Brenner, "On the Semantic Field of Humour, Laughter and the Comic in the Old
Testament," in Y.T. Radday & A. Brenner (eds.), *On Humour and the Comic in the Hebrew
Bible* (Sheffield, 1990), 39–58.

wards individuals or people, but also to reflect the way that this attitude is expressed. The latter matches satire, which in its very nature is a verbal expression of taunt and mockery. This semantic function of לעג is attested in some lyrical verses in which synonyms of לעג appear in the same context.

In a lyrical confession (lament), Jeremiah complains of his being a victim of mockery and reproach:

> I have become a laughingstock all day long;
> everyone mocks me.
> For whenever I speak, I must cry out,
> I must shout, "Violence and destruction!"
> For the word of the Lord has become for me
> a reproach and derision all day long. (Jer 20: 7–8).

In the first bi-colon Jeremiah describes his personal situation by using a pair of synonyms: שחוק (*shoq,* laughter) and לעג (*l'g,* mock). This pair appears in Ezekiel as hendiadys: תהיה לצחק וללעג which literally means: "You shall be to laughter and mockery." The roots *shq* and *l'g* together with their verb and noun derivatives reflect the personal experience of one who was put to shame and feels that the public are laughing at his suffering.[16]

In the second bi-colon Jeremiah discloses the reason for his being scorned and mocked by his audience. It is because whenever he speaks he shouts out "Violence and destruction." From what follows (v 10), it seems that he was disparaged by the audience, who mocked his threat: מגור מסביב ("Terror is all around"), and nicknamed him by this epithet (cf. v 3 and also: 6:25; 46:5; 49:29)[17]

In the third bi-colon Jeremiah complains about the reason for the contempt he suffers, which is his prophetic mission: "the word of the Lord" becomes for him reproach and derision—לחרפה ולקלס. This Hebrew pair of synonyms has a close affinity to the previous pair and belongs to the same semantic field: it expresses the suffering and distress of an individual or a nation (cf. Ps 44:14 79:4) experiencing ridicule.[18]

The affinity between taunt (ridicule) as an attitude and its verbal expression is evident in Isaiah's reaction to the cynical behavior of the leader-

16 *shq* and *shq* are usually regarded as etymological and semantic variants. A. Brenner traced their usage in the Bible and found out that "most of the actual occurrences belong to the contempt ridicule pole." *Ibid.,* 46–52.

17 J. Bright, *Jeremiah* (AB, New York, 1965), 132–133. A.B. Ehrlich, *Mikra ki-Pheshuto* III (New York, 1969), 221–222.

18 On the close affinity of קלס (*qls*) to mockery and derision, see A. Brenner (n. 15), 53.

ship, (אנשי לצון "scoffers," "arrogant rulers" [NRSV] cf. Isa 28:14), who ridicule him and mimic his preaching when he cites their words of mockery:

> Whom will he teach knowledge
> and to whom will he explain
> the message?
> Those who are weaned from milk?
> those taken from the breast?
> For it is precept upon precept,
> precept upon precept (צו לצו)
> line upon line, line upon line (קו לקו)
> here a little, there a little (Isa 28:9–10)[19]

Then he rebukes them using the same unintelligible language and way of speech: "So through barbarous speech—בלעגי שפה—and a strange tongue—ובלשון אחרת—the Lord will address this people." (cf. NRSV) "With stammering lip and with alien tongue He will speak to this people" (v 11).[20]

The reproach by means of discourse, the mockery through the repetition of key words and doubling of phrases used by the object of the mockery, are basic devices of satire. The double repetition of the phrase עלה קרח ("Get along with you, bald" [NRSV]; "Go away, baldhead! Go away, baldhead!") used by the small boys who jeered at Elisha (2Kgs 2:23) testifies to this satirical device.[21]

To the semantic circle of לעג belongs the pair of terms משל ושנינה (NRSV: "a proverb and a taunt"), which appears as a hendiadys in the Deuteronomistic layer of the Bible (Deut 28:37; 1Kgs 9:7; cf. 2 Chr 7:20). It has been pointed out that a note of disdain and irony is reflected in this hendiadys. No wonder that in the course of our study it will become evident that the generic term 'משל' with its variation of meanings and usages in biblical literature depicts the characteristic elements of satire more than any other "genre" in the Bible.[22] The semantic field of לעג with all its variants testifies to the relevance of borrowing the term "satire" for our study. By

---

19 Tur-Sinai rightly pointed to the alliterative connection between the phrases קו וצו and קיא צואה in v 8. See his book *Peshuto shel Mikra* III (Jerusalem, 1967), 79.

20 D. Yellin, *Ḥiqrey Mikra*, VI (Jerusalem, 1939), 20, comments that the prophet used בלעגי deliberately for two reasons: (a) to mock the way they speak in which they distort letters of the words; (b) to introduce the meaning of ridiculous: ridiculous language

21 Elliot (n. 3), 284, quotes this legend as a paradigm for the power of the curse and points to the interrelationship between curse and satire.

22 O. Eissfeldt, *Der Maschal in Alten Testament*, BZAW 24 (1913), 9ff.

using "satire" as the title of our monograph, and "satirical elements" more cautiously throughout the study, we do not impose an alien concept on the literary interpretation of the Bible; we merely explore literary and artistic elements inherent in it while using our modern terminology.

The use of the epithet "political satire" in this study

The apposition of "political" and "satire" is meant to limit the scope of our study to the analysis of biblical texts that relate to political issues. The word "political" is a derivative of the Greek polis and related to the activities of its citizens, referring to their rights and duties in managing their self-rule organizations. Later it was extended to other systems of government and included both internal and external affairs of state.[23] I have purposely refrained as much as possible from dealing with satirical aspects of the relationship between people and God ("religious satire"), and with satirical aspects of the relationship among individuals ("moral satire"). With the appellation "political satire" emphasis is on the use of satire for political purposes in international confrontations or internal affairs. Within this range are also included satirical epigrams and taunts related to the tribal society of Israel prior to the formation of the state. Rivalry, tensions and confrontations among kindred tribes followed by power struggles left their impression in the ironic and satirical note of tribal epigrammatic songs (Gen 49; Deut 33; Jud 5). This ironic note heralds the more sophisticated satire that developed later in the monarchical Israel.

This is the place to define and summarize the elements of political satire which will serve as a working hypothesis for the analysis of the literary units in our study. Not all these elements need to be in evidence in order for a certain unit to be considered a conveyor of political satire.

1. Sordid criticism: this generally reveals a negative and hostile attitude, yet on some occasions reflects a close attachment to the object criticized, as in prophecies of reproach against Israel itself (cf. Isa chaps. 30–31).
2. The criticism is aimed at historical and concrete personalities, institutions, political systems, and mainly tyrants and arrogant, villainous adversaries.
3. The animosity is exposed in some instances by a curse against the tyrant and quite often by the merriment and joy at the sudden downfall of the

---

23 C.E. Schutz, *Political Humor* (London, 1977), 12.

arrogant person. This specifically typifies the prophetic taunt-elegies. Joy
at the sudden destruction of the adversary is the tiny distinction between
satire and irony, and differs substantially from the merriment and laughter that typify comedy.

4. There is no clear-cut division between satire and irony, not even between
   satire and humor. The difference between them is in mood and tone, and
   these are mainly subjective. In humor and irony there is more a mood of
   forgiveness, whereas in satire the dominant tone is that of animosity and
   the insult.

5. Satire exploits rhetoric for its political purpose. It is polemical in its very
   nature, whether conveyed in a historiographical speech, or in parables
   and fables.

6. In many cases the satirist does not reveal the name or the identity of the
   object of the criticism, but he makes use of nicknames, metaphors, allegory and even parody that allude to that object. The use of camouflage is
   applied either out of personal precaution or as an artistic technique.

7. The satirist utilizes the grotesque, the paradoxical, and the absurd to
   sharpen the criticism and taunt. He exploits stylistic and phonetic devices
   such as puns, double entendres, play of sounds (paranomasia, alliteration
   and assonance) for his witty criticism.[24]

In tracing satirical elements in biblical literature we shall gradually proceed from the basic components of the biblical composition—appellations,
midrashic name derivations, epigrams, proverbs, etc., to the more integrated
amalgamated literary units with respect to their structure and form; and from
there to the comprehensive compositions, or corpora.

So the first three chapters of the study are titled according to the generic nomenclature used in the form-criticism of the Bible; the other three
chapters are titled according to the literary-corpus classification used in
the literary and historical criticism of the Bible. As stated above, although
this study has no pretension to being historic and diachronic *per se,* it casts
some light on the evolution that the Bible underwent in terms of usage of
political satire, and its affinity to the major literary trends that signify the
growth of biblical literature.

---

[24] I.M. Casanowicz, *Paranomasia in the Old Testament* (1892, reprinted by "Makor",
Jerusalem, 1971).

2

IRONIC AND SATIRICAL ELEMENTS IN APPELLATIONS AND IN THE LEGENDARY DERIVATION OF NAMES

The linguistic and stylistic components that serve as devices and elements in the Bible for satire, such as nicknames, symbols, allusions, and various forms of paronomasia, antithesis, ambiguity and puns, are not typical of satire alone. They are used in the various genres of biblical poetry. But if they are used to express an attitude of contempt or ridicule aimed at certain people or a certain community, they may be defined as satirical means—the "scourge of slander."[1] However, some of them might at first have been a sort of "genes" from which satire emerged and developed, especially appellations, symbols, antithesis, and puns.

The use of a nickname as a substitute for a name, or at times as an appellative, is known to us all. We are all surrounded by friends who sometimes are called by a pet name, sometimes by a name of opprobrium. In one form or another nicknames are symbols, a sort of code in social communication for expressing the intimate attitude of the close environment (chiefly homogeneous) towards the individual.[2] But only when the nicknames are intermixed with a note of ridicule and scorn towards a certain individual, or point up his or her flaw, may they be defined as satirical.

---

1 The epithet "scourge of slander" is borrowed from Job 5: 21.

2 According to Auden, satire evolves in a homogeneous society, in which common social and ethical values are shared. See W.H. Auden, "Satire," in R. Paulson (ed.), *Satire: Modern Essays in Criticism* (Englewood Cliffs, 1971), 202 ff.

In the following, various forms of scurrilous uses of appellations in the Bible are presented.

1. Appellations from the animal world

It is quite usual—and we find instances in the Bible—for infants to be given names of animals. This kind of naming for human beings is in no way intended to highlight any defect; however, a distinction should be made between names from the animal world given to newborn children because of their magical, symbolic, or totemic[3] significance, and nicknames that become attached to a person at a later stage of his or her life, when their main purpose is to ridicule him or her because of a discernible trait, behavior or physical defect. In such cases, the animal image is usually a term of opprobrium. An example is the metaphor "dog," which is abusive with a political slant. There are instances in early biblical historiography in which the nickname "dog" is explained in a negative sense and its purpose is to characterize the adversary.

a. The metaphorical use of the term "dog," always in the form of a rhetorical question, appears three times in connection with David. This apparently is not by chance, considering that we have here a single style, particularly as regards the political rhetoric that occupies a central place in the historirgraphy of David. In his approach to Saul, David abases his self-esteem, and calls out, "After whom has the king of Israel come out? After whom do you pursue? After a dead dog? After a flea?"[4] (1 Sam 24: 15).

b. Abishai the son of Zeruiah uses exactly the same phrase when he is bent on killing Shimei the son of Gera, who set out to curse David: "Then Abishai the son of Zeruiah said to the king, Why should this dead dog curse my lord the king? Let me go over and take off his head" (2 Sam 16: 9).

c. From the fierce reaction of Abner son of Ner, the strong man in the House of Saul, to the complaint of Ish-boshet, "Am I a dog's head of Judah?" (2 Sam 3: 8), one may perhaps gain an insight into the political signifi-

---

3 B. Porten, "Name, personal names in Israel", *EB* vol. 8, 42, considers the employment of animal names as the most common genus of secular names that was used among the Israelites and the aliens. Most of them belonging to the pre-monarchial era; only one is post-exilic. M. Sister even conjectured that this attests to the "totemic" origin of the names. See his book: *A Study in the Development of Society and Literature in Biblical Times* (Tel Aviv, 1962), 33–37 (Hebrew).

4 M.H. Segal, *The Books of Samuel* (Jerusalem, 1955), 191 (Hebrew); J.A. Montgomery, *The Books of Kings* (ICC; (Edinburgh, 1951), 394.

cance of this "bestial" sobriquet, which indicates a bold attitude and derisive behavior on the part of the holder of high office towards the master.[5]

d. This critical and stinging metaphor-epithet in connection with the behavior of a high political office-holder is also present in the words of
Hazael to Elisha: "What is your servant, who is but a dog, that he should
do this great thing?" (2 Kgs 8: 13). Whether these are the words of Hazael
himself or whether the author—knowing of Hazael's "dog-like" behavior
in causing Israel such great suffering after his ascension—put them in his
mouth to underline the baseness of him who was anointed king by an Israelite prophet, the use of the name "dog" here reflects a critical and
hostile attitude towards Hazael, king of Syria. It is worth adding that the
same expression, "Who is your servant, (the) dog," is known much earlier. It appears as an expression of submission and self-abnegation by the
kings of Canaan in the El-Amarna letters and in Hebrew in the Lachish
letters.[6] It may therefore be defined as a "satirical" term in the political
lexicon of the Ancient Near East.

2. Epithets from the living world in the epigrams on the tribes

In the odes to the tribes in the Bible, animal imagery plays a central part in that the name of the tribe is accompanied by an epithet from
the fauna or from the flora. This symbolizes the qualities or the state of that
tribe. The assumption that the qualities or collective behavior of that tribe
inhere in the eponymous name is linked to the presupposition that these
qualities are innate in the members of the tribe, who are the progeny of one
forefather. In some of them the epithets serve as a grip for irony regarding
the behavior of the tribe, a sort of personification of it, which in conditions
of crisis and war also becomes satire.

a. *Issachar.* In Jacob's blessing, Issachar as the tribal name is depicted
in the following epigram:

5 Segal, (n. 4), 247; M. Garsiel, *II Samuel* (Ramat Gan, 1989), 28 (Hebrew).

6 This very expression appears in Lachish ostracon from the sixth century BCE. See N.H.
Tur-Sinai, *Lachish Documents* (in the renewed and expanded edition of S. Ahituv, Jerusalem,
1987), 31–32, in particular ostracon 5, 127–138 (Hebrew). This phrase appears in earlier documents of El Amarna no. 60, 71 and is used as an expression of self-humiliation and obedience:
see Montgomery, *Kings*, 394, and P.K. McCarter, *I Samuel* (AB; New York, 1984), 384; however, they somehow fail to notice the satirical tone employed in that expression by biblical
historiographers of the monarchial age.

Issachar is a strong ass, crouching between the sheepfolds;
he saw that a resting place was good and that the land was pleasant;
so he bowed his shoulder to bear, and became a slave at forced labor
(Gen. 49: 14)

This characterization of Issachar is obviously not complimentary. חמור גרם namely, an ass with a powerful body,[7] which "crouches between the משפתים which are apparently the saddlebags placed on the ass's back,[8] is not a flattering image in the personification of the tribe, and it contains a trace of ridicule even though the name Hamor in itself has no pejorative connotation.[9] The satirical element is in the antithesis between Issachar's intention of living leisurely and pleasantly ("he saw that a resting place was good and that the land was pleasant") and the actual outcome: "So he bowed his shoulder to bear and became a slave at forced labor." Issachar acquired his ease at the cost of the burden he placed on his shoulder, and therefore merits the epithet "a strong ass." The critical political message is clear also: Issachar became enslaved to the Canaanites in return for "rest" (מנוחה), but in that way the tribe forfeited its patrimony (נחלה). This satirical "blessing," or epigram, reflects censure of Issachar's political conduct, in complete contrast to what is described in the Song of Deborah. Here the tribe wins a blessing for rallying to the call and for its special contribution to the war against the Canaanites: "The princes of Issachar came with Deborah, and Issachar was faithful to Barak; into the valley they rushed forth at his heels" (Jud 5: 15).

b. *Dan.* In the blessing of Moses it is said of Dan: ". . . [he] is a lion's whelp that leaps forth from Bashan" (Deut 33: 22). In Garsiel's view[10] this image is based on Dan's inheritance in Laish (ליש) being a synonym for אריה (lion) (Jud 18: 7, 14, 27, 29). Since the tribe of Dan proved a disappointment in that it did not take up arms against the Canaanites, Deborah taunts Dan through the punning use of the image of a lion's whelp (גור): "Why did he abide with the ships?" (יגור) (Jud 5: 17). The verb יגור in the Bible has two meanings, "live" and "fear," and if the Song of Deborah intended the latter in its barb, then there is here more than a trace of derision and irony. These belong with the other satirical portrayals in the poem, such as the sketch

---

7 S.D. Luzzatto, in his *Commentary to the Pentateuch* (first appeared in Padua, 1871, republished in Tel Aviv, 1965), 197 (Hebrew).

8 Kimḥi in his commentary to this verse.

9 The name Ḥamor (חמור) in itself does not represent a negative meaning, cf. Gen 34: 2; like camel (גמל) it is a very common name among the Arabs.

10 Garsiel, *Midrashic Names in the Bible* (Ramat Gan, 1987) 48 (Hebrew).

aimed against Reuben, who remains "among the sheepfolds to hear the piping for the flocks," while his brother-tribes are fighting the Canaanite enslaver (5: 16–17); and the sketch portraying Sisera's mother awaiting her victorious son's return from the war (5: 28–31), which Kaufman has rightly called a "poem of ridicule and malicious joy."[11]

If in these poems disguised satirical use is made of animal epithets applied to the tribes for the purpose of abuse or ridicule in connection with the set of relationships among the tribes of Israel, it may be concluded that already at an early stage in the history of Israel, possibly prior to the establishment of the kingdom, satire constituted a basic feature in popular composition, and one of the characteristics of the genre known as the "oracles about the tribes."[12] Even those who prefer to regard these examples as irony alone—because they refer to fraternal tribes—and not as satire (glee at the downfall of an enemy), must admit that we have to do here with political irony.

3. Names or appellations

In several narratives in the Bible names appear but it is not at all clear whether they are personal names or appellations; some may even be interpreted allegorically. A number of them are charged with irony or satire. Here are some examples:

a. Much effort has been made in biblical scholarship to identify the kings who were engaged in the war of the enigmatic story in Genesis 14 with historical kings who ruled in this geopolitical region in the first half of the second millennium BCE, known as the age of the Patriarchs. The attempts to identify the four kings—Amraphel, Arioch, Chedorlaomer, and Tidal—according to Amorite, Horite, Elamite and Hittite names, or combinations of names, showed that these names are not necessarily fictional; but it is doubtful that one may draw historical conclusions from this about the event described in the chapter. This is either because of chronological reasons or because there is no epigraphic evidence of an invasion of this sort.[13] Yet no one would consider identifying the names

11 Y. Kaufmann, *The Book of Judges* (Jerusalem, 1962) 145 (Hebrew).

12 J. Bewer, *The Literature of the Old Testament* (New York, 1933), 11ff.; R. Pfeiffer, *Introduction to the Old Testament* (New York, 1948), 275ff.

13 N. Sarna, *Understanding Genesis* (New York, 1970), 111–119; E.A. Speiser, *Genesis* (AB; Garden City NY, 1964), 106–108.

of four out of the five kings of the plain (of Jordan) mentioned by name—Bera (ברע) king of Sodom; Birsha (ברשע) king of Gomorrah; Shinab (שנאב) king of Admah; and Shemeber (שמאבר) king of Zeboim— as actual historical names. Clearly, these are epithets, that is, symbolic names, behind which lies the goal of the biblical author—to condemn the kings of Sodom and Gemorrah and their allies. If we add to these names—invented out of the Hebrew words for hate (שנא), evil (רשע), and wickedness (רע)—the name Bela (בלע), which is presented here as standing for the city identified as Zo'ar (צער; cf. Gen 19: 22), the satirical tendency in etymological and allegorical guise becomes more transparent. True, we are not dealing with "satirical allegory" here, as a specific genre in satirical literature, so termed by Pollard in his study of satire;[14] but certain elements of such a combination are indeed present.

b. Nor did the fortune shine on Cushan-rishathaim, king of Aram-naharaim (Mesopotamia): not politically, as he was vanquished in war by Othniel the son of Kenaz, Caleb's younger brother (Jud 3: 9–10); and not in terms of his historical identity, despite the many attempts to identify him with some historical king.[15] Here we are dealing with an epithet, not a name, and he who applied these epithets held that the first of the oppressors of Israel in the time of the Judges could be nothing other than the archetype of evil (רשעתים, twofold evil), whose kingdom extended over the territory between the Euphrates and the Tigris. (Only in four other places in the Bible does Aram-naharaim appear as the name of a country, and one of them as the seat of Balaam the son of Beor [Deut 23: 5]). He even took pains over formal symmetry, by means of doubling and rhyming the names: Cushan-rishathaim/Aram-naharaim.[16]

c. A satirical note also sounds in the account of the struggle for power in Shechem (Jud 9) between Abimelech and his opponent Gaal the son of Ebed. Garsiel proposed regarding the genealogical name "ben Ebed" (v 26) as a status term (slave) and not as an abbreviated name like Obed, Abdon.[17] Bearing in mind that Abimelech, who reigned over Shechem, is "son of the maidservant" of Jerubbaal (v 18), we see a parallel regarding origins between Gaal, the son of a slave, and Abimelech, the son of

---

[14] A. Pollard, *Satire* (London, 1970), 28ff.

[15] C.F. Burney, *The Book of Judges* (London, 1920), 64–65; A. Malamat, *EJ* 3 (1954), 85–91.

[16] Accordingly the midrashic interpretation of the name in Talmud Babli, *Sanhedrin* 105, 1; see also: Kaufmann, *Judges* 103; R.G. Boling, *Judges* (AB; New York, 1975), 80f.

[17] Garsiel (n. 10) 38–39.

a maidservant; this reflects a politically polemical note of derision and scorn. (The name "Gaal" is discussed in the next section.)

4. Pejorative [Midrashic] name derivations

In certain cases the biblical author overtly produces a derivation of a name for the purpose of censure. Such derivations will be termed "pejorative name derivations," as their aim is to ridicule and smear the bearer of the name by imparting a negative meaning to its true (or at least prevalent) etymological meaning. It is a device of satire in its various manifestations in world literature.

a. *Nabal* (נבל) 1 Sam 25). The aim of the account of the confrontation between David and Nabal the Carmelite is twofold: to magnify and glorify David with his noble qualities, as one who is destined to reign, and to justify his act of taking Abigail, Nabal's wife, as his own wife, on the one hand, and to besmirch and condemn Nabal, the "very rich" man, who sought to humiliate David and withold from him and his men their wages, on the other hand. To this end, it adds character descriptions to Nabal: "The man was churlish and ill-behaved," and the epithet "Calebite" (1 Sam 25: 3). In my view, considering the context, this name is a term of offense: כלבי (son of dogs),[18] and not necessarily the name of his family, Caleb, as it tends to be interpreted.[19] The aim of the account becomes still more evident when the author makes Abigail give the derivation of her husband's name: "For as is his name, so is he; Nabal [i.e., fool] is his name, and folly is with him" (v 25). The original meaning of the name נבל (according to southern Arabic etymology) is "noble," "of good stock," "gracious,"[20] but the aim of the text is reproof, through alliteration and pun. Support for this view is found in the wordplay in Isaiah 32: 5–6: "The fool will no more be called noble . . . for the fool speaks folly and his mind plots iniquity."

The critical and derisive tendency continues in the grotesque account of Nabal's death (vv 36–37): "And Abigail came to Nabal; and, lo, he was holding a feast in his house, like the feast of a king. And Nabal's heart was merry within him, for he was very drunk; so she told him nothing at all

---

[18] The LXX reads "κυνικός," which means dog-like. Accordingly, Ralbag in his commentary: "In his utmost cruelty he is like the dogs that hate their kindred"; and see also: H.W. Herzberg, *I & II Samuel* (OTL; London, 1982), 202.

[19] Rashi, Kimḥi; followed by some modern commentators such as Segal, *Samuel*, 195; McCarter, *I Samuel*, 396.

[20] S. Aḥituv, "נבל," *EB* 5, 746–747; Roth, "נבל," ibid., 394–409.

until the morning light. And in the morning, when the wine had gone out of Nabal, his wife told him these things, and his heart died within him, and he became as a stone." Perhaps here too lies a phonic association between the repeated name נבל (Nabal) and the word נבל (*nebel*), meaning "wineskin." The wine came out of Nabal as from a *nebel*.[21]

b. Similarly, the name Gaal (געל), Abimelech's rival in the struggle for power in Shechem (Jud 9: 26), serves as the object of a masked barb. The name Gaal, from the southern Arabic *ju'al* means beetle. Noth derives it from *ja'lan*, a date that grows in a watered field.[22] Garsiel finds a note of contempt in the words of Zebul, Abimelech's officer, who ridicules Gaal: "Where is your mouth now, you who said, 'Who is Abimelech, that we should serve him?' Are not these the men whom you despised? Go out now and fight with them" (Jud 9: 38). In his view, the word מאסת ("you despised") contains a concealed barb aimed at the name Gaal, which is explained as מאוס, meaning despicable.[23] If his assumption is correct, we have a double ridicule: You, Gaal, the despicable one, go out and fight with the men whom you wish to rule and whom you despised.

c. *Ahab the son of Kolaiah* (Jer 29: 21–23). In the conflict between Jeremiah and his adversaries—the two false prophets, Ahab the son of Kolaiah and Zedekiah the son of Maaseiah—Jeremiah curses them both. For the purpose of the curse he uses the name "Kolaiah" (קוליה), and makes a play on it in various ways: "Because of them this curse (קללה) shall be used by all the exiles from Judah in Babylon: 'The Lord make you like Zedekiah and Ahab, whom the king of Babylon roasted (קלם) on the fire'" (v 22). On the basis of phonic association between קוליה, קללה, and קלה a pejorative name etymology is constructed here, which turns the theophoric name Kolaiah, whose presumed meaning is קוה ליה ("hope in God")[24] into the object of a curse in the name of God, involving roasting in fire. Not by chance did the satirist choose to play on the verb קלה, which is not common in the Bible, instead of שרף, which is usual (32: 20; Deut 7: 5; Josh 6: 24; Jud 18: 27). Moreover, the satirical tendency of contrasting the name is also revealed in the paradoxical use by the prophet of the stylistic formula of blessing for the purpose of a

---

21 On the irony and wit which characterize the whole story, see: M. Garsiel, "Wit, Words and a Woman," in Y. Raddy and A. Brenner (eds.), *On Humour and the Comic in the Hebrew Bible* (Sheffield, 1990), 161–167.

22 M. Noth, *Die isräelitischen Personanennamen im Rahmen der gemeinsemitischen namengebung* (Stuttgart, 1928), 230.

23 Garsiel (n. 15), 39.

24 S. Aḥituv, "קוליה," *EB* 7, 93.

curse: the formula "The Lord make you like . . ." followed by a personal
name appears in the Bible in the context of blessings, for example, "The
Lord make you like Ephraim and Menasseh" (Gen 48: 20).[25] This device
of pejorative name etymology is used principally by the author of Chronicles, who turns it into his particular means for historiosophic and religious
evaluation.

d. *Achan* (עכן). The latter transgressed the injunction (Josh 7) and
is called Achar (עכר) in 1 Chronicles 2: 7, which imparts a negative etymology to the name: "The troubler (עוכר) of Israel, who brought trouble
on Israel by his violation of the sacred ban"; and likewise from the text in
Josh 7: 25: "Why did you bring trouble upon us (עכרתנו)? The Lord brings
trouble on you (יעכרך) today."

e. *Asa* (אסא). According to the Chronicler, there is a direct connection between punishment and sin. A king who has become ill, or who had
died in his prime, has certainly been punished for a sin he committed. If the
sin is not mentioned in the Book of Kings, it is necessary to invent it. Asa
is depicted in Kings as one who did "what was right in the eyes of the Lord,
as David his father had done" (1 Kgs 15: 11), and his illness is mentioned
only as one of old age: "Only in old age was he diseased in his feet" (v 23).
But the Chronicler seeks a religious cause for Asa's illness and finds it
in his sin: "In the thirty-ninth year of his reign Asa was diseased in his
feet, and his disease became severe; yet even in his disease he not seek the
Lord, but sought help from physicians" (2 Chr 16: 12). There seems to be a
disguised pejorative name etymology here, explaining אסא in the sense of
"physician" (from the Aramaic אסיא); behind it lies biting criticism against
one who seeks help in doctors and not in God.[26]

5. Negative historiosophic evaluation

Such an evaluation is also reflected in the eponymous names applied to
various nations that engaged in prolonged conflict with Israel, and against
which resentment was felt.

a. *Edom*. This is the "national" name applied to Esau, who according to
the account was born "all red" (Gen 25: 25). The red color that symbolizes
him appears in the story of the sale of his birthright to Jacob, but there it is

---

[25] Cf. "I shall bring a curse instead of a blessing on myself" (Gen 27: 12); and see M. Weinfeld, "קללה," *EB* 7, 186.

[26] Garsiel (n. 15), 172.

in connection with the mess of pottage: "Let me eat some of that red pottage (therefore his name was called Edom)" (v 30).

But the red is also associated with blood, and the two appear in the context of Edom in the war of the three kings—of Israel, Judah, and Edom—against Moab: "The next morning, about the time of the sacrifice, behold, water came from the direction of Edom till the country was filled with water . . . and the Moabites saw the water opposite them as red as blood" (2 Kgs 3: 20, 22). Actually, in this narrative Edom appears as the ally of Judah and Israel. Its cruel hostility toward Israel was chiefly evinced in the destruction of Jerusalem, which then became a symbol of the enemies of Israel. It is no surprise that the post-exilic Isaiah opens his prophecy on the fall of Edom on a satirical note of malicious joy, using the color red as a description of the blood (נצחם) likened to the red wine in the wine press. This image of blood flowing like wine in the wine press arises from the mention of the Edomite city Bozrah, whose name is reminiscent of the grape harvest (בציר) : "Who is this that comes from Edom, in crimsoned garments from Bozrah (בצרה) . . . Why is thy apparel red, and thy garments like his that treads in the winepress? I have trodden the winepress alone, and from the peoples no one was with me; I trod them in my anger, and trampled them in my wrath; their lifeblood is sprinkled on upon my garments and I have stained all my raiment" (Isa 63: 1–3).[27]

The link of theme and sound between Edom (אדום) and blood (דם) finds clear and forceful phonic expression in Ezekiel's oath of vengeance on Mount Seir (Edom): "As I live, says the Lord God, I will prepare you for blood and blood shall pursue you; because you are guilty of blood, therefore blood shall pursue you" (35: 6).[28]

b. *Moab.* The etymology of the name Moab, which concludes the tale of Lot and his daughters in the cave (Gen 19: 30–38), is disputed by commentators on the basis of the etiological tendencies they find in the account as a whole. Most derive it from מאבי אב (ἐκ τοῦ τιατρός μου in the LXX). Some interpret it as an expression of the pride of a mother who has conceived by her father,[29] and others regard the entire story as an Israelite fabrication (if not exactly satirical), deriding Moab and Amon for their origins through incest.[30] There are also those who derive the name Moab from

27 Luzzatto in his *Commentary to Isaiah,* 612, claims that the names that appear in this prophecy were deliberately exploited by the prophet for punning and other devices of humorous effect.

28 R. Weiss, *Mi-Shut ba-Mikra'* (Jerusalem, 1976), 22 (Hebrew).

29 H. Gunkel, *Genesis* (Göttingen, 1969), 217.

30 A. Dillmann, *Genesis II* (Edinburgh, 1897) 113.

the Arabic *wa'aba,* meaning "to be ashamed," giving the sense of "he who caused shame by his birth."[31] The story itself is not a satire, but its insertion into the ethnological framework of Genesis reflects a later, isolationist, historiosophic tendency in the history of Israel. This was aimed principally against intermarriage with Moabites and Amonites.[32]

c. *Babylon.* The legend behind this name (בבל)—"because there the Lord confused (בלל) the language of all the earth; and from there the Lord scattered them abroad over the face of all the earth," which concludes the account of the Tower of Babel (Gen 11: 1–9)—in no way accords with the meaning of the name in Akkadian, bab-ili, "gate of the gods."[33] We have here a case of reversal of meaning, a "pejorative name etymology." However, the satirical tendency is reflected not only in the midrash of the name but in the entire narrative (see Chapter 3 below).

6. The use of antithesis or double entendre for the purpose of satire

These serve as devices for ridicule, and are much used in riddles, comedies and satires. They permit camouflage of the barb through suggestion based on a meaning that is the opposite of the selfsame word—a kind of point and counterpoint. The Sophists and the poets of Greece and Rome (Aristophanes, Demosthenes, Cicero, and others) widely employed these means in their political polemics.[34] The following are a few expressions of double entendre containing a satirical note, intimating what the poet really has in mind.

a. In the string of "Woe" prophecies, Isaiah taunt-elegizes the revelers in Zion: "Woe to those who rise early in the morning, that they may run after strong drink, who tarry late into the evening till wine inflames them" (Isa 5: 11). Usually the verb ידליקם (inflames them) is interpreted to mean that the wine will set them alight, burn them.[35] From the double meaning of

31 J. Liver, "מואב," *EB* 4, 708.

32 Z. Weisman, "Etnology, Etiology, Genealogy and Historiography in the Tale of Lot and His Daughters (Genesis 19: 30–38)" in *Sha'arei Talmon, Studies in the Bible, Qumran and the Ancient Near East Presented to Shemaryahu Talmon,* eds. Michael Fishbane and Emanuel Tov (Winona Lake, Indiana, 1992), 43–52 (Hebrew).

33 L. Oppenheim, "בבל,"*EM* 2, 10, relying on Akkadian etymology.

34 I.M. Casanowicz, *Paronomasia in the Old Testament* (1892), 14, where he mentions examples from Greek and Roman poetry.

35 Rashi: "burns in them"; Kimhi: "inflames them to fulfil all their desires"; Luzzatto, to *Isaiah,* 74 follows his clue and elaborates his further: "It was the wit of the prophet to allude, in one word ידליקם to their other abominations" (Hebrew).

the verb דלק ("burn", "ignite"), and also רדף (pursue), it seems correct to interpret ידליקם (following Ehrlich and on the basis of the parallel רדף/דלק in Lam 4: 19),[36] in the sense of "will pursue them" (and compare Gen 31: 36; 1 Sam 17: 53). In this way a parallel is created between the two hemistiches, which contains an irony: in the morning they pursue wine and at night the wine pursues them. Yellin was indeed right to regard the use of double entendre in the verb ידליקם as quite intentional by the prophet;[37] and it seems to me that the intention is satirical.

b. The wordplay with the different meanings of לא דבר (a nothing) and לו דבר (a city in Transjordan), with only phonic identity between them, and also the different meanings of the name Karnaim, enables us to perceive the satirical note in the prophecy of Amos: "You who rejoice in Lo-debar [a nothing], who say, 'Have we not by our strength taken Karnaim [horns] for ourselves?'" (6: 13). Lo-debar is the name of a city in eastern Transjordan (2 Sam 9: 4–5; 17: 27).[38] Karnaim is also a city in eastern Transjordan (1 Macc 26: 43); "Ashteroth-karnaim," Ashteroth in the Karnaim region Gen 14: 5.[39] These two cities were apparently conquered by the kingdom of Ephraim—a political achievement in itself. By a slight change in the vowel letters of the name לו דבר from לו to לא Amos turns the political gain which the men of Samaria so vaunted to ridicule and scorn.[40]

7. Artistic skills in Laments

The use of different wordplays (alliteration, paranomasia, etc.) as features of satire (Chapter 1, section 3, above) is present in elegiac odes also. Medieval commentators already discerned this literary manifestation. Regarding the lament in Micah 1: 10–16, Kimḥi observes: "The poets' and elegists' way of speaking in their laments and songs is דרך צחות [devices of style, mainly figures of paronomasia]." Ibn Ezra adopts a similar approach in his interpretation of Micah 1: 14. Certainly they saw the connection between devices of style (דרך צחות) and the genre (elegy), but they did not

---

36 A.B. Ehrlich, *Mikra ki-peshuto*, III, 13, proposes to amend "ידליקם" (hiphil) to "ידלקם" (qal), corresponding to "ירדפם"—"will chase them"; already Jonah Ibn-Janaḥ, in his book *Sepher ha-Shorashim*, made this observation (see B.Z. Bacher's edition, Berlin, 1896, photocopied in Jerusalem, 1966).

37 D. Yellin, *Ḥiqrey Mikra* (Jerusalem, 1983), 258–259 (Hebrew).

38 Z. Kallai, "לא דבר, לו דבר" *EM* 4, 409–410.

39 B. Oded, "קרנים", *EB* 7, 277–278.

40 R. Weiss, (n. 28), 187; N. Rosel, *Amos* (Israel, 1990), 198 (Hebrew).

adequately plumb the nature of the genre in terms of its politically satiric nature. In these elegiac verses the poet's ironic attitude is revealed, elegizing the object of his ode while giving the impression of assuming that the crisis and the calamity that have visited the people are retribution for their behavior. Sometimes the lament is mixed with a kind of glee at the distress of the object of the elegy. This impression arises from the ancient "taunt of the bards (הַמּוֹשְׁלִים)" on the fall of Moab (Num 21: 27–30). It apparently served as the core for the prophetic taunt elegies against Moab by Jeremiah (chap 48) and by Isaiah (chaps 15–16), which are intermixed with features of political satire (see chapter 5 below). At times it is evident that the barbs in the prophetic elegies are aimed at Israel itself; then the prophet's ambivalent attitude to his people finds expression in tragic irony.

The elegiac taunt in Micah 1 uses many varied forms of the artistic devices, which highlight and sharpen the prophet's ambivalent attitude to the destruction and the disintegration that has struck (or will strike, if we interpret this elegy as a warning of imminent danger[41]) the cities of the Judean plain and the environs of Jerusalem, apparently in the wake of Sennacherib's expedition. On the one hand, identity is felt with the suffering of his people, as expressed in the phrase in verse 8, and that in verse 9: "It [the wound] has reached the gate of my people"; on the other hand, one hears in his words irony and censure against the "delighting" cities of Judah that encircle the beseiged capital. The irony is felt especially in the use he makes of punning, whose essence is not only phonic but also conceptual (plays of words), a device termed *zimud* (juxtaposition) by Moshe Ibn Ezra in his work *Shirat Yisrael,*[42] namely juxtaposition of words similar in sound but different and even antithetical in meaning. The elegy ends with a call to the Daughter of Zion: "Make yourself bald and cut off your hair, for the children of your delight; make yourself as bald as the eagle for they shall go from you into exile" (v. 16). The maternal personification of Jerusalem concludes the elegies on the other settlements of Judah, in all of which the settlements appear in female personification. It is expressed in the epithet "she who inhabits" adjoined to the names of the cities and the settlements: she who inhabits Shaphir, she who inhabits Zaanan, she who inhabits

---

41 J.M. Smith, *Micah* (ICC, Edinburgh, 1911) 51; M. Seidel, *The Book of Micah* (Jerusalem, 1976), 7 (Hebrew). A different view which rejects any relationship between this prophecy and the Assyrian invasion of Judah is expressed by J. Licht, "Micah," *EB* 4, 886 and in S. Wargun's article in *Sepher Baruch Ben Yehuda* (Tel Aviv, 1981), 259–280 (Hebrew).

42 Moshe Ibn-Ezra, *Sepher ha-'Iyyunim weha-diyyunim 'al ha-shira ha-'Ibrit* (ed. A.S. Halkin; Jerusalem, 1975), 239–240.

Maroth, she who inhabits Lachish, she who inhabits Maresha; and it is also expressed in verbs in the feminine gender—עברי חלה, יצאה,—that sub-sequently match the feminine metaphorical usage in verse 7 concerning Samaria, which ends, "For from the hire of a harlot she gathered them, and to the hire of a harlot they shall return."

It is reasonable to regard the localities surrounding Jerusalem in these verses as "the children of your (Jerusalem's) delight" (v 16), and the puns on their suffering as a kind of derision, even with a trace of malicious plea-sure: the cities of Judah are racked by pain, like a woman in labor, on ac-count of the conqueror's onslaught, and their "delights" have become their loss and their bereavement.

This picture with its female personification and its ironic elements is akin to that appearing in Jeremiah's elegiac prophecy regarding the Daugh-ter of Zion, although lacking the personal lyrical expression of "the prophet of destruction":

> At the noise of the horseman and archer every city takes to flight;
> they enter thickets; they climb among rocks;
> all the cities are foresaken, and no man dwells in them.
> And you, O desolate one,
> what do you mean that you dress in scarlet,
> that you deck yourself with ornaments of gold,
> that you enlarge your eyes with paint?
> In vain you beautify yourself.
> Your lovers despise you; they seek your life.
> For I heard a cry as of a woman in travail,
> anguish as of one bringing forth her first child,
> the cry of the daughter of Zion gasping for breath,
> stretching out her hands,
> "Woe is me! I am fainting before murderers" (Jer 4: 29–31).

The extreme transition from elegy (empathy) to mockery (irony) verg-ing on contempt (satire) is achieved through the passage from the heart-breaking description of the foresaken city (v 29) to direct speech spoken to its female figure: "And you, O desolate one, what do you mean," etc. (v 30). The reader cannot but be struck by the similarity between the female character of the lustful woman (probably "daughter of Zion" in v 31), whom he addresses directly in the second person, and Jezebel, known for her "har-lotries" and her "sorceries [that] are so many" (2 Kgs 9: 22), whose punish-ment is described so cruelly, if not cynically: "When Jehu came to Jezreel,

Jezebel heard of it; and she painted her eyes, and adorned her head, and looked out of the window . . . And he said, Who is on my side? Who? [Who are you? Who?] Two or three eunuchs looked out at him. He said, 'Throw her down.' So they threw her down; and some of her blood spattered on the wall and on the horses and they trampled on her" (2 Kgs 9: 30–33). This, however, occurred not before she had managed to welcome him with a greeting laden with satire: "Is it peace, you, Zimri, murderer of your master?" (v 31).

The distinction between elegy and fable, between tragic irony and satire, lies in nuance, and it is so fine that only language in all its flexibility is capable, by means of shades of syntax and its wealth of images, of bridging them.

❦ 3 ❧

SATIRICAL FABLES IN POLITICAL CONFRONTATIONS

The word *mashal* appears in the Bible as the term for various literary forms not easily linked by any common denominator.[1] It actually provides the title of one of the Wisdom books in the Bible.[2] The wide use of *mashal* to denote different literary forms, such as types of maxims, aphorisms and riddles, moral poems and taunt elegies, may indicate common roots in the ancient oral composition, but it hinders the definition of the *mashal* as a special genre in itself.[3]

Yet the sense of "image," "likening one thing to another," as found in Aramaic, Arabic and Akkadian, goes some way toward explaining the origin and essence of the word.[4] The form nowadays termed *mashal* as generally defined in literary criticism (fable and parable) is in fact not given this name in the Bible, even though it exists there: Jotham's fable (Jud 9: 8–15), Nathan's fable of the little ewe lamb (2 Sam 12: 1–4), Jehoash's fable of the thistle and the cedar in Lebanon (2 Kgs 14: 9–10), Isaiah's fable of the vineyard (5: 1–9), and to some extent Isaiah's fable of the plowman (28: 23–29).[5]

---

[1] S. Abramsky, "*mashal*" (Hebrew), *EH* XXIV, 631–632; L. Mowry, "Parable," *IDB* III, 649ff.

[2] M. Haran "*mashal*" (Hebrew), *EB* V, 548–553.

[3] E. Nourse, "Parable," *ERE* IX (Edinburgh, 1917), 628–631.

[4] S. Shabib, "*mashal*" (Hebrew), *EH* XXIV, 628; O. Eissfeldt, *Der Maschal im Alten Testament* (Giessen, 1913); *BDB*, 605.

[5] D. Kimḥi, in his Commentary to Isaiah 28, 23; A. B. Ehrlich, *Mikra ki-Pheshuto* III (New York, 1969), 60.

Similar to these are the allegorical fables of Ezekiel: the eagle and cedar (17), the lioness and her cubs (19), and his likening of the king of Egypt to a cedar in Lebanon (31). These literary units are undoubtedly fables, as they use a tale connected with the plant and animal world allegorically or metaphorically to provide a moral for a person or for a specific community of people. Sometimes a threat or a curse against the object of the fable or of the moral is added.[6] Precisely in these fables, not those explicitly termed *meshalim* in the Bible (e.g., the Balaam oracles, Num 23–24), where the curse element is evident, there are features of political satire whose barb is hurled at the treacherous behavior or despotism of the king, and withering criticism is aimed at misrule in the context of actual political events. Not by chance in all these fables are the subjects of the message personages of the highest classes; this attests to the fable as a literary form representing the cultural elite; it is not so "popular" as is generally held.

1. The fable of Jotham (Jud 9: 7–20)

Few apparently would dispute that there is a leaning toward political satire in Jotham's fable. The features characterizing it as a paradigm of political satire are primarily its belonging to the literary genre of fable, which from antiquity to the present has served in world literature as the instrument and garb for severe criticism of unhealthy social manifestations and of rivals in real political struggles (not merely as a moral).[7] Attached to it were formal and rhetorical (stylistic) means, also found in other kinds of literary genres, which aided the artist (the fabulist) to transmit in dramatic forms his satirical message to his audience. Among these devices there are, for example, the graded number sequence of three and four with complete contrast between the three and the fourth, the repeated refrain and the poetic rhythm. These are factors fostering the reception of the message, which was meant to be delivered orally, and they help us understand its special meanings. So much is agreed; but from this point on, views are divided among scholars and commentators going in different, or even contradictory directions, and they cannot be ignored in the attempt to probe the essence of the satirical meaning of this passage. The differences center mainly on the following questions:

---

6 On the affinity between *mashal* and *kelala* (curse) see Eissfeldt, *Maschal,* 52ff.

7 A. Pollard, *Satire* (London, 1970), 30 ff., cites examples from Aristophanes (5th century BCE), Jonathan Swift (1667–1745) and George Orwell (1903–1950). M. Hodgart, *Satire* (1969), 24 ff., cites Aesop's Fables and the fables of La Fontaine as models for satirical works.

a. Against whom, or what, is the satire aimed?
b. What is the relationship between the fable and its application, and what does this imply concerning the use of the fable in Jotham's apologue?
c. What is the nature of the fable and its *Sitz im Leben*?
d. What are the historical and social circumstances reflected in it?

These questions will guide us in our interpretation of the fable, and will help us to draw conclusions regarding its characteristic satirical properties. These may serve as criteria for defining the quality of other fables in the Bible as a type and of political satire in the Bible as a phenomenon.

a. Against whom or what is the satire aimed?

The biblical narrator presents Jotham's speech as addressed to the "men of Shechem" who made Abimelech their king. The appeal in verse 7, "Listen to me, you men of Shechem," follows smoothly from what is related in verse 6. The sarcasm that closes Jotham's speech (vv 16–20) is directed at them, as is the curse he invokes at the end: "But if not, let fire come out from Abimelech, and devour the citizens of Shechem, and Bethmillo" (v 20a). The curse is realized in the continuation of the story; at the end of it the narrator emphasizes this fact, as a moral accompanied by a theological touch: "and God also made all the wickedness of the men of Shechem fall back upon their heads, and upon them came the curse of Jotham the son of Jerubbaal" (v 57). But although Jotham's words are meant for the "men of Shechem," the major accusation they contain is trained on Abimelech, who killed his seventy brothers, the sons of Jerubbaal, so that he might rule Shechem alone. The charge is expressed in the continuation of the curse against the "men of Shechem": "and let fire come out from the citizens of Shechem and from Beth-millo, and devour Abimelech" (v 20b). At the end of the narrative, in chiastic order, the lesson regarding Abimelech is highlighted: "thus God requited the crime of Abimelech, which he committed against his father in killing his seventy brothers" (v 56). For all that, it is true to say that the satire is not aimed directly at Abimelech, the sponsor of the killing, who is the one deserving of the curse,[8] but against the "men of Shechem," who worked to make Abimelech king; hence, the charge of murdering the sons of Jerubbaal is brought against them (in Jotham's reproof: v 18).

---

[8] U. Simon, "The Parable of Jotham (Judges IX, 8–15): The Parable, Its Application and Their Narrative Framework." *Tarbiz* 34 (1965), 1–34 (Hebrew).

The accusation and the accused are evident: the ingratitude of the men of Shechem, who acted against Jerubbaal in a manner he did not deserve (vv 17–18). The political lesson is evident: betrayal begets betrayal and wickedness is the reward of wickedness. Whoever has been party to the spilling of innocent blood will pay with his blood, and he will be utterly devoured by the fire that he himself helped to ignite.

b. The relationship between the fable and its application

If that is the satire and that is its target, why did Jotham need the fable of the trees? Could he not have delivered his reproof, with all the bitterness and sarcasm contained in it, as well as the curse that closes it, without having to resort to a fable?

Clearly, the fable is meant to play a part beyond the public censure and beyond the direct curse. Its functions may be rhetorical, to capture the attention of the listeners and to convince them to alter their position; or it may serve to transmit a further ideological message, one not included in the reproof and with implications over and above that particular political event of the power struggle in Shechem. An indication of the first reason is found in the opening of Jotham's speech, "Listen to me, you men of Shechem, that God may listen to you" (v 7),[9] which implies that Jotham expects his words to fall on attentive ears. Yet the opening does not accord with the continuation of the reproof, which ends in a curse (vv 17–20).

The use of "God" in the opening of the speech matches the use of the word in the repeated chorus in the fable, spoken by the fruit-bearing trees. For example, the olive: "Shall I leave my fatness, by which gods and men are honored, and go to sway over the trees?" (v 9, and cf. vv 11, 13). But it appears nowhere in the words of censure and the curse spoken after the telling of the fable (vv 17–20).

An indication of the second reason may be seen in the discrepancy between the fable and the application in Jotham's apologue, especially regarding the facts that the narrator presents as the setting of the polemic. According to them, the initiative for the kingship came from Abimelech, not from the trees, as in the fable. It was not preceded by approaches on the part of the men of Shechem to others to accept the kingship, nor is it anywhere intimated that the latter rejected it because they regarded it as

---

9 The usage of the generic epithet of God *elohim* (vv 7, 9, 13) shows close affinity with Wisdom literature in the Bible.

profitless for gods and men, and a deviation from their true and useful purpose in life, as in the fable of the trees (cf. vv 1–6). In other words, while the satire in the fable is aimed at kingship as a social idea and regime, the barbs in Jotham's satire of reproof are concrete and personal, and are shot at the amoral and treacherous behavior of the "men of Shechem" and their bloody plot with Abimelech to seize the rule over Shechem.

On the basis of this inner tension between the parts of the unit (the fable and the moral) it is possible to grasp the debate among different commentators as to the satirical point of the fable. Some, having recourse to the "fable" itself (vv 8–15), and distinguishing it from the moral, hold that the fable is a very keen satire against the institution of monarchy, and even a negation of it in principle.[10] Others, relying on the existence of a primary link between the fable and the moral, argue that the fable itself does not indicate a fundamental negation of monarchy as an institution, for monarchy as such is viewed positively in the Bible; it is a criticism against the stupidity of the people, who offer the rule to a dangerous and unscrupulous man, unfit for the office.[11] Between these two extremes there are those who find both in the fable and the moral a negation of a concrete reign in the particular historical circumstances of Israelite society at the time, but not negation of monarchy in principle as a socio-political institution.[12]

However, there is no need to decide between the two extreme positions; another explanation is possible, which will ease the tension between the fable and the moral, and obviously between the political satire deriding the institution of monarchy and the sharp satirical barbs thrust at historical figures in an actual struggle for rule.

The key to such an explanation lies in Gutman's position, based on various sources in classical world literature, especially Greek: "Wherever fables with political content have come down to us, the sources usually relate the content in a style attesting that the fable was known in ancient times and was adapted to the actual needs of the moment."[13] This generalization also holds for Jotham's fable, if we see its inclusion in Jotham's speech as the adaptation of a "universal fable," which indeed had an in-

---

[10] M. Buber, *Malkhuth shamayim* (Jerusalem, 1965), 65 (Hebrew); H. Tadmor, in *'Iyyunim be-Sepher Shophtim* (Jerusalem, 1971), 323 (Hebrew); Y. Zakovitch, "For Three. . . and for Four," *The Pattern of Numerical Sequence in the Bible* (Jerusalem, 1979), 244f. (Hebrew).

[11] Y. Kaufmann, *The Book of Judges* (Jerusalem, 1964), 201 (Hebrew).

[12] Simon (n. 8), 21–23; I. Abarbanel, in his commentary on *Nebi'im Rishonim* (Jerusalem, 1955), 123.

[13] J. Guttman, "Jotham's Fable," in *'Iyyunim be-Sepher Shophtim* (n. 10), 315.

dependent existence, in order to suit the specific needs of the polemic.[14] Such adapations are not foreign to biblical literature whose roots lie in oral tradition. The integration of fables, elegies, and independent works into polemical rhetoric for the purpose of an actual political struggle is found in many places in the Bible.

c. The nature of the fable and its Sitz im Leben

The word "fable" (*mashal*) is nowhere mentioned in "Jotham's fable," and its application here is infuenced by its use in medieval literature. There is no doubt that it is a fable as this genre is conventionally defined. Nor is it the only one of its kind in the Bible, not even the only one used for political satire.

Until the beginning of the twentieth century Jotham's fable was thought to be the most ancient in world literature.[15] However, it may be presumed that the "genes" and motifs characterizing it as such predated it in one form or another in the ancient east.[16] The assumption that the birthplace of Jotham's fable is Canaan is no more than a surmise, as is the assumption that its parentage and birth lie in political debate in Israel at the time of the Judges just before the establishment of the monarchy.[17] Kaufmann's statement that Jotham's fable is "a complete innovation in the literature of parables . . . For the first time a fable appears as a means of moral and political reproof,"[18] is still not certain. Lack of knowledge of a "progenitor" of the fable does not prevent scrutiny of the functional, structural and formal qualities of Jotham's fable to ascertain its situation in life and its satirical tendencies with respect to politics.

Jotham's fable is set in a speech of reproof, or a polemic of sociopolitical nature. Fables are applied for this purpose elsewhere in the Bible, for example, 2 Samuel 12: 1–13; 2 Kings 14: 9–10; Isaiah 5: 1–6; and Ezekiel 17. The fable is related in a certain historical circumstance, and serves

---

14 Guttman, ibid., even compares the introduction of Jotham's speech (v 7) to that of Kalimachus to his audience.

15 Guttman, ibid., 311–315.

16 The use of fables in political contexts is well attested. Examples from Mesopotamia can be cited from the 18th century BCE, such as the letter of the king Shamshi-Addu to his son Yamash-Addu, *ARM* 1, 15.

17 Simon, (n. 8), 24: Jotham's fable is a specifically Israelite fable, faithfully reflecting the specific problem of the end of the era of the Judges.

18 Kaufmann, *Judges*, 202.

the fabulist as an allegorical means for achieving a concrete outcome. The nature of this outcome is evident from the introduction to the fable and in the dramatic transition to the moral voiced by the reproving orator.

In form, structure and style the fable is an independent literary unit, being different from the introduction that precedes and the conclusions that follow it. In its form, Jotham's fable is a poetic work. In sequential structure it fits the numerical graded model of three and four, a pattern that appears in the concatenations of Wisdom sayings (Pro 30: 15–17, 18–20, 21–23) and also of prophetic oracles (Amos 1: 3–6).[19] Here the graded numerical sequence of three and four is antithetical (which highlights the contradiction), the fourth appearing as the absolute opposite of the three that precede it.[20] The bramble, which is not a fruit-bearing tree, but a lowly thorn bush, appears as the complete contrast to the three fruit-bearing trees, the olive, the fig and the vine, and its response to the request by the trees that it reign over them is quite contrary to the response of the others. It is possible that the order of the first three also represents a descending degree, if we consider the age, produce and abundance of their leaves.[21]

The poetic form of the fable is also evident in the rhythmic repetition of the same phrases that constitute the leitmotiv and are a kind of chorus in the dialogue between the trees and the candidates for kingship over them. The repeated request of the trees, "Come you, and reign over us" (vv 10, 12, 14), and the reply of the fruit-bearing trees, "Shall I leave my. . . . and go to sway over the trees?" (vv 9, 11, 13), mark the opening and closing of each stanza of the fable. The fable does not have a clear-cut ending of a closed circle. Its elliptical conclusion (v 15) leaves its lesson regarding the kingship to the judgment of the hearers. In this respect, it is similar to the "riddle" form, which seems to approximate it in type,[22] being used by the riddle-maker as by the fabulist (Ezek 17) as a means of pointing the way, overtly or by intimation, to the listener and activating his intellectual faculties to infer and draw conclusions by comparison (or alternatively by contrast).[23]

19 A detailed study of this numerical pattern is found in Zakovitch's dissertation (n. 10).

20 H. L. Ginsberg, "On the History of the Graded Number Sequence" (Hebrew), in: *Minhah le-David* (ed. S. Assaf, B. Dinaburg and S. Klein, Jerusalem, 1935), 78–82.

21 This explanation does not necessarily contradict that offered by Zakovitch.

22 Eissfeldt, *Maschal* (n. 4), 9–10, points to semantic parallels in Hab 2: 6; Ezek 17: 2.

23 Z. Weisman, "Patterns and Structures in the Visions of Amos," *BM* (*Beit Mikra*) 39 (1969), 40–57 (Hebrew); see especially 46–47.

d. The use of metaphor from plant life in Jotham's fable

The metaphorical and allegorical employment of flora is important for understanding the special nature of Jotham's fable. The biblical literature is rich in metaphors and images connected with the plant world. Two opposite directions in their employment may be distinguished: one is likening a person to a plant so as to characterize his appearance, his qualities and his status. (For example, "The righteous flourish like the palm tree and grow like a cedar in Lebanon" [Ps 92: 13]; "As a lily among brambles, so is my love among maidens" [Cant, 2,2]; "Your mother was like a vine in the vineyard, transplanted by the water" [Ezek 19: 10–14].) The other is likening a plant to a person, that is, personification. (For example, "And all the trees in the field shall clap their hands" [Isa 55: 12].) A similar use to this is found in the taunt elegy against the king of Babylon: "The cypresses rejoice at you, the cedars of Lebanon" (Isa 14: 8; and see Chapter 6 below).

In Jotham's fable both directions are followed. On the one hand, there is personifcation of the trees and their likening to humans; this occurs in the opening: "The trees once went forth to anoint a king over them"; in the dialogue between all the trees ("and they said to . . .") and the trees that are offered the kingship ("Shall I go to sway over the trees?"); and in the conclusion, with the speech of the bramble, "If in good faith you are anointing me king over you . . ." (v 15). On the other hand, the fate of the humans is compared to the fate of the trees. In the fable, this is found in the ominous reply of the bramble: "But if not, let fire come out of the bramble and devour the cedars of Lebanon" (v 15); in the moral, it is found in Jotham's reproof: "But if not, let fire come out from Abimelech, and devour the citizens of Shechem" (v 20). This is the sole connecting link between the fable and moral with respect to style, for in other respects the lack of a match between them is notable.[24]

The allegorical interpretation, which finds two aspects of the same unit in the fable and in the moral, attempts to explain Jotham's fable as an equation, with symmetrical reflection of the characters as mirror-images. The true image is that found in the moral, and the mirror-image is that found in the fable. This explanation thereby misses the paradoxical quality of the

---

24 J. M. Myers, *The Book of Judges* (IB II), 754: "Herein lies the lesson of the fable. Trees taking refuge in the shade of the bramble, which boasts a protection it is powerless to give, is the height of absurdity. On the other hand, the worthless bramble may harbor a fire which can sweep the destruction even of the mighty cedars of Lebanon."

fable, and obviously its satirical significance. Those who distinguish entirely between the fable and the moral overlook the essential affinity between them, without which there is impairment of the actual significance, which is the essence of any fable (e.g., the fable of the vine in Ezekiel 15). Therefore, a synthetic approach is needed, which, while distinguishing the fable from the moral, still seeks the connecting point between them through which they are cross-fertilized.

e. Two-way satire

The personification in the fable, trees ready to anoint a king over them, points to the disguised criticism: See what became of the trees, which wanted to act like humans and set themselves up an institution like that of humans. They are uprooted, they sway, and their end is to be devoured by fire. The personification of the trees here, as in other poetic works, is not allegorical but a metaphor used by the poet, and it includes both observation and a moral lesson. The objects that appear in the fable are introduced from the very start, with their representational significance, as metonyms, so that the moral is not an "interpretation" of what is shown on its manifest level, but a specific reference on another level. The message in the fable is that the fruit-bearing trees are aware that if they cease their natural activity, giving forth fruit, and instead "sway over the trees," that is, are uprooted from the soil and wander among the trees,[25] the bounty they bring to the world and the pleasure derived from them by God and humans will cease, as, of course, will their own pleasure.

But the thorny, fruitless bush conditions its agreement to reign over the trees with stipulations that cannot be met: "Come and take refuge in my shade"—when it is not even able to shade its own roots, but on the contrary is prickly and dry enough to send them up in flames. The message therefore is political: it refers to the set of relationships associated with self-rule. It is satirical because it turns the independent trees into subjects taking shelter in the threats of the most inferior of them. The process of anointing the king thus reaches its paradoxical—even absurd—conclusion: free choice turns into slavery and a blessing into a curse. What was the reply of the trees to the threats of the bramble?—the fabulist does not tell us. Were they perhaps persuaded by its threats that there was no use in imitating humans and placing a king over themselves? Or did Jotham, too, who adapted this fable

---

25 Simon (n. 8), 2, 20.

to the purpose of his speech, perhaps expect that under the influence of the fable the "men of Shechem" would reconsider setting up a king over them? Clearly, the fable itself is a keen satire against monarchy, for if someone is found who agrees to reign he is not likely to bring benefit but the opposite—he is liable to cause calamity.

Jotham uses the alternative, unfinished ending of the fable, "if in good faith. . . but if not" (v 15) for his own immediate political needs, after his chances of convincing the men of Shechem have faded. He turns the metaphor into an equation; and the satire in the fable, directed against monarchy as an artificial invention foreign to the laws of nature, becomes a polemic whose barbs are aimed at those who anointed Abimelech, the spiller of his brothers' blood. He converts the threat by the bramble at the end of the fable (v 15b) into a curse that will befall both Abimelech and those who made him king (v 20); this he achieves by reiterating with bitter and pointed scorn the condition contained in "if you have acted in good faith and honor" (v 16)[26] and the phrase "let fire come out . . . and devour."

Thus, and in keeping with the use of other fables where the moral accompanies observation and experience, Jotham converts the satirical fable against monarchy into a satirical polemic against a king who usurps the rule. The fable preceded the conversion, but whoever used it cited it for the purpose of the moral lesson. The transition of the fable into an actual political message is achieved by means of the word "now," which is used in other fables in the Bible, to mark the passage from the fable to its application, particularly the actual outcome deriving from it (cf. 2 Sam 12: 10; Isa 5: 6). The word "now" also serves as a technical term in the political communicative style, signifying the passage to the practical point of the message in a speech or a letter.[27] A priori, there is no match between the fable and moral, and in each of them the satire is addressed to a different recipient. But a posteriori, they do not contradict. In a certain sense they even complement each other, for in the end the first attempt to assume the monarchy, made by Abimelech, with the encouragement and support of the men of Shechem, failed, not only because of the moral failure of the "first" king and the capriciousness of his supporters, but also because the willingness had not yet ripened in the men of Israel to yield their natural freedom in exchange for enslavement to an arbitrary and profitless regime.

---

26 Simon, 18, deals thoroughly with this phrase.

27 2 Kgs 18: 20, 21, 25; 5: 6; 10: 2; Ezra 4: 11, 17. And see L. Loewenstamm, "Mikhtaw," *EB* IV, 966–974.

f. The historical and social background of the fable

The attempts made to find a socio-historical underpinning for the fable, on the basis of the anti-monarchial ideology it expresses, have been no more than guesswork.[28] Those who have sought its actual link with the history of Israel in intra-biblical testimony follow contrary directions with regard to the epoch. On the one hand, some connect its anti-monarchial ideology to the negative attitude to monarchy in the prophecy of Hosea (whom they consider the first of the prophets to oppose the monarchy as an institution); these date the fable to the second half of the eighth century BCE, the period of moral and political decline of the kingdom of Israel. They also attribute to this period Gideon's negative reply to the "men of Israel" (Jud 8: 22), and the negative attitude to establishing a monarchy in Israel in Samuel's words to the people (1 Sam 8; and cf. I Sam 12).

These scholars assume that the ideology of negating the monarchy developed only after the weaknesses of the monarchy had become manifestly clear and in consequence of its failure as an institution. In fact, only the later editors (the Deuteronomists) projected this negation backward to antedate the establishment of the monarchy in Israel. Despite the identity of outlook between the fable and the historiographic and prophetic sources we have cited regarding the monarchy, there is an essential difference between them, namely, the absence in the fable of any national-religious argument regarding the monarchy as a sin against God; by contrast, Samuel considered the people's demand for a king to be set over them as a betrayal of God's grace and a refutation of God's kingship.

Likewise the prophet Hosea: "I will destroy you, O Israel; who can help you? Where now is your king, to save you. . . Those of whom you said, 'Give me a king and princes'? I have given you kings in my anger, and I have taken them away in my wrath" (13: 9–11; and see also 8: 4). Jotham (and, if you will, the ancient fabulist) regarded monarchy only as crass stupidity and suicide. This essential difference is what makes the anti-monarchial fable a satire.

Other scholars have tried to attach the anti-monarchial fable to the end of the period of the Judges, and to find in it an echo of the debate that arose in Israel over the passage to the system of an established monarchy. They, too, however, ignore the fact that the fable, with its universal sapiential qualities, does not suit the theocratic anti-monarchial ideology concomitant

---

28 A. Malamat, *Toledoth 'am yisra'el* I (Tel Aviv, 1969), 76–77 (Hebrew).

with the establishment of the monarchy in Israel and which found expression in the historiographic and prophetic sources mentioned above. That is, the fable does not come from the same creative milieu as the theocratic anti-monarchial ideology. It represents different groups; its milieu is in the Wisdom circles. In its pragmatic and universal qualities it reflects knowledge and life experience beyond defined territorial and national boundaries. As such, it suits various societies at various historical periods and in various geographical locations, whose common denominator is opposition to exchanging beneficial natural liberties for stark power suffused with the peril of annihilation. Therefore, those who seek to place the anti-monarchical ideology of the fable in the social and economic setting of the regime of the Judges in Israel overstep the mark, and largely disregard the independent and universal status of the fable as a witty and sophisticated sapiential work.[29]

In this sense, making the fable a part of the narrative historiographic corpus is like making the "Judgement of the King" (1 Sam 8: 11–17), which also is an independent unit, part of the description of the dispute between Samuel and the people over the monarchy. Like the latter, this fable serves as a typological example, and even though it reflects ancient conditions, it should not necessarily be identified with a specific and defined experience in the history of Israel. Thus, there is justification for the caution displayed by Tadmor, who stated that "from the typological viewpoint an ancient setting is reflected here that conforms with the transitional periods—the days of the formation of the monarchy."[30] Even more care is called for in fixing a definite historical point for the fable.

It is otherwise regarding the application of the fable (the so-called moral), which serves the purposes of the narrator of the political Abimelech episode. It is imbued with a note of satire aimed at the "men of Shechem," whose support for Abimelech's enthronement and whose betrayal of him were apparently actual historical events. It should be recalled in particular that this city had an earlier tradition of a Canaanite monarchy.

2. The Fable of Jehoash (2 Kgs 14: 8–10; 2 Chron 25: 17–19)

The main qualities that characterized Jotham's fable are also represented in miniature in the fable of Jehoash.

---

29 G. F. Moore, *Judges* (ICC; Edinburgh, 1958), 246.
30 Tadmor (n. 10), 322–323; see also B. Mazar in the same volume, 327–328.

a. Here, too, there is personification of trees, expressed in the spoken communication among them and the application to plants of a set of relationships typical for human society. It is the marriage proposal: "A thistle in Lebanon sent to a cedar in Lebanon, saying, 'Give your daughter to my son for a wife'" (v 9ab).

b. Its elliptical ending: "And a wild beast of Lebanon passed by and trampled down the thistle" (v 9b). The cedar's reply to the proposal by the thistle is not stated here, just as in Jotham's fable the trees' reply to the threats of the bramble is not told.

c. The independence of the fable and its secondary attachment to the literary unit in which it is set, demarcated by the opening that precedes it, "And Jehoash king of Israel sent word to Amaziah king of Judah" (v 9aa), and the reply in direct speech by Jehoash to Amaziah that follows it, "You have indeed smitten Edom, and your heart has lifted you up" (v 10). The extraction of the fable from the framework of the negotiations being conducted between the two rival kings just eases the flow of the reading and the understanding of the exchange of political messages that preceded the military confrontation between them.

d. The tension between the fable (v 9) and the moral in verse 10 is self-evident, deriving as it does from the complete absence of accord between them; and it raises a similar problem to that discussed in connection with Jotham's fable: the relationship between the fable and its moral. It is no surprise, therefore, that here, too, differences emerged among interpreters of the meaning of the fable. On the one hand there is Rashi's allegorical and historical exposition, which likens the thistle in Lebanon to Shechem the son of Hamor, the cedar to Jacob, and the wild beast that tramples the thistle to the sons of Jacob who came upon the slain (cf. the story of Dinah, Gen 34). On the other hand, there are those who deny any connection between the fable and the moral.[31]

Here also there is a fable from the plant and animal world, which apparently had an independent existence and was borrowed for the requirements of a political polemic. The barbs of its satire are aimed at Amaziah, who felt the urge to spark a war against Jehoash, king of Israel, who was more powerful than he. This adoption of the fable was accomplished through the two-way metaphorical use of personification. On the one hand, the plants of

---

31 Ehrlich, *Mikra ki-Pheshuto* II, 364; and also N. H. Snaith, *IB* III (New York, 1954), 262: "Since the story is a parable and not an allegory there is no need to seek to identify the wild beast."

Lebanon were likened to people, wishing to enter into a marriage bond for political purposes (v 9). On the other hand, the differences in external power of the rival kings were compared to external differences in height between the plants: the cedar, which is lofty and represents strength and grandeur, against the mean thistle, which is trampled by the "wild beast"—(a third element included in the fable, which stimulates guesses as to whom, or what, the fabulist aimed at).[32]

The connection between these two directions, and of course between the fable and the moral, is the thistle, and as Rashi states in his commentary, "It is an image of contempt that he likened him to the thistle." The image of "the cedar on Lebanon" in this fable is introduced as a contrast, to emphasize the lowliness and worthlessness of the thistle, and to a certain extent it is parallel to the fruit-bearing trees which appear as a contrast to the bramble in Jotham's fable. "Cedars of Lebanon" also appear unexpectedly at the end of Jotham's fable (Jud 9: 15), but they play no central role in the drama itself, serving as a kind of common symbol for the two fables. Thus, we return to the "genes" from which the politically satirical fable developed: the image for the purpose of ridicule and derision, emphasis on the absence of logic by means of contrast and polarization of opposites.

"Cedars of Lebanon" served as a reservoir for many similes in the Bible, some of them also allegorical (cf. Ezek 17). The satirical use of the simile of the cedar in this fable is reminiscent of its use in Jeremiah's reproof of Jehoiakim, king of Judah: "Do you think you are a king because you compete in cedar?" (Jer 22: 15). This rhetorical taunting question appears in the middle of a taunt elegy on the fate of Jehoiakim (vv 13–19), and somewhat impairs its consistency.[33] For the purpose of a polemic against Jehoiakim was there an implant of a prevalent metaphor here, the likening of the good king to the cedar by the prophet?[34] Or was it perhaps relocated here from the fable of Jehoash about the thistle and the cedar? In any event, this polemical rhetorical question well matches the fable of Jehoash, and complements it. The text may be understood thus: You, the thistle (Amaziah)—will you reign (can you continue your rule), when you dare to compete with the cedar (with me, Jehoash)?!

[32] Simon, 12.

[33] A different division of the unit is found in R. P. Carroll, *Jeremiah* (OTL; London, 1986), 426ff., who distinguishes between the "owe saying" (vv 13–15a) that closes with a satirical question: "Do you think you are a king that you compete in cedar?" where the force of the question could be: "Are you playing at being a king that you compete in cedar?" and vv 15b-17 that follow it.

[34] Cf. Ehrlich, *Mikra ki-Pheshuto*, III, 225–226, who rejects the proposal to read "Ahaz" (following the LXX) instead of "Erez."

—— ℬ 4 ℭ ——

ELEMENTS OF POLITICAL SATIRE
IN BIBLICAL NARRATIVE

The feature common to the two literary units considered in this chapter, the account of the Tower of Babel (Gen 11: 1–9) and "Is Saul also among the prophets?" (1 Sam 19: 20–24), is very general. Therefore, the term "narrative" has been chosen for the chapter heading. Common to them both, apart from their being transmissions of events or occurrences that befell particular people, is etiology: the purpose of the accounts, as is attested through the concluding formulation "therefore," is to explain the origin of a name or a popular proverb. The differences between the two episodes are great and need not be set out in detail here. Briefly, in terms of the distinction generally applied by scholarship to the types of biblical narrative, the first of the two stories belongs to the etiological legends, while the second is a popular tale. A further difference concerns their literary topography: the first merges into the universal ethnographic framework of the beginnings of humankind set forth in chapters 1–11 of Genesis; the second forms a part of the texture of Israelite historiography, relating to the beginning of the monarchy in Israel mostly described in 1 Samuel.

1. Elements of political satire in the story of the Tower of Babel

The story of the Tower of Babel (Gen 11: 1–9) was already deemed a satire by some of the modern commentators on Genesis. Cassuto describes it, albeit with some hesitation, as ". . . a kind of satire against what was considered magnificence and glory in the eyes of the Babylonians, a sort of

parody of what they were accustomed to say and relate."[1] N. Sarna finds
that a general air of satirical hostility to pagan notions pervades the story,
with respect to the concepts, mythology and religious forms of paganism;[2]
G. von Rad infers from the story that "God's movement must therefore be
understood as a remarkable satire on man's doing;"[3] and E. Speiser considers the account "criticism of man's folly and presumption."[4]

However, beyond the universal satirical screen of the tale lies an Israelite historiosophical tendency, whose barb is directed against Babylon
as a world superpower, and with which Israel kept a historical account. We
base this exposition on a literary analysis of the tale, including its materials
and formal components, and on its historical topology, which rests principally on biblical sources.

*a. The etiological nature of the story and its link with
the ethnological framework*

A link connects the story called "The Tower of Babel," or "The Generation of Separation" (Gen 11: 1–9), to the account entitled "The Table of
the Nations" (chapter 10) that precedes it, even though it differs entirely
in tendency, nature and literary form.[5] Using genealogies, the Table of the
Nations describes the division of humankind that remained after the flood,
namely, the sons of Noah, into peoples, countries and languages, as a natural genealogical process. The story of the Tower of Babel is intended to
explain why humankind spread over the earth and their language became
confused, its underlying assumption being that previously "the whole earth
had one language and the same words." At first sight, the account is still un-
aware of the division of humankind into peoples, languages and countries as
listed in the Table of the Nations.[6] In spite of differences in content and style
between these two units, a thematic connection between them is evident,
without, for the moment, our determining whether the account of the Tower
of Babel (11: 1–9) is earlier than the Table of the Nations, or whether it is

[1] U. Cassuto, *A Commentary on the Book of Genesis, Part II: From Noah to Abraham*
(Jerusalem, 1974[6]), 154–169 (Hebrew).

[2] N. M. Sarna, *Understanding Genesis* (New York, 1970), 76.

[3] G. von Rad, *Genesis* (OTL; London, 1966), 143–148.

[4] E.A. Speiser, *Genesis* (AB; Garden City NY, 1964), 74–76.

[5] Sarna, *Genesis*, 64ff.

[6] J. Skinner, *Genesis* (ICC; Edinburgh, 1930[2]), 224; J. Sasson, "The 'Tower of Babel'
as a Clue to the Redactional History," in: *The Bible World* (New York, 1980), 211–219.

later and was inserted into the ethnological-genealogical framework (chaps 10, 11: 10–32) only at the redaction stage. It is apparent that the account of the Tower of Babel, as an etiological legend, is tendentious. Unlike the Table of the Nations, which depicts the map of ethnic, linguistic and geographical distribution naturally and impartially, with no value judgments, the narrator of the human dispersal in the story of the Tower of Babel expresses his opinion as to why a revolutionary change occurred in human history. In this sense it is to some extent like other etiological narratives of the beginnings of humankind (Gen 1–11).

b. The unity of the story

Although "The Tower of Babel" is the common title of the story, the two connected nouns in the name are regarded by several commentators as secondary and as not representative of the true essence of the story— "Babel" because it is like the application of midrashic names at the end of other etiological episodes;[7] and "tower" because it is distinct from the "city" (vv 4–5). The juxtaposition of the two nouns is regarded as a combination of two different recensions (the latter in fact being the first)[8], or at least a combination of two separate motifs—one, the spread of humankind (vv 8, 9b); the other, the confusion of language (vv 7, 9a).[9]

It is noteworthy that even if the story was composed from the combination of different versions, or different motifs, in the form before us it is an integral story, with greater literary and ideological force than if each of the two motifs had remained independent. This is because the merging of the motifs makes fiercer and sharper the confrontation between humankind and the divinity, which forms the core of this legend. The confrontation is between earth, presented here as the personification of humankind— "Now the whole earth had one language and the same words" (v 1; cf. v 9: "the language of all the earth")—and the divinity, presented here anthropomorphically—"And the Lord came down to see the city" (v 5; also "And the Lord said. . . So the Lord scattered. . . the Lord confused. . . the Lord scattered them"—vv 6, 8, 9). The divinity is even presented in one instance as a collective unity, parallel to that of humans, as indicated by the sentence spoken by God: "Come, let us go down, and there confuse their language"

---

7 I. L. Seeligmann, "Aetiological Elements in Biblical Historiography," *Zion* 26 (1961), 114–169 (Hebrew).

8 H. Gunkel, *Genesis,* (Göttingen, 1969), 92ff.

9 C. Westermann, *Genesis 1–11,* (London, 1984), 535ff.

(v 7), parallel to what is spoken by men: "Come, let us make bricks . . ." (v 3; also, "Come, let us build ourselves a city . . .," v 4).[10]

In the confrontation that occurs, the "city" and the "tower" serve only as symbols. They represent the spontaneous desire of the human race to build its world for itself independently and unrestrained. Obviously, they arouse the suspicions and fears of God that humankind's united initiative will limit his absolute rule on earth. The attempts to separate two different recensions of the story, the dispersion of humankind and the confusion of its language, or the city and the tower, limit and blur the confrontation; it is precisely the tower, with "its top in the heavens," and which can approximate man to God (cf. Jacob's ladder, Gen 28: 12), that here constitutes a decisive factor in the clash between them, and also a principal reason for the dispersal of humankind "upon the face of the whole earth" (v 4). The confrontation as the central axis of the story is also attested by the structure of the narrative and the relationship among its various component parts.

c. The structure of the story and its artistic form

Different commentators have pointed out the complex chiastic structure[11] of the story and its artistic form.[12] The first half recounts the actions of humans (vv 1–4), ending in a declaration of their intent (v 4b); the second half (vv 6–9) describes God's response to this initiative, but in the reverse order to theirs: first, God's intention (vv 6–7), then God's action is expressed (vv 8–9). Verse 5 is a kind of connecting link, or a bolt joining the two parts set opposite each other. In the two parts, especially in the discussion regarding humans, wordplays are present, based on alliteration and assonance: הבה (v 7) as against הבה (v 3); ויפץ (v 8) as against נפוץ (v 4); and even in the etymology of the name: "Therefore its name (שמה) was called Babel" (v 8), as against "and let us make a name (שם) for ourselves" (v 4).

Yet it is doubtful that those who draw conclusions from this as to the unity and integrity of the entire story are correct.[13] It is hard to ignore the fact that at least verses 1 and 9b are the work of a composer who blended the story into the framework of primeval history. Still, there is

---

10 The building of a city is mentioned before, in Gen 4: 17.

11 J. Wenham, *Genesis 1–15* (WBC 1, Texas, 1987), 235: "It is possible also to see the narrative as a palistroph, or extended chiasmus."

12 J. P. Fokkelmann, *Narrative Art in Genesis* (Amsterdam, 1975), 11–45.

13 Contra Cassuto, *Genesis* 158–162, and Fokkelmann (n. 12), who followed him in this respect.

no doubt that the artistic structure attests to a complete literary design, not a mere patchwork.

d. The ideological significance of the story

The discussion of the story opened with the statement that the tale is tendentious, but what the tendency is, and what the ideological significance reflected in it is, are a subject of debate among old and modern commentators. The dispute centers on the question of the relationship between the punishment meted out to the "Generation of Separation" and the sin it committed. The almost universally accepted assumption is that the members of that generation did sin, and there is no punishment without sin.[14]

Against those who argue that here there is a sin against God and deduce the sin according to the punishment, Abarbanel argued[15] that if there is a sin here, it is a sin of humankind against itself, against its natural purpose. In his terms, it is the desire for artificial things and luxuriousness. Nevertheless, he too views God's reaction as punishment for an act by humans and he regards them as interdependent: the sinning humans were punished spiritually: God confused their language and scattered them over the face of the earth. Westermann[16] offers a similar interpretation, although he uses modern imagery. He applies the term "metropolis" to characterize the revolutionary transformation that has taken place in human history with the building of the "city." However, he sees the principal shift in the introduction of the motif of building a tower with its top in the heavens. With the tower humankind's desire reaches the point of realizing its grandeur with vast enterprises. Although this desire is not directed against God, and it is entirely a desire imprinted in humans themselves, it contains the danger of their bursting out of their natural limitations and threatens their existence.

A different explanation of the conflict between humans and God in this story, negating the conventional assumption of sin and punishment, was proposed by B. Jacob.[17] He discarded the view that there was any sin in the acts of the "Generation of Separation"; this, at least, was not their initial intention. Following Ibn Ezra and Ralbag, he interpreted their actions as an

---

14 See, for example, Talmud Babli, *Sanhedrin* 109a.

15 I. Abarbanel, *Perush ha-torah* (a photographed copy of the Warsaw edition of 1862) (Jerusalem, 1954), 33f.

16 Westermann, *Genesis,* 554.

17 B. Jacob, *Das erste Buch der Tora—Genesis* (Berlin, 1934), 300ff.

effort to survive. They did not wish to ascend to heaven and to succeed God, but to survive on earth—by consolidation. Obviously, God's reaction is not a punishment, for it is not the scattering of a people dwelling in its land, but the spread of humankind throughout the world. This conclusion may follow inevitably from the purpose that God intended for humans, and it may be the realization of the blessing God bestowed on them: "Be fruitful and multiply, and fill the earth" (Gen 1: 27; 9: 7);[18] otherwise there would have been no reason or need for the creation of so wide a world. Their attempt to build a city for themselves that would contain all humankind was a sort of infringement of the divine plan of populating the great world, and this entailed the response of God, who prevented it.

It is not sin and punishment, therefore, but a conflict between the intentions of two unequal forces. This is what makes the deed of humans ridiculous. God is not angered by human action, for it is not immoral. God simply laughs at and mocks them for their vain attempt to achieve their desires. Benno Jacob thus reached the conclusion that the account before us is a sharp irony against humankind; he interpreted it as divine irony: "He who sits in the heavens laughs; the Lord has them in derision" (Ps 2: 4).[19] But if this is irony, it is nothing other than tragic irony of human beings against themselves, their efforts to realize their desires being in advance doomed to failure and to the contrary result: humans wished to unite for the purpose of ensuring their existence, and were scattered by the decree of God. All the world spoke one language and used the same words, and God confused their language.[20] Might there even be here an indirect criticism of God, who created the human in his image, and gave him dominion over the works of his hands (Ps 8: 7)? Yet precisely when humans have activated their God-given faculties which distinguish them from beasts— language (v 1), technological capability (v 3), purposeful thinking and memory (cf. v 4: "and let us make a name for ourselves")—God is filled with concern because "nothing that they propose to do will now be impossible for them" (v 7).

---

18 B. Jacob, *Genesis,* 301; however, Ibn Ezra preceded him in this observation: see his comment on Gen 11: 7–8, "And the Lord scattered them, and it was for their benefit . . ." (Hebrew).

19 B. Jacob, Genesis, 302; cf. also G. von Rad, *Genesis,* 145; and see: A. Richardson, *Genesis I–IX* (London, 1953), 124ff.

20 The clue to the distinction among different types of irony, and "tragic irony" in particular, in I. M. Kikawada's article "The Shape of Genesis 11:1–9," in J.J. Jackson and M. Kessler (eds.), *Rhetorical Criticism* (Pittsburgh, 1974), 29–30.

The chief ideological import of the story lies in the "confrontation," for the confrontation arose when humans tried to realize the image of God in themselves in a contrived unity: "one people and one language," "a tower with its top in the heavens," "and let us make a name for ourselves." Yet it is actually God who reacted in a way common to humans: he who dwells in the heavens goes down to see the city and the tower, hears their language, and is filled with dread and jealousy lest he lose his exclusive rule because of their consolidation. And he even speaks in the plural form, as they do. God's reaction cannot therefore be explained on theological grounds, as many commentators hold, arguing that the "Generation of Separation" was punished because of its sin. The characters in the story are not deniers or challengers of God, who is not even mentioned in their speeches. This confrontation is not like that in the passage "The kings of earth set themselves and the rulers take counsel together against the Lord and his anointed" (Ps 2: 1ff); or like that described in Ps 14: 1–2, which contains a similar motif: "The fool says in his heart, 'There is no God.' They are corrupt, they do abominable deeds, there is none that does good. The Lord looks down from heaven upon the children of men, to see if there are any that act wisely and seek after God."[21] So if irony is present in the story, it is a two-way irony, born out of a paradox: humans and God have exchanged their roles. This interpretation, much as it concurs with the inner sense of the narrative, does not accord with the ending. This refers mainly to verse 9, which concludes the account with an etiological and etymological explanation, expressing the name Babylon (בבל) in the confusion (בלל) of languages and ascribing the scattering of humankind to this geographical and historical center. By means of this verse, there is a shift from paradoxical irony to political satire and a leap from primeval existence to historical reality.[22]

e. From irony against humankind to political satire against Babylon

Various scholars observed that hidden in the midrashic derivation of the name "Babel"—"because there the Lord confused (בלל) the language of all the earth"—is a satirical sting aimed against the mighty Babylonian empire; yet they interpreted it differently. Those who regarded this passage as an integral part of a consistent, entire narrative expounded the whole story accordingly and attributed its origin to an Israelite author. Cassuto

21 Cf. the parallel in Ps 53: 1–2.
22 Westermann, *Genesis,* 534ff.

went far in this direction, explaining the entire story as an Israelite parody of the account of the Babylonians: "You called your city Babylon the Gate of God (bab-ili) and your tower 'the house of the foundation of heaven and earth,' and you did not know that only God himself, in his own glory, and no man can determine where the Gate of God is, and you did not know that the heavens are God's and only the earth did he give to men . . ."[23] Thus, his satirical-parodic interpretation bound the name "Babel" with the building of the tower and with the sin of paganism, in keeping with his view of the unity of the narrative and the unity of the Torah.[24] He went still farther in as-cribing the account historically to suit his perception of the ancient origin of the Torah, calculating the historical setting of the composition of the story as the time of the destruction of Babylon after it fell to the Hittites, in the second half of the second millennium BCE.[25]

But Cassuto's assumption is untenable. Babylon did not face destruc-tion after its overthrow by the Hittites; even in the days of its decline it was the capital of the kings of Kassite Babylonia. His exposition certainly does not explain why the scattering of humankind was the outcome of its en-deavor to build a city and a tower for itself in Babylon.

Several of the critical scholars took a similar path in quest of ancient Babylonian remnants in this story. They posited that the Israelite author was acquainted with Babylonian literary sources. In particular, they meant the Babylonian account of the creation, the *Enuma elis*, in which they found parallels to the story of the building of Babylon and the tower whose top was in the heavens,[26] although in the Babylonian account of the creation the temple was built as Marduk's sanctuary, and not for the defense of humans against their dispersal over the face of all the earth, as in our story. These

---

23 Cassuto, *Genesis*, 157.

24 Cassuto, *The Documentary Hypothesis and the Composition of the Pentateuch* (Jeru-salem, 1961) (Hebrew).

25 Cassuto, *Genesis*, 158.

26 *Enuma elis*, tablet IV, lines 55–58:

> When Marduk heard this/ Brightly glowed his features like the day/ 'Construct Babylon, whose building you have requested/ Let its brickwork be fashioned. You shall name it The Sanctuary.'

See also lines 62–64:

> They raised high the head of Esagila equaling Apsu./ Having built a stage-tower as high as Apsu./ They set up in it an abode for Marduk, Enlil (and) Ea.

The citations are from J. B. Pritchard *ANET* [2] (Princeton, 1969), 68–69.

scholars indeed exercised greater caution in determining the relationship between the Babylonian literary materials and the writer of the account in Genesis, as they did in dating the historical background of the author. Speiser estimated that the biblical narrator employed Babylonian materials and data[27] for the purpose of his criticism of humans' folly and presumption, and gave them his own interpretation. This narrator should be identified with the "Jahwist,"[28] whose literary work is usually dated not before the time of the monarchy in Israel.[29] Sarna argues that the Bible deliberately "chose" the city of Babylon and its famous temple of the god Marduk as the focus "of a satire on paganism, its concepts, its mythology, and its religious forms."[30] When the Bible "chose" to settle accounts with paganism, he does not state. Might it be only later, in the time of the post-exilic prophet Isaiah (the second), the great exemplar of the polemic against paganism?

Westermann rejected the view of scholars who attributed the origin of the story to Babylon, and also of those proposing an Israelite source for the story because they saw it as a polemic against Babylon. He believed that both extreme opinions had fallen into methodological error by making Babylon the focus of the story, which it was not.[31] In his view, the core of the tale was humanity, and like other narratives about the primeval history of humankind (Gen 1–10) it cannot be stated with certainty where it was created. The fact that no parallels have so far been found for the story among the neighbors of Israel indicates that it was designed in Israel, and that it certainly underwent a lengthy process orally and in writing until it attained its present form.

Still, he hesitates to give a clear opinion as to when the story was composed, and does not venture to suggest a different author from the one to whom the story is attributed by the documentary hypothesis, namely, the "Jahwist."[32] But in his discussion of the purpose of the narrative and its ideological point, he indicates an ideological-religious link between the motif of "the tower with its top in the heavens" and the mockery of Babylon

---

[27] E.A. Speiser, "Word Play on the Creation Epic's Version of the Founding of Babylon," *Orientalia* 25 (1956), 317–323.

[28] Speiser, *Genesis,* 74.

[29] Speiser, *Genesis,* Introduction, xxviii.

[30] Sarna, *Understanding Genesis,* 76.

[31] Westermann, *Genesis,* 540.

[32] Westermann, *Genesis,* 541, disagrees with Eissfeldt, who ascribed the story to L (a pre-Jahwistic layer); however, he agrees that it had originated long before it was fashioned by J.

in the prophecies of Isaiah (14: 13–14) and Jeremiah (chaps 51, 53) concerning the wish of the king of Babylon to ascend to the heavens and to be like the supreme being. But he drew no conclusions from this link regarding the historical and cultural background—none, certainly, regarding the political circumstances on whose account the story's author aimed his barb at Babylon. It stands to reason that if Isaiah, to whom is ascribed the taunt elegy against the king of Babylon (see below, chapter 6),[33] and Jeremiah (chaps 51, 53) hurl their arrows at Babylon, this provides a historical explanation associated with the rise of Babylon as a world power and with its role in respect of the nations of the world in general and Israel in particular.

This in itself indicates (according to the prevailing outlook of Bible scholarship) a far later period than that when the "Jahwist" was active. It is still more important that the historical and political lesson of the rise of Babylon to world power is reflected satirically in the story of the Tower of Babel. It is that Babylon, with its desire to center the unification of the entire world on itself, that was the very power that exiled peoples from their lands and scattered them across·the face of the earth. Its rule led to the confusion of languages and a medley of tongues, when it mixed different peoples and languages within its area of dominance.[34] Likely, if not decisive, evidence of this may be found in the prophecies of Jeremiah against Babylon. In them the abrupt switch from the prophecy at the beginning of the reign of Jehoiakim son of Josiah (Jer 27) to the prophecies on the destruction of Babylon (chaps 50–51) is most evident. In the prophecy in chapter 27 the king of Judah is commanded, in the name of the Lord of hosts, God of Israel, to serve Nebuchadnezzar king of Babylon, whom God installed over all the lands and over all the beasts of the field. In the divine command, which declares that "it is I who by my great power and my outstretched arm have made the earth with the men and animals that are on the earth and I give it to whomever it seems right to me" (v 5), God gives world dominion to his servant the king of Babylon, and he warns his chosen

---

[33] On questions concerning the historical setting of this elegy and whether or not it was composed by Isaiah, see below, chapter six.

[34] Kramer pointed out a Sumerian parallel to the confusion of languages (in the biblical story of the Tower of Babel) in the Epic of Enmerkar (ca 2000 BCE). See his articles "Man's Golden Age: A Sumerian Parallel to Genesis 11:1," *JAOS* (1943), 191–192 and "The Babel of Tongues: A Sumerian Version," *JAOS* 88 (1968), 108–11. Yet he himself was aware of the fundamental difference between the two stories. While the reason for the confusion of languages in the Sumerian epic is the rivalry between the two gods Enki and Enlil, in the biblical story it is among the people.

people, Judah, not to rebel against this king but to bring their neck under his yoke (v 12).[35]

Some years later, following the bitter historical experience of world rule by Babylon, especially the destruction of Jerusalem and the Temple and the exile of Judah from their land, Jeremiah prophesied the destruction of Babylon. In an elegy, which contains more than a trace of malicious joy at the great crisis that visited Babylon, he laments,

> "How the hammer of the whole earth is cut down and broken! How Babylon has become a horror among the nations! I set a snare for you and you were taken, O Babylon, and you did not know it; you were found and caught because you strove against the Lord" (50: 23–24).

In contrast to the prophecy in which Jeremiah called in the name of the Lord to all the peoples to serve the king of Babylon (chap 27), now he exhorts them to

> "Flee from the midst of Babylon, let every man save his life! Be not cut off in her punishment for this is the time of the Lord's vengeance, the requital he is rendering her. Babylon was a golden cup in the Lord's hand, making all the earth drunken; the nations drank of her wine, therefore the nations went mad. Suddenly Babylon has fallen and been broken," etc. (vv 6–8).[36]

It is doubtful whether Jeremiah was acquainted with the story of the Tower of Babel, but the lot of the peoples of the earth was dependent on the world centrality of Babylon. The confusion that Babylon caused, just when the peoples placed in it their expectations, reflected so equivocally in Jeremiah's prophecies, probably served as a historical experiential anchor for the story of the "Generation of Separation" in Babylon. In a more concrete way the connection was preserved between the tower whose top was in the heavens and God's judgment against Babylon in Jeremiah's prophecy: "Though Babylon should mount up to heaven, and though she should fortify her strong height, yet destoyers would come from me upon her, says the

---

[35] Opinions are divided as to the authorship and the dating of this prophecy. Y. Kaufmann, *The History of the Religion of Israel*, 456–457 (Hebrew), considers it an authentic prophecy of Jeremiah and dates it to the beginning of Jehoiakim's reign (604 BCE). By contrast, R. P. Carroll, *Jeremiah* (OTL, London, 1986), 531f., ascribes it to a later period.

[36] There are contradictory opinions about the relationship between this prophecy and the prophecy of chapter 27: see Kaufmann, n. 35, on the one hand, and Carroll, n. 35, 814–817, on the other.

Lord" (51: 53). A similar motif appears in a more developed and biting way in the taunt elegy of Isaiah (Isa 14: 12–20).

Apparently, therefore, the story of the "Generation of Separation" in Babel should be ascribed to the historical setting of the end of kingdom of Judah. The satirical element present in the story does not, indeed, detail the historical events of the period. It is veiled, more being hidden than revealed, and in the manner of satire it clings to symbols. The choice of "Babel" as the place from which humans were scattered and where the languages were confused is not fortuitous. Even if it lacks the criticism and judgment in terms of morality and values found in the prophecies of Isaiah and Jeremiah, the symbol remains: the Tower of Babel, the symbol of the failure to unite all humankind, a source of misunderstanding between humans and the centerpoint from which the peoples are scattered. At this is aimed the hidden satirical barb of the biblical author, who in the depiction of the primordial history of humankind reflected his own historical experience.

2. Between irony and satire in a popular tale: "Is Saul also among the prophets?"

The popular proverb "Is Saul also among the prophets?" appears in two different narratives describing Saul's prophecy among a band of prophets. One is in 1 Samuel 10: 10–12, the other in 1 Samuel 19: 20–24.

In this discussion, which attempts to discern satirical elements in the popular legend, main interest lies in the account of Saul's prophesying at Naioth (1 Sam 19: 20–24). But this cannot be pursued without a consideration of its relationship with its parallel in 1 Samuel 10: 10–12. Both accounts end with an etiological explanation commencing with "therefore," followed by the saying in the form of a question "Is Saul also among the prophets?" The relationship between them has merited various explanations, which may be grouped around two main approaches. One is that the two stories refer to the same saying but are independent; each of them made its own use of it for its own purposes and with its own leaning, without being aware of the other.[37] The second, and preferable perception, is that the narrator of Saul's prophesying at Naioth (1 Sam 19, 20–22) was familiar

---

37 H. Gressmann, *Die älteste Gesichtsschreibung und Prophetie Israels* (Göttingen, 1921), 82; J. Strudy, "The Original Meaning of 'Is Saul also among the Prophets?'" *VT* 20 (1970) 207–213; N. H. Tur-Sinai, *Ha-lashon We-ha-sepher* (Jerusalem, 1960[2]), 233–237 (Hebrew).

with the story of his prophetic seizure at Gibeah (1 Sam 10, 10–12) and adapted it to his own goals.[38] Naturally, the creative milieu of this story differs from the first, which is earlier.[39]

a. Differences in function and tendency between the two stories

The first story is a main link in the description of Saul's introduction to his destiny as God's anointed (1 Sam 10: 1–16). His "prophesying" (*hithnab'uth*) among a band of prophets at Gibeath-elohim serves as a sign that God is with him (vv 5–7). It is connected with the metamorphosis which in anthropological language may be termed "rebirth," in biblical language being "turned into another man" (v 7). That is, the coming of the spirit of God generates a change from the naive youth portrayed in the story of the search for the asses (chap 9) to the war-leader (*nagid*) over the people of Israel.[40] The prevailing tone of the story is one of favor towards Saul. Samuel, having instructed Saul with signs after anointing him with oil (10: 2–7), separates from him immediately (10: 9), so that in the scene of the prophesying itself he plays no part at all; but in the scene of the "prophesying" in the second story he plays an active part—"Samuel standing as head" over the prophesying prophets (19: 20). The climax of the prophetic experience, the coming of God's spirit upon Saul and his prophesying among the band of prophets, is accompanied by an etiological anecdote concerning the astonishment created by his prophesying among all those previously acquainted with him: "The people said to one another, 'What has come over the son of Kish? Is Saul also among the prophets?'" (v 11).

This astonishment should not be interpreted[41] as bewilderment at how a man of Saul's standing can attach himself to a band of prophets of inferior status,[42] but as just the opposite, as others explain it—as surprise at the honor that has fallen to Saul's lot, he being found worthy to enter the

---

[38] H. P. Smith, *The Books of Samuel* (ICC, Edinburgh, 1961), 181; P.K. McCarter, *I Samuel* (AB; New York, 1984), 331.

[39] M. Buber ascribes the first etiology, which is the older one in his view, to a tradition that favored Saul; he ascribes the later etiology to fanatics close to the House of David. See his book *Darko shel Mikra* (Jerusalem, 1978), 204f. (Hebrew).

[40] Z. Weisman, "Anointing as a Motif in the Making of the Charismatic King," *Biblica* 57 (1976) 378–398.

[41] *BDB*, 209: "Often questions, expressed in a tone of surprise, or put rhetorically . . ."; see also Strudy (n. 37), 210.

[42] M. H. Segal, *The Books of Samuel* (Jerusalem, 1964), 78 (Hebrew); H. W. Herzberg, *I & II Samuel* (OTL; London, 1982), 86.

company of the prophets.[43] But the astonishment, which is not without a trace of irony, is connected to Saul himself, and stems from the sudden transformation that has occurred with his prophesying in the company of the prophesiers, characterized by loss of previous identity, an event that to his acquaintances appears as an extreme change in his image.[44] It is not by chance, therefore, that the details describing his prophetic frenzy in the second story and which have been interpreted as derisive and mocking— "And he too stripped off his clothes," "and he lay naked all that day and all that night" (19: 24)—are absent from the first story (10: 10–12). Despite the irony in the first anecdote of his prophecy (which actually seems to have originated in the circle of his friends and acquaintances), it is remote from the tendency to belittle his worth and to denigrate his authority as king, as is expressed in the parallel story.

A different tone, not devoid of a satirical barb, pervades the second anecdote. This is evident in both the popular tale itself and the context. Saul the king, who wishes to kill David (19: 1ff), is caught up unwillingly among a company of prophets prophesying before Samuel at Naioth in Ramah. He is obliged to go there himself after three delegations of messengers he sent failed in their attempts to bring David to him, "and they also prophesied" (19: 20, 21). There is no hint that David, who fled from Saul, was also among the prophesiers. Saul's prophesying in these circumstances is not a sign of his being chosen for a divine mission to his people, but symbolizes his failure as the anointed king before the prophet Samuel, who had turned his back to him, and his abasement in his lying naked before Samuel (v 24). The rift between him and Samuel had not healed and the two had not met since the parting at Gilgal (15: 34–35); therefore, there is more than a grain of ridicule in the fact that the meeting between them this time occurs with Saul being in a state of absolute senselessness as a result of his prophesying before Samuel, "and lay naked all that day and all that night" (19: 24).

But that is not all: David succeeds in escaping Saul yet again, apparently after witnessing the shameful scene in which the king strips off his clothes and lies naked before the old prophet who spurned him. Buber, not surprisingly, regards this account as "a base act of wickedness" and concludes that "the editor of this version was one of the fanatics of those close

---

43 Thus Kimhi in his commentary on this saying in I Sam 10: 12 (Hebrew).

44 S. Abramsky, *Samuel* (Enc. 'Olam ha-Tenakh) (Jerusalem & Ramat Gan, 1985), 103 (Hebrew).

to the House of David, who wished to add still more ignominy to David's enemies."[45] McCarter considers the story a parody containing an attempt by the author to add Samuel to David's supporters, and expressing contempt towards Saul.[46] The qualities and means described above form the elements of a political satire whose background is known to us from the narratives on Saul and David, and the extreme personal contrasts between them are captured by the keen eye of the expert storyteller. This popular tale constitutes a link in this conflict. It represents a kind of literary rather than rhetorical polemic (as, for example, in the speeches of Abigail and of David himself) against the legends of the grace of the choice of Saul as God's anointed and king over Israel.

b. The political background of the narrative

The origin of the narrative is in the struggle of David and his supporters against the House of Saul, and its aim is to entrench David's status as king over all Israel. The political tendency is to legitimize David's position as ruler instead of Saul. This tendency is reflected in two aspects of the tale: on the one hand, David wins the protection and support of the prophet Samuel, the anointer of kings, who frustrates Saul's intent to capture him and thereby allows him to realize his goal and attain the rule in his stead. On the other hand, Saul is exposed in all his weakness as one unable to control even his close servants, or indeed himself. This characterization of Saul as one who has lost his charismatic authority to the advantage of his young rival is present in other stories about the conflict between them. It finds marked expression in Saul's recriminations against his servants who were standing about him (22: 6–8). But while these recriminations contain a tragic note—a king betrayed by his close servants despite the gifts he has showered on them—in our tale there lurks a satirical note against Saul, who is incapable of imposing his will, not only because his servants have submitted to the authority of Samuel, who turned his back on him, but also because he himself lay naked before Samuel (v 24). This state of insensibility is what allows his young, sharp-witted rival to slip from his grasp. No great imagination is required to reconstruct the scorn of the gossip-hearers: "See what is he who rules us! Shall such a one as he reign over us?"

---

45 Buber, (n. 39), 205.

46 McCarter, 1 Samuel 331: "This account . . . can be read as a kind of parody of 10:10–12."

The confrontation between Saul and David has shifted from the overt real and rational sphere to the the hidden psychopathological and chaotic sphere, evinced in Saul's madness. The spirit of God that came upon Saul on his being chosen for God's mission as the first king in Israel (1 Sam 10: 1 ff) is replaced by an evil spirit (16: 14ff). He who is invited to cure him of the evil spirit is no other than David, who acquired the spirit of God when he was anointed secretly by Samuel (16: 1–13). The polar contrast evident in the account of the confrontation between them, born out of Saul's madness, has also inflitrated our story. True, the spirt of God visits Saul again— "And the spirit of God came upon him also, and as he went he prophesied" (19: 23). But this is not the same prophesying in the spirit of God as in the first story, which heralded his selection and which stimulated his activity as leader, with Samuel's encouragement: "Do whatever your hand finds to do, for God is with you" (1 Sam 10: 7); or when he aroused the poeple to war against Nahash the Ammonite (11: 6). Here the prophesying leaves him helpless and insensible, as if the spirit has departed from him. There the prophesying stimulates him to act, as if the spirit has entered him.

David's flight to Gath (21: 11–16) is also a popular tale. Some hold that it is the direct continuation of the popular story of 19: 19–24.[47] It seems that the play of literary contrast between Saul and David goes on. David pretends madness: "So he changed his behavior before them and feigned himself mad . . ." (21: 14). In all likelihood he imitated the prophesiers, and was saved. He is clever and succeeds in obtaining what he wants, even at a moment of serious crisis. Saul goes mad without wishing it and fails to realize his plan. If this is not actual satire, at least irony is not lacking here.

---

47 Smith, *Samuel,* 201f.; Herzberg, *I & II Samuel,* 182.

ᚹᛟ 5 ᚲᛉ

ELEMENTS OF POLITICAL SATIRE
IN THE PROPHETIC LITERATURE

By its nature, the prophetic literature, perhaps more than any other literary division of the Bible, required satirical devices. In the first place, this is on account of its rhetorical quality—the prophet addresses his audience with direct speech with the goal of convincing them of the truth of his message.[1] In this respect the prophetic literature differs from the literature of the Torah, whose essence is the promulgation of commandments and instructions delivered directly from God to the people. In particular, it differs from the psalm literature, in which the human being in his distress turns to God, prays to God and extols God's works and greatness. It is true that in part the wisdom literature also is delivered directly from the preacher to the listener, and thus contains rhetorical elements, but these are largely devoid of satirical features and the bitter diatribe attached to the actual social and religious struggle in concrete historical and political circumstances. The role of the prophet as the assailer at the gate, who inveighs against manifestations of social and political corruption, frequently to the accompaniment of threats and even curses against the institutions and leaders of society, puts him in need of a polemic redolent with scorn, irony and wit. These characteristics, by our definitions, are the elements of political satire.[2] A basic condition of

---

[1] The growth of "rhetoric" is generally ascribed to classical Greece, see: S. Shabib "Rhetoric," *Encyclopaedia Hebraica*, vol. xxx (Jerusalem, 1975), 987 (Hebrew). However, some of its characteristics may be found in the prophets' speeches, several centuries earlier.

[2] On the use of rhetoric in political satire see: *The Satirist's Arts*, ed. H.J. Jensen (Bloomington, 1972) ixff.; M.D. Fletcher, *Contemporary Political Satire* (London, 1987), ixff.

all political satire is criticism aimed at actual events and directed at a specific target.

This distinction mainly applies when the prophet turns his prophecies towards other nations, particularly gentile despotic kingdoms that have grown corrupt in their ways and have brought destruction upon other peoples, especially Israel.[3] Against these, too, theological and political criticism frequently dons satirical garb. In the transition from delivery of the prophecies, which were spoken orally, to their formulation in writing it often happened that the direct connection between particular prophecies and their historical context weakened or broke altogether; this circumstance obviously hinders us from clearly defining the actual object of the censure, namely, the historical personage or the circles at whom the prophet aims his barbs or the concrete target of the satire. Therefore, in such cases our satirical interpretation will rely on literary and structural probabilities more than on firm historical evidence.

Our guiding principle in the analysis of these prophecies is based on the distinction made by the Sages between prophecy that "was necessary for its own time and for generations," and so became preserved in writing, and prophecy that was useful only for its own time, and has not been preserved (B. Megillah, 14a). By this means we shall try to discover the relationship between the single historical moment of the prophecy and the deviation and changes that occurred in it when it proved "necessary for generations." It is possible that the satirical elements imbedded in it at the time of its creation were "adapted" and explained differently in the elaborate process of its becoming "necessary for generations." In this respect, form criticism may direct us, at least regarding the definition of the genres, in our quest for the primary connection between the satirical nature of the prophecy and its generic origin.

Devices of political satire are present in many prophecies differing in kind, but they are especially frequent in two: the "Woe" prophecies[4] directed at the nations and also inwardly; and the *mašal* elegies, that is, taunt elegies,[5] which characteristically are dirges with a satirical note both in socio-religious and political polemics directed within Israel; and in prophecies concerning the nations. Each type constitutes a kind of sub-genre in itself, and both lie within the overall genre known as "prophecies concern-

---

3 E. Jenni, *Die politischen Voraussagen den Propheten (AThANT* 29, Zürich, 1956).

4 W. Janzen, *Mourning Cry and Woe Oracle (BZAW* 125, 1972).

5 O. Eissfeldt, *Der Maschal im Alten Testament (BZAW* 24, Giessen, 1913).

ing the nations."[6] In addition, not completely separate from these two in terms of their genetic-literary origins are the *mašal* forms commonly known in literary theory as fable and parable.[7] These appear principally in internal Israelite prophetic polemics, the first especially in the prophecy of Isaiah (5, 1–7) and the second in Ezekiel (chaps 15, 17, 19).

1. Taunt elegies in the prophecies concerning the nations

We have chosen the compound term "taunt elegies" as a means of defining prophecies which have in common elegiac elements, whether in content or in form, but also the quality that differentiates them from the usual elegies, which is their being a *mašal* in the sense of a taunt elegy.[8] Only in two of the prophecies concerning the nations does this quality appear by name: Isaiah 14: 4[9] and Habakkuk 2: 6. It is true that *mašal* appears in Micah 2: 4 in the title of the elegy, but this is not a prophecy against the nations. The other prophecies included in this category, even though the caption *mašal* does not appear at their beginning, are taunt elegies against the nations which some, on account of this quality, indirectly ascribe to "*mošlim* poetry," such as the prophecy concerning Moab in Isaiah 15–16 and its duplicate in Jeremiah 48: it has been attempted to identify their common source as the ancient song of the *mošlim* on the fall of Moab in Numbers 21: 27–30;[10] and the double prophecy concerning Edom (Oba 1: 1–11; Jer 49: 7–16). The term *mošlim* is taken from Numbers 21: 27, which itself does not shed much light on who the *mošlim* were, what was characteristic in their activity, and what in their poetry singled them out. Kaufmann defined their poetry as "mantic and magical in its nature," recounting historical events in Israel and in the nations—it "exulted, wailed, scorned, blessed and cursed," and so "it expressed the feelings of the poet towards these events." He regards this poetry as the archetype of ancient Hebrew poetry that evolved over the years and was absorbed in the classical works of prophecy.[11] It is not apparent from his definitions whether he considered

---

6 Y. Hoffman, *The Prophecies against Foreign Nations in the Bible* (Tel Aviv, 1977) (Hebrew).

7 M. Haran 'משל' *EB* 5, 548–553; S. Abramsky 'המשל במקרא' *EH* 24, 631–2.

8 H. Jahnow, *Das Hebräische Leichenlied im Rahmen der Volkerdichtung* (Giessen, 1923).

9 The LXX reads θρῆνον (lament) instead of משל and in Mic 2:4 the same term is used for נהי.

10 M. Diman-Haran, "An Archaic Remnant in Prophetic Literature" (Hebrew) published originally in *BIES* 13 (1946/47), 7–15.

11 Y. Kaufmann, *Toldoth ha-Emuna ha-Yisraelit* III (Jerusalem-Tel Aviv, 1964), 43.

the *mošlim* to be Israelite poets in origin and pre-classical Israelite seers in function. From what is told of the early Israelite prophets in the Bible in the sporadic prophecies attributed to them, there is no evidence of this. The only early prophet to whom *mešalim* were ascribed in the Bible was of non-Israelite origin, namely, Balaam ben Be'or (Num 23: 7, 18; 24: 3, 15, 20, 21, 23); moreover, in the series of mantic- magical "fables" (*mešalim*) attributed to him there are no elegiac elements, except, perhaps, for the last fable which opens with the lament "Woe" (אוֹי with aleph and not הוֹי).[12] It is thus doubtful if it is possible to generalize a definite literary archetype and relate it to a definite creative milieu on the basis of terms labelled *mašal* and *mošlim*, which the Bible itself uses for a variety of purposes in an inconsistent manner.

We have prefaced our discussion with these methodological comments to qualify the use of the term *mašal* in the following as a particular pattern of ancient *mošlim* poetry, but without committing ourselves in advance to the historical and literary conclusions that have become attached to them.

Thus, in the analysis of the prophecies against the nations that we have placed under the rubric of this compound term, the question will indeed arise once more about who the elegist is, who is his audience, and what is the elegist's attitude to the nation, or the ruler, whom he elegizes. Beyond this, occasionally it will be asked if the prophet and the elegist are the same person, or if the prophet has converted the elegy of the early authentic elegist to his own later theo-political tendency and has made satirical, or possibly even parodic, use of it.

2. Political satire in the prophecy concerning Moab (Isaiah 15–16; Jeremiah 48)

Several theories have been posited on the basis of a comparison between the two (partly) parallel versions of the prophecy concerning Moab in Isaiah 15–16 and Jeremiah 48. Among the various hypotheses that may explain the duplication, the preferred basic possibility is that both Isaiah and Jeremiah based themselves on an early source.[13] The differences among scholars who adopt this approach mainly concern the nature and era of this early source and purposes and methods of its adaptation by the prophets of the scripture. To this one should add, and in this case only in respect of this

12 G. Wanke, "אוֹי" und "הוֹי" *ZAW*, 78 (1966), 215–218.
13 Y. Hoffman (n. 6), 196.

double prophecy, that in Jeremiah's prophecy on Moab there is a parallel version, or even quotation, of an archaic song on the fall of Moab ascribed to the *mošlim* that appears in Numbers 21: 27–30. Haran (then Diman)[14] relies on this song to conclude that this is the early source which both Isaiah and Jeremiah used in the oracles concerning Moab; or put in our terms, they both based themselves on "an ancient remnant of this pre-Israelite poetry that may be called *mošlim* poetry." He reached this conclusion despite the absence in Isaiah's prophecy of any quotation from this early song, except for names of settlements in Moab mentioned in both of them. However, the "triple cord" that he spun "will not soon be severed" and the assumption of the existence of an ancient source from the *mošlim* poetry from which both Isaiah and Jeremiah drew their prophecies concerning Moab has been a basic assumption in the explanation of this prophecy.[15] As the ancient poem about Moab in Numbers 21: 27–30 has an elegiac nature—"Woe to you, O Moab! You are undone, O people of Chemosh!" (v 28)—and the double oracle on Moab in Isaiah and Jeremiah also includes elegiac features, although lacking the formal features of the elegy "Woe" (אוי or הוי), the assumption became entrenched that the elegy originally was a taunt elegy of the *mošlim*. Abarbanel refers to this approach in his commentary to Numbers 21: "He gave proof of this from the words of the *mošlim*, the ballad singers who composed poems and sacred hymns about the ancient wars which are written in the Book of Wars of the Lord, as mentioned above (v 14). They composed songs and proverbs in honor of Siḥon when he conquered Moab so that it would endure as a proverb and a taunt; the song and the sacred hymn are 'Come to Heshbon . . .'"[16]

Thus, Abarbanel as long ago as the Renaissance period clearly recognized the *Sitz im Leben* of the "*mašal* elegy," well before this tie was known to modern scholars. Yair Hoffmann systematically and analytically traced the early elegy on which Isaiah and Jeremiah constructed their prophecies. He made a textual comparison, isolating the common core in the two prophecies from the later prophetic accretions, and thereby reached a conclusion similar to Haran's: the ancient nucleus common to the two prophecies is an elegy which at least at first was a Moabite dirge, and which the prophets of Israel used at a later period, each in his own way, weaving it

---

14 See above, note 10.

15 Y. Hoffman, 196; Duane L. Christensen, *Transformations of the War Oracle in Old Testament Prophecy* (Ann Arbor, 1975), 5.

16 I. Abrabanel, *Perush ha-Torah* (Warsaw, 1862; reprinted Jerusalem, 1954).

into their prophecies against the nations. He diverges from Haran (Diman) only in respect to the historical setting of this elegy.[17]

However, if we are dealing with an original Moabite lament, where lies the barb typical of the prophetic taunt elegy? Is it only in the Israelite prophetic additions? Or were there already present in the archaic lament ridicule, irony, and malicious joy, these being the clear-cut features of political satire, in which case it is unlikely that its author was a Moabite?

Let us then first turn our attention to the song of the *mošlim* on the fall of Moab in Numbers 21: 27–30, this, according to the theory we have cited, being the "genus" from which the prophetic oracle concerning Moab developed.

A. The song of the moslim on the fall of Moab (Numbers 21, 27–30)

The biblical author most probably had important reasons for introducing the poem into his historiographic account of the conquest of the land of Sihon "from Arnon to Jabbok" by the Israelites and their settlement "in all the cities of the Amorites, in Heshbon and in all its villages" (vv 24–25). Their juridical-political aspect may be learned from the negotiations between Jephthah and the king of the Ammonites (Jud 11: 12–28).[18] It is reasonable to assume that the song of the *mošlim* was inserted here in order to vindicate Israelite settlement in territories of the land of Moab: from the outset the Israelites had been commanded by God not to cross these borders as Moab had been given as a possession to the sons of Lot (Deut 2: 8–10); so the pretext given for Israelite settlement here is that these lands had fallen to Israel in his war against Siḥon king of Heshbon, and in fact it was the latter who had captured them from Moab. Rashi and his grandson Rashbam also explain the term *mošlim* in this historical and literary context as referring to Balaam and Be'or (his father), who were active witnesses to the events that then took place.

The song of the *mošlim* itself consists of two parts: one is a call to establish Heshbon, the city of Sihon, whence went forth the fire that devoured Moab (vv 27–28); the second is an elegy on the loss of Moab and his heritage and the capture of his sons by the king of the Amorites (vv 29–30). From both these parts this is evidently not a Moabite elegy. The first part

---

17 Y. Hoffman, 197–199, argues against Haran and Kaufmann who ascribed the elegy to the pre-settlement period of Israel; he dates it in the 8th century BCE.

18 Y. Kaufmann, *Sepher Shophtim* (Jerusalem, 1964), 214–222.

opens with an invitation to "Come to Heshbon," and expresses joy at the victory of Siḥon over Moab. Noth, who considers this opening the purpose of the entire song, therefore tends to attribute it to the Israelites.[19] But it is not certain that this can be proven from the poem itself, whose protagonist is Sihon, while Israel is not mentioned at all, and neither is the Lord his God. But nor is the second part of the elegy a dirge by Moab on the loss of his land and the fall of his sons and daughters captive to Sihon, but is in fact an anti-elegy (or elegiac parody) in that it ridicules the people of Chemosh, who (the antecedent is apparently Chemosh the god of Moab) "made his sons fugitives and his daughters captives to the Amorite king Sihon" (v 29); this is likewise the interpretation of Rashi, and especially Ramban (Nachmanides). It seems to me that the satirical barb indeed lies more in the elegy than in the first part of the poem, and the "elegist" here does not share Moab's grief but actually gloats over it.

If in fact this *mošlim*'s elegy served as a nucleus for the elegiac prophecy of Isaiah and Jeremiah concerning Moab, it did not evolve from the Moabites. It is doubtful if Isaiah even knew it, as it is not cited at all in his prophecies. Jeremiah does cite it at the end of his oracle (or anthology of oracles) concerning Moab (48: 45, 46), but without its opening "Come to Heshbon, let it be built, let the city of Sihon be established"; nor do certain details preserve their form, having become corrupted or substituted. This is perhaps on account of the time span separating them. Even the satirical arrow shot at Chemosh, who made his sons fugitives, is substituted in Jeremiah's version by "for your sons have been taken captive." Considering that the elegy, with its modifications, was inserted at the end of the collection of Jeremiah's prophecies concerning Moab, before its closing verse "Yet I will restore the fortunes of Moab in the latter days" (v 47), we get the impression that the ancient elegiac ode weakened and lost its edge in the passage to the anthology of prophecies concerning Moab in the book of Jeremiah.[20] However, the main key to our question whether the satirical barb is present in the ancient elegy, or only in the use made of it by the prophets, lies in the ancient elegy whose isolation and reconstruction have been attempted through comparison of the prophecy on the destiny of Moab in Isaiah 15–16 with its parallels that form part of the prophecy concerning Moab in Jeremiah 48.[21]

---

19 M. Noth, *Numbers* (OTL; London, 1980), 164–165.

20 Diman (n. 10), 14.

21 See the comparative table in Hoffman's book, *Isaiah* (Jerusalem, 1986), 84; and see also his book (n. 6), 186–187.

The guiding principle in Hoffmann's reconstruction is that the same stanzas present in both prophets, even with textual variations, were originally an ancient elegy concerning Moab. Now the ancient elegy that he reconstructed is devoid of the satirical barb present in the song of the *mošlim*, aimed at the powerlessness of Chemosh to protect his sons and daughters, which we quoted above (Num 21: 29). Chemosh is not mentioned in it at all, not even as he to whose temple they come to lament, and naturally there is no mention of the Amorite king Sihon. The satirical barb in the elegy stanzas common to the two prophets pours scorn upon the pride and haughtiness of Moab, which may be interpreted as the direct cause of his precipitous collapse, along the lines of "Pride goes before destruction, and a haughty spirit before a fall" (Prov 16: 18). Jeremiah, unlike Isaiah, interprets the pride and insolence as a sin against God: "I know his insolence, says the Lord" (v 30); and "Make him drunk, because he magnified himself against the Lord" (v 25). In Isaiah mention of Moab's pride and insolence (16: 6) is connected with his appeal to the daughter of Zion to give shelter to the refugees of Moab (16: 1–4). The reference to his pride is perhaps meant to explain the rejection of the appeal by the daughter of Zion, or, alternatively, the reverse: it is a satirical barb cast against Moab that Judah did not harbor hostility towards him for his insolence but granted him shelter.

Although the theme of Moab's pride appears in both prophecies, and in almost identical language, the problem arises as to whether indeed it is part of the ancient elegy: the elegiac account of the mourning and wailing that cover Moab's entire domain, delivered in indirect speech, is suddenly interrupted by direct speech, and in the plural: "We have heard of the pride of Moab." This interjection is not identical either in content or form with the elegist's direct speech in the singular, "My heart cries out for Moab" (Isa 15: 5; cf. Jer 48: 36, also Isa 16: 9, 11; and Jer 48: 31–32), which is repeated like a refrain between the stanzas of the elegy. Clearly, the declaration "We have heard of the pride of Moab," laced with irony, was not made by the Moabite elegists but, to the contrary, by those who justify the calamity that befell the Moabites for their sin of pride. It does not reflect a collective national lament but the scorn of a political rival who has taken the opportunity to settle historical accounts with the Moabites. If this statement did in fact belong to the Moabite elegy from its creation, before it was applied by Isaiah and Jeremiah in their oracles, there is room to consider whether the elegy did not constitute a sort of parody, or fable elegy, from its beginnings, namely, the "song of the *mošlim*" sung by those who rejoiced at

the fall and destruction of Moab; these, moreover, might have been Israelites or Moab's enemies from a different nation, for the Israelite religious
element is missing from the version in Isaiah.

But even if we regard the above-quoted theme, which does contain
an element of political satire, as a secondary tier constructed upon the
original—after we detach it from the elegy—it is doubtful that we will be
left with an authentic Moabite folk-lamentation. Several characteristic components are missing: for example, the complaint to God, a description of the
cruelty of the foe, and the cry for vengeance against him.[22] At first sight the
expressions of identification by the first-person speaker that accompany
the stanzas with a lyrical note—"My heart cries out for Moab," etc.—would
indicate that the elegist shares in the pain of the sufferers, but even this lyrical incursion may be interpreted in two ways: as the words of the Moabite
elegist voicing his empathy with the collapse of his country and people;
or alternatively, as those of the taunting poet, making a show of grief at the
Moabites' distress, but with the satirical and parodic note of glee at it. These
two contrasting possibilities in fact find expression in the interpretations of
early and modern commentators.

Against Rashi's commentary to Isaiah 15: 5, which finds sympathy in
the Israelite prophets with the distress of the nations of the world, we encounter the commentary by Luzzatto, who considers the phrase "My heart
cries out for Moab" a kind of parody.[23] In keeping with Rashi, and contrary
to Luzzatto, is Sawyer, in his commentary to this text: he regards the elegy
on Moab not as a parody but as straightforward and genuine.[24] Hoffmann
takes a middle position between the two sides: in Isaiah he interprets these
lyrical expressions by the prophet as "participation in Moab's distress, in
contrast to the malicious joy that is evident in Jeremiah's prophecy."[25] It
seems that this distinction was influenced more by the general tone invest-
ing Jeremiah's prophecy, which is composed of different oracles (unlike
Isaiah's), than by the original elegy that he sought to reconstruct.

The possibilities of divergent interpretations of the elegist's direct
speech exacerbates the problem still more: Do we have here an authentic
Moabite elegy that was subverted by the Israelite prophet into a satire

---

22 H. Gunkel, *Einleitung in die Psalmen* (ed. J. Begrich, 1933); Tigay, "Lament," *EM* 7,
139–141 (Hebrew).

23 Luzzatto, *Isaiah* (Padua, 1855, reprinted in Jerusalem, 1967), 198.

24 J.F.A. Sawyer, *Isaiah* I (Edinburgh, 1984), 152–153.

25 Y. Hoffman, *Isaiah*, 86.

against Moab, or was the satirical prophecy against Moab camouflaged as
an elegy from the outset?

B. *An oracle concerning Moab (Isaiah 15–16)*

The heading מַשָּׂא מוֹאָב (15: 1), followed by the name of a nation or
its land, is repeated at the opening of Isaiah's prophecies concerning the
nations (chaps 13–23). Only in one case does it appear at the opening of a
prophecy concerning Judah, "An oracle concerning the valley of vision"
(22: 1). The framework of the collection of prophecies concerning the nations, which opens at 13: 1, also contains the "taunt against the king of
Babylon" (14: 4), which is preceded by the verb "and you will take up"
(וְנָשָׂאתָ). The phrase "to take up a taunt" with different inflections of the verb
from the root נשא appears in other cases in the Bible in which a taunt elegy
is presented in one manner or another, such as Micah 2: 4; Habakkuk 2: 6,
and also the oracles of Balaam in Numbers 23: 7ff. The verb נשא fulfills a
similar function also with respect to the lamentation.[26] Only once does it
appear in relation to "oracle" (מַשָּׂא),[27] despite the derivative connection between the verb נשא and the noun מַשָּׂא. It is doubtful if it can be determined,
on the basis of these references, that the use of the noun מַשָּׂא serves to imply
elegy and *mašal,* and that the oracles of Isaiah concerning the nations
should, on account of the indirect link we have described, be interpreted as
taunt elegies.

The ending (16: 13–14) is distinct in content and style from the oracle
itself in that it is prose and in that it distinguishes between the ancient message "the word which the Lord spoke concerning Moab in the past" (v 13)
and the updated prophetic message "and now" (v 14). According to this
distinction—and at this stage it is immaterial if the ending should be ascribed to the prophet himself[28] or to a later redactor[29]—the oracle that appears between the title and the ending, namely 15: 1–16: 12, is the word of
the Lord "in the past." This distinction serves as the basis for the opinion of
most commentators that this oracle is in essence an ancient elegy on Moab.

However, if we accept as true the testimony in the prophetic ending
that "this is the word which the Lord spoke concerning Moab in the past,"

---

26 Cf. Amos 5:1; Jer 7:29; Ezek 19:1, 26:17, 27: 2, 32, 28: 12, 32: 2.

27 2 Kgs 9: 25.

28 According to Kaufmann, *Toldoth ha-Emuna ha-Israelith* III, 47.

29 According to G.B. Gray, *The Book of Isaiah I–XXXIX* (ICC; Edinburgh, 1962),
273–78, 295.

where does the word of the Lord appear in the elegy? Throughout the entire prophecy in Isaiah, as distinct from its duplicate in Jeremiah, not once does a message in God's name appear explicitly, except, of course, in the ending itself. If we start with the assumption that the entire prophecy is the word of the Lord by the very fact of its inclusion among Isaiah's prophecies, then we are not dealing here with an ancient Moabite elegy unless we distinguish between two speakers: the Moabite elegist and the Israelite prophet who bends the elegy into a prophecy of doom concerning Moab. This indeed is the approach of modern commentators, and it is based principally on the distinction between the descriptive elegiac account itself in indirect speech and the expressivist attitude to the events described in first-person direct speech.[30]

A further distinction between two strata in the prophecy is perceived in the lack of stylistic uniformity in the oracle itself, especially between the rhymed poem and the prose sentences inserted into it. The tendency is to regard the latter as secondary elements.[31] It transpires, therefore, that those who distinguish between an ancient Moabite elegy and the use made of it by the prophet for his purposes tend first of all to attribute the prose sentences to the prophet. As for the poetic lines in direct speech and in the singular, opinions are divided. Some ascribe all of them to the prophet, and some distinguish between the lyrical expressions of the elegist, for example, 15: 5; 16: 9, 11, and the prophetic message in 15: 9b, which in their view is the word of God spoken by the prophet. In particular, to the prophet is attributed the stanza distinct in content and style in 16: 1–5, in which an empathetic or ironic appeal is sounded, apparently to the daughter of Zion, to give shelter and refuge to the fugitives and outcasts of Moab.[32]

To answer the question we posed at the beginning of the discussion, we must make maximal use of the relevant literary and formal aspects that have been considered, as well as those that have not been adequately scrutinized. To interpret the prophecy, whose textual difficulties are so many, we shall focus on those relevant to our concern.

C. The structure and components of the elegy

In form, we have here a single elegy, opening with rhymes of descending dirge meter, the first indicating the troubles that befell Moab:

30 Gray, 271–273.
31 Cf. Gray, 272.
32 Gray, 285 considers the paragraph 15: 9b-16: 5 as a "prophetic interpolation."

Because Ar is laid waste in a night / Moab is undone // Because Kir is laid waste in a night / Moab is undone.

The second presents Moab's reaction to the catastrophe:

He (Moab?) has gone up הבית and Dibon / to the high places to weep[33] // over Nebo and over Medeba / Moab wails."

The elegy also ends with two rhymes (16: 11–12) that differ in nature and form. The first, in poetic meter (16: 11), is a lyrical chorus closing the elegy itself and returning us to the opening line (15: 1): "Therefore my soul moans like a lyre for Moab / and my heart for Kir-heres (compare "Moab" and "Kir" in the opening line). The second, which is prose in form and prophetic in nature (16, 12), "And when Moab presents himself, when he wearies himself upon the high place, when he comes to his sanctuary to pray, he will not prevail," returns us to the second line of the opening (15, 2). In this way it closes the cycle of the elegy on a prophetic-satirical note. Luzzatto was correct in his interpretation here: "This matches what he said above—'He has gone up and Dibon to the high places to weep'."[34]

Unlike its manner of insertion into Jeremiah's prophecy, here the elegy itself is divided into two main parts, 15: 1–9 and 16: 7–11, by the prophetic message in direct speech at 16: 1–4. In it the prophet urges the daughters of Moab who seek shelter from the enemy, to turn to "the mount of the daughter of Zion," and he urges the daughter of Zion to be a refuge for them. Hoffmann attributes this message also to Isaiah on stylistic grounds.[35] However, it is possible that verses 1 and 2 were transposed, and verse 2 should be moved to the elegy in chapter 15, after 15: 8, as Duhm suggested;[36] or, in our view, after 15: 9, which would create continuity of the speech by the prophet, who places himself as a link between the fugitives of Moab and the daughter of Zion. The transposition of 16: 2, which in some way spoils the continuity and begins with the word והיה ("and it will be"), typical of a prophetic message, would continue the prophecy begun at 15: 9 spoken in direct speech and representing, albeit not explicitly, the words of God; this is how the "reconstructed" prophecy would read (following the *KJV*):

---

33 Because of the unclear syntax of the colon many efforts have been made to restore the original text, such as: הבת "daughter" instead of הבית "the house." See, e.g., Sawyer (n. 24), 150: "The daughter of Dibon has gone up. . . ."

34 Luzzatto, in his commentary to *Isaiah*, 207 (Hebrew).

35 Hoffman (n. 6), 192.

36 B. Duhm, *Das Buch Jesaia* (*GHAT;* Göttingen, 1914), 103–104.

Yet I will bring more upon Dimon
Lions upon him that escapeth of Moab, and upon the remnant of the land
For it shall be, that as a wandering bird, cast out of the nest,
So the daughters of Moab shall be at the fords of Arnon.

In form we have here a prophecy of doom, with no reason not to ascribe it to the prophet who reveals God's intention without mentioning his name explicity. The sudden transition from the elegy depicting the event and the public experience in indirect speech to a prophecy in direct speech occurs when the account reaches its climax: "For the waters of Dimon are full of blood" (15: 9a). If indeed "Dibon" has been substituted here by "Dimon" for the purpose of alliteration,[37] then satirical use has been made of the elegy in order to turn it into a prophecy of doom. The כִּי ("for") that opens the prophecy is different in nature and function from the כִּי preceding it in the prophecy, in which it opens seven of its lines. The prophetic message all at once discloses that the prophet does not identify with the suffering of Moab, contrary to what might appear from the empathetic experiential account, chiefly the lyrical outpouring accompanying it in the first person, "My heart cries out for Moab" (v 5); it is made, in fact, to settle accounts with him: all the suffering undergone by Moab is still not enough, and "even more" may be expected. Therefore, whoever identifies the prophet with the elegist must necessarily also conclude, with Luzzatto and others, that even the lyrical expression found in this part of the elegy (v 5), and repeated in the second part (16: 9, 11), is merely contrived, and in truth the prophet does not sympathize with Moab in his troubles but actually ridicules him.[38]

On the other hand, a distinction may be drawn between the prophetic message and the lyrical, ecstatic expressions in the first person: the lyrical expressions of sympathy with the suffering of Moab may be ascribed to the elegist who with body and soul agonizes over the fate of his people. All the more so, if we note that these lyrical expressions are a refrain echoing at the end of every stanza of the elegy, although it is difficult to reconstruct the stanzas with certainty. This possibility matches the (auto-suggestive) poetic dynamic of a national elegist, whose descriptions of the mourning and wailing stir him to give direct empathetic and ecstatic expression to his

---

37 Luzzatto, *Isaiah* 200: Dimon (דִּימוֹן) is Dibon and the prophet used it for paranomasia with blood (דָּם).

38 Luzzatto, *Isaiah*, 200, and see also note 23.

personal lament. This assumption is likely in view of the fact that the lyrical refrain, with only slight variations, also appears in Jeremiah (48: 31, 36, and cf. Isa 16: 7, 11). In keeping with the basic principles set out at the beginning of this discussion, this attests that these lyrical outbursts belong to the common source used by both prophets.

As for the artistic structure of the elegy, the use of a refrain as an integral part of it is a well-known device. In this elegy one can trace the passage from the descriptive stanzas, which mostly open with the word כי ("for"), not as a causal conjuction (15: 1a, 1b, 5b, 5c, 6a, 6b, 8a, seven times in all—which deserves note), to the personal lyrical refrain beginning with the phrase על כן ("therefore"). This recurs in Jeremiah 48: 31, 36, 37, and in Isaiah 16: 9, 11. It is also possible that the first refrain in Isaiah (15: 5) preceded the phrase על כן, and it should be transferred from verse 4 to the beginning of verse 5, which would read "Therefore my heart cries out for Moab . . ." Such a transposition not only does not break the continuity and rhythm of verse 4 but actually facilitates it.[39] Still, a distinction should be made between this and the על כן at the start of verse 7, which is prosaic in function—"Therefore the abundance they have gained and what they have laid up they carry away over the Brook of Willows"—and is meant to indicate recompense. Hence, it should apparently be interpreted as the prophet's reaction to the compensation that Moab deserves, and not as a description of the catastrophe by the elegist.

The parallel expression in Jeremiah 48: 36 may be similarly understood. In neither the elegy in Isaiah's prophecy nor the parallel section in Jeremiah does this prose sentence fit its context. In Isaiah it follows verse 6b, describing a drought that struck the land and breaking the continuity between verses 1–6b and verse 8, which portray the wailing and the deep mourning that beset Moab after its rape by the foe. Indeed, verse 6b is absent in Jeremiah, and of verse 7 only the first part is present, and in a different place. It is in fact difficult to explain how this comment became woven into the elegy, appearing in Isaiah as well as Jeremiah, albeit with considerable differences.

A similar and more acute difficulty arises in connection with the direct speech in the plural in Isaiah 16: 6:

> We have heard of the pride of Moab, how proud he was;
> Of his arrogance, his pride, and his insolence—
> His boasts are false

---

39 Gray, *Isaiah*, 280, indeed noticed it, but hesitated to draw a conclusion from it.

A speech repeated in slightly different form and in an obviously polemical prophetic style occurs in Jeremiah 48: 29–30:

> We have heard of the pride of Moab—he is very proud—
> Of his loftiness, pride, and his arrogance,
> And the haughtiness of his heart.
> I know his insolence, says the Lord;
> His boasts are false, his deeds are false.

This theme in its dual versions is touched with a note of satire. The
plundered, aching Moab suddenly appears as an object of criticism, if not
scorn. Moab's pride, notorious among many ("We have heard"), is brought
up precisely in the dreadful crisis that has struck it, as Luzzatto perceptively
observes: "'We have heard': Until now we have heard him boasting, now
we shall hear him wailing."[40] Some see this motif as the reasoning behind
the sin for which he was punished. But since the motif is common to the
two prophecies (except for the addition of the direct intervention in God's
name in Jeremiah—"I know . . . says the Lord"), it is regarded as part of the
ancient elegy cited by both Isaiah and Jeremiah. However, according to the
opening "We have heard" in the plural, which is unique in this elegy, and
also on account of the note of criticism reflected in it against Moab, it is
hard to ascribe it to an early Moabite elegist who spoke the entire elegy and
especially the expressions of personal lyrical identification contained in it.
     This difficulty remains even in the wake of attempts to interpret this
verse in Isaiah (namely 16: 6) as a reply by the dwellers in Zion to the request by the fugitives of Moab for shelter with them;[41] such attempts bind it
to the prophetic section attributed to Isaiah and not to the ancient elegy, yet
the same expression is repeated in Jeremiah not in a like context. Jeremiah
cites it while expanding it from the entho-political to the theo-political
frame of reference: "I know, says the Lord . . ." (v. 30). This motif of
Moab's pride and his enmity towards Israel, accompanied by a curse of
God against him, appears in another prophet contemporary with Jeremiah,
namely Zephaniah 2: 8–10; and the account-settling Moab may expect at
God's hands is depicted satirically in another prophecy of Isaiah (25:
10–12). It should therefore be seen as an Israelite prophetic theme growing
on historical soil and influenced largely by the political relations between
the two nations.

---

40 Luzzatto, *Isaiah,* 205.
41 See, e.g., Kraus *Commentary on Isaiah* (Budapest, 1904), 16 (Hebrew).

It seems to us, therefore, that the theme of pride in Isaiah's prophecy on Moab is not a direct continuation of the elegy on the plunder of Moab in the first part, 15: 1–9, nor a response of the dwellers of Zion to the fugitives of Moab (16: 2–4). It is the opening of another taunt elegy concerning Moab, whose essence is a heartrending cry at the destruction caused to his vineyards that were his source of pride, and at God's termination of the treaders' joy at the wine presses (16: 7–10); this may be understood from the use of the transitive verb השבתי ("I have hushed") in the first person in verse 10.[42] The fact that this section of the elegy (or as we term it, taunt elegy) appears almost in its entirety and in similar order in Jeremiah, while the first part is quoted only piecemeal in different places of his prophecy, speaks for our assumption of its poetic autonomy and not, as is usual, for its being the continuation of the same elegiac poem. The differences between the two elegies are attested by further signs, such as the sparse use of the word כי as the opening of stanzas in the second elegy (twice only, as against seven or eight times in the first); and the inconsistent use of the elegiac meter that characterizes the first elegy. True, the second, like the first, continues with the use of "Moab" as a male national personification, but only marginally. The main thrust of the cry concerns "the vine of Sibmah," a name twice repeated in the brief elegy, which may be interpreted as an allegory and a metaphor for the female national personification, Moab. The allegorical usage serves the satirical tendency of this taunt elegy.

Thus the so-called "elegy concerning Moab" unfolds before us in its two aspects, as two facing mirrors. The one is a Moabite elegy within which the satirical reactions of the Israelite prophet echo; the other is an Israelite taunt elegy, which from the outset is meant to settle accounts with Moab, proud that its "shoots passed over the sea," and within which lines of a Moabite elegy are heard, applied by the prophet in a metaphorical and parodic way.

D. The satirical tendency of Isaiah, compared with Jeremiah, in the double prophecy concerning Moab

Our conclusions from examination of Isaiah's prophecy concerning Moab, and from its comparison with the parallel in Jeremiah, do not wholly match the conclusion reached by Hoffman, who on the basis of this comparison stated that "noteworthy is the element of sharing in Moab's distress

---

42 Cf. The parallel colon in Jer 48: 33.

that characterizes Isaiah's prophecy, in contrast to the gloating that emerges from Jeremiah's prophecy, about a century later."[43] Isaiah's prophecy, with its use of the ancient Moabite elegy, is also laced with satirical tones reflecting a kind of malicious joy at Moab's downfall also, but these are more concealed and perhaps more restrained than those in Jeremiah.

There is no doubt that the motifs typifying the oracles of doom against the nations are more marked in Jeremiah's prophecy than in Isaiah's.[44] The first of these is the direct speech in God's name which appears in the title of the prophecy and accompanies the calamities that visit Moab (Jer 48: 1,8, 10, 12, 15, 25, 26); but only once does this occur in the section regarded as the ancient elegy on Moab (v 30, discussed above). The calamities are connected with God's judgment on Moab, through which the leitmotiv of the elegy reverberates: ". . . that Moab is laid waste and judgment has come upon the tableland" (vv 20–21). The destroyer who executes God's judgment is commanded and cursed with these words: "Cursed is he who does the work of the Lord with slackness; and cursed is he who keeps back his sword from bloodshed" (v 10). The judgment is explained as a consequence of the sins of Moab against God (v 26) and against Israel (v 27).[45] His fate is sealed: "Moab shall be destroyed and be no longer a people because he magnified himself against the Lord" (v 42). The judgment of the people of Moab does not omit the place of Chemosh, their god (v 7); and the "people of Chemosh" are mentioned in the stanza parallel to the song of the *moslim* in Numbers 21 (cf. Jer 48: 46 with Num 21: 29)—a theme quite absent in Isaiah's prophecy. It seems that Jeremiah's prophecy is not uniform, but a kind of anthology of prophecies on Moab.[46] This is particularly evident in the different use of the personification of Moab. While at the start of the prophecy the female personification appears (vv 1–9), as is typical of most of the prophecies concerning the nations, in the other parts the male personification predominates. This is similar to the case in Isaiah's prophecy and it distinguishes the ancient elegy as well as the song of the *moslim* about Moab.

The expressions of anger and pleasure in vengeance that characterize Jeremiah's prophecies against Moab and which may be explained by the

43 Hoffmann, *Isaiah*, 86 (Hebrew).

44 Hoffmann, (n. 6), 208; R.P. Carrol, *Jeremiah* (OTL; London, 1986), 796.

45 Carrol, *Jeremiah,* 789.

46 See "Oracles against Moab, Jer. 48: 1–47 (LXX 31:1–44)" in D.L. Christensen's monograph (n. 15), 234–245.

historical circumstances of Israelite-Moabite relations in his time do not appear in Isaiah's prophecy. They are attenuated to intimations of a satirical nature. Perhaps precisely in this way they offer us insight into Isaiah as a political satirist who allows his victims to speak for themselves in their own words, into which he stealthily inserts his satirical barbs.

——— ഇ 6 ഗ ———

A TAUNT ELEGY ON THE KING OF BABYLON (ISA 14: 4–21)

The marvelous integration of content and form, of rhythm and meter, of realism and surrealism, of elegy and grotesque into a single ode is only one of the fine qualities that make this taunt elegy a masterpiece of biblical poetry. These features contribute substantially to its presentation as a paradigm, to the extent that it may be stated with certainty: We have here a taunt elegy, and perhaps more than any other genre, it serves as artistic dress for political satire in the Bible.

The taunt and the features of its content and form

The taunt, as attested by its prefatory statement, "you will take up this taunt . . . ," opens in verse 4 with the typical elegaic word of a dirge "How."[1] It is directed at a particular person, designated by the title "the king of Babylon," in contrast to many other instances, particularly in prophecies against the nations, when it is directed at a nation or a national personification.[2] The personal object of the taunt, whose name is not stated explicitly, is characterized throughout the stanzas of the poem: he is spoken of in the third person (vv 4–7), he is addressed directly in the second person (vv 8–12, 15–20), and what he said in his heart is quoted in direct speech (vv 13–14). The natural conclusion of the poem, therefore, seems to me to be verse 20,

---

[1] 2 Sam 1: 19, 25, 27; Jer 9: 18; Zeph 2:15.
[2] Isa 13—against Babylon; 15–16—against Moab; cf. Jer 48 and Num 21: 28–30; 23 against Tyre.

in which he is still addressed directly and accounts with him are settled by a fierce admonition. But unlike other interpreters, I do not entirely discount the possibility of including verse 21, which refers to his sons, even though its style is diluted with prose and its rhythm alienates it somewhat from the poem proper.[3]

The focus of the satire on one character, the object of the elegy, contributes greatly to the artistic unity of the poem as a whole even as the writer carries us from one scene to the next, from one reacting crowd of onlookers to another, from the realistic sphere (vv 4–7) to the surrealistic (vv 9–11), and from the world of spirits in Sheol to the mythical and astral sphere (vv 12–14).

Regarding the poem's structure, five stanzas are usually distinguished,[4] although they are not symmetrical in structure and rhythm and may be better defined as scenes. The first scene takes us in an instant from the description of the tyrant and oppressor to the reaction of the surrounding universe to his fall: peace and quiet suddenly descend with his extinction: "The whole earth is at rest and quiet." Then at once there is an outburst of joy: "They break forth into singing" (v 7), expressed through personification of the cypresses and the cedars of Lebanon, which rejoice at the fall of their hewer, and which emit their sigh of relief in direct speech to him: "'Since you were laid low, no hewer comes up against us.'"

The second scene brings us from the cosmos to Sheol, from realistic and elegiac description to surrealist and dramatic. The dramatic setting in Sheol, where the leaders of the earth and the kings of the nations welcome their oppressor, is, like the preceding scene, characterized by direct speech laced with irony addressed to him by the former victims of his aggression. The lyrical speech of the leaders of the earth in Sheol is longer than that of the trees on the heights of Lebanon, and more sarcastic in its descending dirge rhythm (3:2):

> You too have become as weak as we!
> You have become like us!'
> Your pomp is brought down to Sheol,
> the sound of your harps;
> maggots are the bed beneath you,
> and worms are your covering. (vv 10b–11)

---

3 J.F.A. Sawyer, *Isaiah* vol. I (Edinburgh, 1984), 145.

4 G.B. Gray, *The Book of Isaiah* (ICC; Edinburgh, 1962 [1912]), 248–250; O. Kaiser, *Isaiah 13–39* (OTL; London, 1980), 33.

We return from the dramatic encounter in Sheol to the satirical elegist, who resumes his poem with the opening word "How," but this time the fall is more astonishing—"How are you fallen from heaven"—and the elegy's hero is entitled by epithets from the astro-mythological realm: "O Day Star, son of Dawn!"[5] The addressed protagonist is still no other than the one in the previous scenes, as are his acts of despotism, but here an additional aspect is highlighted, and this becomes the focus for the poets' censure and ridicule. This is his god-like pride and his ambition of dominion even in the heavenly world. With a series of verbs—"I will ascend," "I will set . . . on high," "I will sit," "I will make myself like," accompanied by cosmic and mythological images, he expresses his ambition in a soliloquy: to ascend to heaven, to set his throne above the stars of God, and to make himself like the Most High. And here at the peak of his desires occurs the radical reversal from his ascent above the heights of the clouds to his descent to Sheol. This is the climax and the turning point in the universal drama centered on the "King of Babylon." Here too is the peak of the sarcasm of the prophetic elegist, who pinpoints the reversal perfectly through the adversative conjunction "but": this transforms the first-person monologue he has placed in the king of Babylon's mouth into the sealing of his ultimate fate in the second person: "But you are brought down to Sheol, to the depths of the pit."

The last scene brings us back to the political and historical domain of the beginning of the poem; it is all ridicule and irony at the stupendous fall of the despot. Some locate this scene in Sheol also, and see it as the continuation of the reception there, described in verses 9–11.[6] This irony finds a witty expression spoken by the chorus looking on at his ruin: "'Is this the man who made the earth tremble, who shook kingdoms, who made the world like a desert and overthrew its cities?'" (vv 16–17). It ends with rejoicing over the retribution in the tyrant's fate, with words spoken directly to him: "All the kings of the nations lie in glory, each in his own tomb; but you are cast out, away from your sepulchre, like a loathed untimely birth" (vv 18–19); its epilogue is a moral: "Because you have destroyed your land, you have slain your people, May the descendants of evildoers nevermore be named!" (v 20).

---

5 Sawyer believes that the name *Helel ben Shahar*, "Daystar, son of Dawn," a satirical name given to the king, is made up of two more Canaanite deities (n. 3), 144–145.

6 H. Barth, *Die Jesaja Worte in der Josaizeit* (WMANT 48, Neukirchen-Vluyn, 1977), 129.

Satirical devices in the taunt elegy

The satirical devices of the taunt elegy are evidently based on the use of
mythological motifs and concepts from Canaanite literature that apparently
were converted into sarcastic images by the prophet, who blended them into
the soliloquy of Day Star, son of Dawn: for example, "the Most High,"
"the mount of assembly," "in the far north," "the heights of the clouds."[7] We
have already considered several of the satirical means in earlier chapters,
such as irony, expressed as extreme contrast between the overweening conceit of the hero of the elegy and his nonentity and quietus that come about
with his sudden decline and fall. In this elegy the irony assumes a dramatic
and grotesque expression, whose acuteness increases from scene to scene.
In the first scene, the cypresses and cedars of Lebanon rejoice at his calamity, these having been the victims of the great hewer: "'Since you were
laid low, no hewer comes up against us'"; in the second scene, all the kings
of the nations rise from their thrones to greet the one who tyrannized them
with unrelenting persecution, and say to him, "'You too have become
as weak as we! You have become like us! Your pomp is brought down to
Sheol . . . maggots are the bed beneath you, and worms are your covering'";
in the third, in which occurs his fall from heaven to hell, from "the heights
of the clouds" to "depths of the Pit," "those who see you" look on, witnesses
to the fall of the despot (similar to the use of "all who saw you" in the taunt
elegy of Ezekiel against Tyre [Ezek 28:17–19]),[8] and point in astonishment:
"Is this the man who made the earth tremble, Who shook kingdoms?"
The most pointed satirical barb is the demonstrative pronoun הזה האיש ("Is
this the man?"), especially when this appears as the antithesis and counterweight to the astro-mythological title describing him at the peak of his
haughtiness as a god, "Day Star, son of Dawn." The use of epithets, whether
for the purpose of disguise or to extend meaning from the personal and
individual to the typical and universal, is an important tool in the hands of
the satirist.

Another important element is the secular character of this taunt, in
which the rise and fall of the despot are not explained as due to any divine
intervention, although religious significance may reasonably be deemed to
inhere in the attribution itself to the prophet Isaiah and in the explanation
apparently added by a glossator ascribing the fall of the oppressor to the

---

[7] R. Alter, *The Art of Biblical Poetry* (New York, 1985), 147; Barth, 131–135.
[8] Gray, *Isaiah*, 257.

fact that "the Lord has broken the staff of the wicked" (v 5).[9] The more explicit divine intervention is in the extreme reversal in the fate of the despot and of his victims, the more it detracts from the immanent satirical significance of the elegy. The reversal is then presented as heavenly punishment of the man for his sin, while the satire naturally aims to ridicule the feebleness of the man, who through his arrogance and unbridled ambition brings about his own eclipse. Nor is it impossible that the secular form of the elegy is an outcome of the parodic modeling of the dirge, which in itself, by its nature in the Bible, is secular: the divinity is not mentioned in dirges (see David's dirge over Saul and Jonathan and his dirge over Abner). From beginning to end this satire against the king of Babylon is an exemplar of the taunt elegy, whose connection with the model of the dirge is only formal, that is, in its structure and form; it is unconnected with respect to mood and the essence of the experience.

The historical figure in the taunt

The identity of the protagonist at whom this taunt is directed is important for an understanding of the nature of political satire in the Bible. The argument that it is irrelevant to investigate which ruler was the target of this satire, and that its significance lies in its ahistoricity and its hero's being the archetype of the ruler who pretends to godhood,[10] misses the special substance of political satire in the Bible. On the contrary: the personal element is vital for comprehending the roots of political satire, which in its essence draws from the political experiences and events of the period and is directed at real historical figures, although at times and for various reasons it masks its particular intentions.[11] There is great uncertainty among scholars and commentators as to the historical background of the satire and the identity of the hero. The "king of Babylon" in the title is a most difficult reference, a political element that does not fit into the historical setting of Isaiah's prophecy. The historical encounter between the kingdom of Judah and the kingdom of Babylon only occurred close to the destruction of Jerusalem, about a century after Isaiah's prophecy, which reflects mainly the centrality and hegemony of Assyria in the region. So if the taunt was indeed

9 Gray, *Isaiah*, 247 and 252; Kaiser, *Isaiah*, 28, n. 9 and 30.

10 R. Alter (n. 7), 150.

11 Charles E. Schutz, *Political Humor* (London, 1977); M.D. Fletcher, *Contemporary Political Satire* (London, 1987).

meant for the "king of Babylon," it has to be attributed to a prophet later than Isaiah. There are also grounds for this conclusion in the redactive aspect of the book.

The taunt elegy against the king of Babylon continues the prophecy on the collapse of Babylon in chapter 13, which certain signs indicate as being far later than the time of Isaiah (e.g., 13:17). Some traditional exegetes dismiss the gap in history, assuming that the prophet was able to foretell the future. By contrast, many other scholars date the composition of the taunt to the sixth century BCE. They deny Isaiah the authorship of this taunt, as well as other prophecies that do not fit into Isaiah's historical vista, without naming another prophet as its writer. The reverse direction regarding the time of the composition and its author was indicated by Kaufmann, who attributed both the taunt and the prophecy on Babylon in chapter 13 to Isaiah. He argued that the taunt was not against the king of Babylon but against the king of Assyria (Assyria was confused with Babylon by the writer, who knew that the kings of Assyria sometimes assumed the title "King of Babylon"). At the same time, Kaufmann does not consider the taunt an original work by Isaiah but only a reworking of an earlier poem.[12]

Winckler was the first to point out the historical setting of the taunt on the basis of the Assyrian document K 4730, known as "The Sin of Sargon," in which Sennacherib relates the strange manner of the death of his father Sargon, who also entitled himself "King of Babylon," without burial in his house. Winckler noted the similarity between details of Sargon's death in the Assyrian document and the end of the taunt in Isaiah: the decease of the tyrant king, who did not secure a fitting burial like other kings, and who was cast out of his sepulchre like a "loathed untimely birth" (vv 19–20). On the basis of this resemblance Winckler concluded that the taunt elegy had to do with the fate of Sargon II, king of Assyria (722–705 BCE), whom he identified as the target of the taunt. A later editor re-addressed it against the king of Babylon through the heading (v 4).[13] (Some leading Assyriologists believe that Winckler has gone too far in making this identification.[14] But many scholars and commentators tend to support his assumption that it is

---

12 Y. Kaufmann, *Toledoth ha-emunah ha-Yisraelith* vol. 3 (1964), 179 (Hebrew).

13 H. Winckler, *Altorientalische Forschungen* I (1896) 410ff. Recently this document was published in *State Archives of Assyria* Bulletin, III (1989) by Prof. Tadmor and Prof. Parpola under the tile "The Sin of Sargon and Sennacherib's Last Will."

14 Tadmor and Parpola, 4 indicate the pioneering contribution that Winckler made, followed by their comment: "Perhaps over-audaciously, he combined the motif of the unburied king with Isaiah 14: 14–20."

Sargon, Sennacherib's father, who is the protagonist of Isaiah's taunt elegy, and therefore one may not deny Isaiah, in whose time the fall and mysterious death of Sargon occurred, its authorship.[15])

Let us not be unduly hasty in identifying the "king of Babylon" in the taunt with Sargon II—particularly as Sargon appears by name in the caption to another of Isaiah's prophecies against the nations, and actually with the title King of Assyria, not King of Babylon (20:1). Note, moreover, that Sargon's sin in the Assyrian document was the establishment of a new capital in Dur-Sharrukin, on which account the priests apparently refused him a proper burial: in Isaiah's taunt elegy it was his despotism and his haughtiness towards nations and God. Still, it may be presumed that the historical event linked to the unusual death of Sargon (705 BCE), as well as events and historical experiences associated with the tyrannical methods of the kings of Assyria in its aggrandizement as a world power, are reflected in the portrayal of the tyrant in Isaiah's satire. Whether Sargon was the direct target of the satire or whether he was incorporated in a more "synthetic" paradigmatic figure in terms of his historical components, when Assyria's world hegemony was replaced by the despotic regime of Babylonia, with which Judah also—and principally—kept a historical account, the author, or a later editor, had no difficulty in relating this satire against the king of Babylon.[16] Nevertheless, I would not discard entirely the possibility that from the outset the prophet-satirist (e.g., Isaiah) disguised the object of his taunt elegy and used the title "king of Babylon" (which Sargon also assumed) without explicitly naming him, as the satire ends with a curse against the king and his house (vv 20–21).[17]

The literary affinity of the taunt to Isaiah

For historical reasons, as indicated above, we cannot dismiss the possibility that the elegy was directed against Sargon II, king of Assyria; similarly, for literary reasons, we cannot dismiss the possibility that its author was Isaiah.

The lexical-stylistic criterion should be introduced here. Various commentators aver that in view of the style and motifs of the taunt elegy, Isaiah

---

[15] H.L. Ginsberg, "Reflexes of Sargon in Isaiah after 715 BCE," *JAOS* 88 (1968), 47–50. A.S. Herbert, *Isaiah 1–39* (Cambridge, 1973), 102.

[16] Gray, *Isaiah* 252; Sawyer, *Isaiah* 143; Barth (n. 6), 135–141.

[17] Sawyer, 145 relates the curse to all evildoers and their descendants, similar to the ending of the Song of Deborah (Judges 5: 31).

should not be excluded as its possible author. Ginsberg indeed drew up a
table comparing idioms and expressions in this elegy with other prophecies
whose ascription to Isaiah is undoubted.[18] The stylistic parallel between the
taunt elegy and two other satirical poems of Isaiah against the king of Assyria (10:5–19; 37:22–29) may attest to the possibility that Isaiah was the
author of the taunt elegy.

Another important characteristic of Isaiah's style is the use of the
construct before prepositions. In this taunt elegy this occurs twice: מכת בלתי
סרה "with unceasing blows" (v 6) and יורדי על אבני בור "who go down to the
stones of the Pit" (v 19). A similar usage is found in 9:1—יושבי בארץ צלמות
"the people who walked in darkness" (cf. also 19:8; 30:18). These account
for a considerable number of Gesenius' examples of the use of the construct
in the prophetic-poetic style.[19]

Epilogue

At least two more taunt satires, from which citations have been quoted
above, appear in the collection of Isaiah's prophecies, and both refer to
Assyria: one is directed to Assyria (10:5–19), and the title "The King of
Assyria" is explicitly stated (v 12); the other is a caustic satire against Sennacherib, king of Assyria (37:22–29). In addition to these, features of political satire appear in other prophecies of his, directed both inwards (especially the "Woe" prophecies [5:8–25; 10:1–4; 28]) and outwards, in the
prophecies against the nations. His wide use of satire in his prophecies
in international political contexts makes him also a natural contender for
the authorship of this taunt. Furthermore, the wisdom-ironic theme in Proverbs 16:18, "Pride goes before destruction, and a haughty spirit before a
fall," which also appears in this satire, characterizes other satirical poems of
Isaiah. Hoffmann's argument that this motif appears in his prophecies in a
historiosophic-religious sense, while in this satire that nuance is absent, is
certainly true, but it is not decisive.[20] The satire is set in a prophetic framework where the historiosophic-religious meaning of God's intervention in
the fall of the tyrant is taken for granted (14: 3, 22–23, and perhaps also
vv 24–27, referring to Assyria).

18 See note 15, the list of parallels is on p. 53.
19 Gesenius-Kautzsch, *Hebrew Grammar,* 130a.
20 Y. Hoffman, *The Prophecies against Foreign Nations in the Bible* (Tel Aviv, 1977),
81–85 (Hebrew).

On the other hand, if this is taken as proof that Isaiah used an earlier satirical poem for the purpose of his prophecy, as Kaufmann holds,[21] then one must seek a political-historical circumstance prior to Isaiah that gave the anonymous poet grounds for writing that satire. It is doubtful that a historical situation like that reflected in the "satire" can be found in the history of this geopolitical region earlier than the world rule of Assyria. Moreover, there is no other "Assyrian-Babylonian" king whose fate matches that presented in the poem. So what is to be gained from the search for an anonymous author to replace the prophet known by name?

[21] See note 12.

—— ℬ 7 ℬ——

POLITICAL SATIRE IN THE "WOE" PROPHECIES OF ISAIAH AND HABAKKUK

About forty prophetic units in the prophetic literature open with the elegiac word "Woe" (הוי), accompanied by a name or an epithet. In this sense they represent a special literary pattern in the prophetic literature, at least regarding the style of communication between the prophet and the object of his prophecy. But also with respect to the prophetic message itself, most of these units share a polemical censorious tendency, and, in not a few cases, a political message couched in satirical terms. At times this is directed at external enemies, nations or kings of nations, called by name or described by attributes, as in certain of the prophecies concerning the nations in Isaiah (10: 5; 17: 12; 18: 1; 33: 1), the prophecies of Nahum (3: 1), Habakkuk (2: 6, 9, 12, 15, 19), and Zephaniah (2: 5); at times it is aimed at internal political and social factors, as in Isaiah (5: 8ff.; 10: 1; 25: 1; 29: 1; 30: 1; 31: 1), Amos (5: 18; 6: 1), Jeremiah (22: 18; 23: 1 [against the kings of Judea]), Ezekiel (13: 3, 18; 34: 2) and Zephaniah (3: 1).

Because of the exclamatory "Woe" that begins these prophetic units, there is a tendency to seek the roots of this literary model in the elegy for the dead, and testimony to this is found in 1 Kgs 13: 30, Jer 22: 18; 34: 5, and to some extent in the "Woe" in Amos 5: 16. But even if the prophets borrowed the introductory word "Woe" from an elegy for the dead, it still cannot be inferred from this that the Woe prophecies themselves are elegies, owing to their other literary features.[1] On the contrary, it seems that the prophets made satirical use of the elegiac "Woe" for purposes of a polemic

---

[1] J.W. Whedbee, *Isaiah and Wisdom* (Nashville, 1971), 88.

against domestic enemies and rivals, the elegy generally being replete with scorn and derision, and usually ending with a vision of catastrophe accompanied by the utterance of a curse. Thus, it is immediately possible to sense that what sounds like an elegy is nothing other than malicious joy.[2] In this respect, and with respect to the formal stylistic mode, a distinction should be drawn between the meaning of "Woe" in this pattern and that in the construction "Woe is me" (אוֹי לִי), also found in several prophecies (Isa 3: 9; 6: 5; 24: 16; Jer 4: 13; 6: 4; 10: 19; 13: 27; 15: 10; 45: 3; 48: 46; Ezek 16: 23; 24: 6, 9; Hos 7: 13; 9: 12). Most of these cases express genuine fear.[3]

It is highly doubtful if these formal and polemical qualities are enough to define a genre in itself; moreover, there are differences in content and form among the various units included in this pattern. In this it is no different from others in the biblical literature, which, on the one hand, have distinguishing features and, on the other hand, features in common with different patterns. From analysis of various Woe prophecies, especially in Isaiah, it emerges that this pattern perhaps more than others is characterized by a satirical note, to the extent that the "Woe" commencing these prophecies may be termed the "satirical Woe," not merely the "polemical Woe."

1. "Ah (הוֹי) Assyria, rod of my anger . . ." (Isa 10: 5–16)

A. Definition of the type and context of the prophetic unit

At first sight, the opening word הוֹי would seem to determine the generic relationship of this prophecy to the Woe prophecies. However, this opening, which is present in about forty prophecies in the Bible, about half of them in Isaiah,[4] is insufficient in itself to characterize this prophecy in terms of its content and form. Moreover, the debate over the origin of the Woe prophecies and their nature as an independent genre is still ongoing.[5] Even though the expression "Woe" is in origin a word of lament for the dead, as attested in 1 Kgs 13: 30 and Jer 24: 18, this poetic prophecy, like other Woe prophecies, lacks the content and formal elements typical of the elegy. Derision, however, is not lacking in it, so it may be seen as a

---

2 H.J. Krause, "hoj als prophetische Leichenkalge über das eigene Volk im 8 Jahrhundert," *ZAW* 85 (1973), 15–46.

3 G. Wanke, "אוֹי" und "הוֹי", *ZAW* 78 (1966), 215–218.

4 E. Gerstenberger, "The Woe-Oracles of the Prophets," *JBL* 81 (1962), 249–263; and see especially W. Janzen, *Mourning Cry and Woe Oracle* (Berlin and New York, 1972) with selected bibliography.

5 R.J. Clifford, "The Use of 'Hoy' in the Prophets," *CBQ* 27 (1966), 456–464.

striking example of Isaiah's political satire; but the name "taunt elegy" warrants caution.

Definition of the unit in terms of its extent is likewise difficult, on account of its structural complexity and its inner inconsistency, evident in the prose seam in verse 12 that intervenes between the two poetic speeches. But the difficulty is chiefly due to the combination of prophetic stanzas on "the remnant of Israel" (vv 20–22, 24–26) with prophetic stanzas on Assyria and its downfall (vv 16–19, 27–34), involving multiple transitions from poetry to prose and from direct speech to indirect speech.[6] The definition of the extent of the unit leaves the prophecy without an ending, in that it does not include the punishment invoked against Assyria. Here it departs from other Woe prophecies, which usually conclude with a declaration of the punishment due to their object, the word "therefore" signifying the passage from the reproof to the penalty. It is true that afterwards a description of the punishment does appear, opening with the word "Therefore" (vv 16–19), which certain commentators consider the direct continuation of the unit. Yet the description does not match the account of Assyria's sin either in content or in style.[7]

Regarding style, it may be argued that the depiction of the impending destruction of Assyria on the territory of Israel in the prose passage opening with "Therefore" (v 24) contains words from which are derived the metaphors used for Assyria at the opening of the prophecy—שבט (rod), אפי (my indignation) (v 25), and also מטה (staff) and זעם (anger) (vv 24–26), and so it has a link with sin; but this stylistic link, even if it attests to a single author of these units, is still not enough to indicate that this passage is the direct continuation of the poetic unit, and it is doubtful that it ever was the original ending of the prophecy. For these reasons it is preferable to consider the two pairs of double rhetorical questions in verse 15 as the organic ending of the poetic prophetic unit.[8] In terms of its structure, the rhetorical ending returns us to the beginning. In this way a concentric structure emerges, a poem opening with the metaphors "rod of my anger" and "staff of my fury" (v 5), and ending with a repeat of these metaphors ("rod" and "staff") in the rhetorical questions in verse 15; verse 12 divides the poem into two stanzas.

6 G.B. Gray, *The Book of Isaiah* (ICC, Edinburgh, 1962), 194–5; O. Kaiser, *Isaiah 1–12* (OTL; Philadelphia, 1983), 230 ff.; H. Barth, *Die Jesaja-Worte in der Josiazeit* (WMANT 48, 1977), 17ff.; B.S. Childs, *Isaiah and the Assyrian Crisis* (London, 1967), 41–42.

7 Barth, *ibid.*, 18 and also 28–30.

8 Childs, *ibid.*, (n. 6) 41–44.

The problem of defining the prophetic unit as to type and content is augmented by the problem of its literary context and its place in the framework of Isaiah's prophecy. Although the prophecy refers to Assyria, it was not included in the collection of prophecies concerning the nations (Isa 13–23): it continues the series of prophecies concerning Israel, principally those linked with the confrontation between Israel and Assyria. This is on account of its location, but also on account of the inner dialectic link between the role of Assyria as a world power and the fate of Judea and Jerusalem, which finds expression at the beginning of the poem: "Against a godless nation I send him, and against the people of my wrath I command him" (v 6, and cf. 9: 18: "Through the wrath of the Lord of hosts").[9] This link appears explicitly in the prose bridge in the middle of the poem (v 12), and also in verses 17 and 24, which speak of the downfall of Israel and Assyria.

Opening with a "Woe" followed by a name and attributes, the prophecy also belongs to the group of Woe prophecies in Isaiah (5: 8–10, 11–17, 18–19, 20, 21, 22, ending at 10: 4), although it differs from them in its object and its structure. It is linked by association and alliteration to the ending of the Woe prophecy that precedes it—the repeated refrain of God's judgment, "For all this his anger (אפו) is not turned away and his hand (ידו) is stretched out still" (10: 4)—by means of the metaphors appearing in the opening: "rod of my anger" (שבט אפי) and "staff of my fury" (מטה זעמי) (10: 5).[10] Another connection by association and alliteration in these two prophecies is between verse 2 ("that widows might be their spoil (שללם)/ and that they may make the fatherless their prey [יבזו]) and verse 6 ("to take spoil (לשלל שלל) and seize plunder—(ולבז בז) . . .")

B. Formal and structural aspects: The structure and inner integrity of the unit

In structure and form this prophetic unit is characterized as a polemic in poetic meter uttered by God. Although the entire speech is a dispute with Assyria (or the king of Assyria), it is not addressed to him in direct speech,

---

9 Y. Hoffman, *The Prophecies against Foreign Nations in the Bible* (Tel Aviv, 1977) 304 (Hebrew), claims that this prophecy differs in its character from the prophecies against foreign nations.

10 Childs (n. 6) 41, n. 125, indeed pointed out this link, but did not connect it with the likeness in sound.

but put to him in the third person: "and his rod . . . I send him . . . I command him . . . but he does not so intend . . ." So too is the rhetorical question formulated as a metaphor and directed against him at the end of the unit (v 15). In the framework of the poetic-polemical argument, two boastful speeches of Assyria are quoted: one in verses 8–11, apparently with editorial emendations in verses 10–11;[11] the other by the king of Assyria (vv 13–14). These speeches, put in the mouths of Assyria and its king (for satirical purposes, as we shall see below), are also spoken in poetic meter and direct speech. Some phrases are uttered in the third person; these seemingly are God's words for the purpose of his polemic against them: "For he says" (v 8), "for he said" (v 13).

Several commentators assert that the prose of verse 12 that separates the poetic speeches of Assyria was added by a later redactor; they also surmise that at first a single unbroken speech of the king of Assyria was quoted in the prophecy.[12] Obviously, the first half of verse 12—"When the Lord has finished all his work on Mount Zion and on Jerusalem"—is not spoken by the first-person speaker. The stylistic change from a rhythmical sentence to one with complex syntactical structure, likewise attests to this. Also the content, namely, the punishment that God will bring down on Assyria because of its haughtiness (the second part of v 12), being set for a specific time (the first part of v 12), testifies to the secondary nature of the sentence in that it imposes on the time at which the dialogue is taking place the time of the editor. It is doubtful whether the second part of verse 12, opening with direct speech by the speaker—"I will punish the arrogant boasting of the king of Assyria and his haughty pride"—should also be regarded as part of the secondary addition; not only in content, but in syntax and meter, too, it is no different from the style of the unit as a whole. And as it appears in the Masoretic text, it does not match the first part of the verse. To be sure, if we delete the first part of the verse and leave the second part as it is, there will be a gap between it and what precedes it (v 11); this has prevented many commentators from separating the two parts of verse 12 and has caused them to read instead of "I will punish" in the first person, "He will punish" in the third person,[13] in order to accommodate the two parts of the verse. But it is possible that the later redactor modified the connecting link

---

11 Gray, Barth and Kaiser in their commentaries (*ibid.*, n. 6) to these verses.

12 B. Duhm, *Das Buch Jesaia* (Göttingen, 1914) 99f. Childs, *op. cit.* 41, rejects this surmise.

13 Based on the version of LXX.

that perhaps once existed between two speeches of Assyria, or expanded it. In any event, the literary analysis proposed by several commentators that omits verses 10–12 as being secondary editorial processing, and the start of verse 13—"For he says"—as being a connective repetition, does not succeed in reconstructing a seamless speech by Assyria.

The dramatic effect of the polemic, although produced by quotation and not by direct dialogue, gains from the separation between the two rounds of polemic, one in verses 5–11 and one in verses 13–15. The first cites Assyria's intentions regarding the destruction of Jerusalem as a way of destroying many nations. It begins with a conditional clause, "For he will say" and ends with the future tense, "I shall do to Jerusalem and her idols" (v 11). The second round quotes Assyria's boasting about his deeds in the past tense: "For he said . . . I have done it . . . I have understood . . . and I have removed . . . and I have brought down . . . I have gathered." The first turns on his obsession to destroy and master nations; the second on his haughtiness against his dispatcher, God. The two rounds of the polemic, each representing the conflict between the true maker of world history and one who pretends to being such, are structured as a chiasmus; the first begins with God's words (vv 5–7) and ends with Assyria's words (vv 8–1); the second opens with the words of the king of Assyria (vv 13–14) and ends with the words of God (v 15).

C. The satirical tendency

1) Use of the opponent's speeches for the purpose of the polemic against him

The prophecy itself opens with the word הוֹי, and unlike most of the prophecies with this opening, here the word is followed by the personal name "Assyria" accompanied by two metaphors in the construct form: "rod of my anger" and "staff of my fury." By this means, and in combination with the possessive pronoun, Assyria is made into the instrument of the speaker, God. The opening of this prophecy differs from the other Woe prophecies of Isaiah and other prophets, in which הוֹי is immediately followed by epithets unconnected to any personal name and without a link back to the speaker, mostly in the form of the active participle with the definite article. It may only be said that the common feature of this "Woe" and the others is its rhetorical polemical application. If indeed those seeking the literary roots of the cry "Woe" in the elegy for the dead are right, then an extreme change has taken place and the prophetic usage has transformed it dramatically and radically from an expression of pain over a man's death to one of scorn at a man's pride and arrogance—from identification to ridicule and sarcasm.

In the discussion of the "Fable"-elegy there was some profit in tracing the roots of the ancient elegy that the prophet turned parodically into a taunt-elegy (see the discussions on the "fable" of the king of Babylon [Isa 14: 4–20][14] and on the elegy on Moab [Isa 15–16]);[15] but with this prophecy concerning Assyria there is none, nor any likelihood at all of finding such roots. If there is a parodic component in this Woe prophecy it exists in the boasting speeches of the king of Assyria with the purpose of ridiculing him. The prophet places in the mouth of Assyria, who is the object of his criticism, those very words that make him liable to God's judgment. In this way Assyria's vaunts in direct speech turn into a sort of self-incrimination by the accused that incurs his judgment. The prophet took the "materials" of his speeches from the vainglorious descriptions of the kings of Assyria known from Assyrian records on their military campaigns and victories and on the cities of the kingdoms that fell to them.[16] But he subverts them, mainly in the second speech, when he turns the proud words of the Assyrian king regarding nations and kingdoms to haughtiness with respect of God. The sarcastic satirical note that accompanies the Assyrian king's hubris—"By the strength of my hand I have done it, and by my wisdom I have understood . . ."—is meant to pour scorn on his delusion that the source of his mastery in the world arena is his strength and his wisdom as a ruler, while in fact he is a tool in the hands of God, the true master of world history. Since Assyria's speeches are cited for the purpose of the polemic, they serve the polemicist's tendency, as is already evident from the chiastic order of the two rounds of the polemic noted above.

Accordingly, God opens and closes the polemic. The speeches of Assyria, even though they reflect actual historical and political events, are not quoted to serve the purposes of history: the goal is historiosophic. The transition from the historical event to its lesson is expressed chiefly in the second round of the polemic, whose agenda has to do with identifying who is the true governor of history. The hubris of the Assyrian king, who relates his deeds in the sphere of world history to his strength and his wisdom, and

---

14 See above, Chapter Six.

15 See above, Chapter Five.

16 J.B. Pritchard, *ANET*, 282–284 Tiglath-Pileser III; 284–287 Sargon II; 287–288 Sennacherib.

who does as he pleases throughout the world—"And I have removed the boundaries of peoples and have plundered their treasures" (v 13)—places him in direct confrontation with God, who in the prophet's conception is the one who sets boundaries for peoples (cf. Deut 32: 8: "He fixed the bounds of the peoples"). In the polemic, God does not dispute the historical facts as described in the boasting of the Assyrian king in his first speech; on the contrary, he allows him to expand the account of his actions on the world scene, in order to prove to him, in the end, that what he portrays as his successes and "the fruit of the greatness of his heart" originate in the divine plan, that as king he is nothing but an instrument in the hand of the true maker of history. He achieves this by means of rhetorical questions that conclude the polemic (v 15).

2) The use of rhetorical questions and wisdom fables

The rhetorical questions, even when containing a sapiential metaphor borrowed by the prophet for the purpose of his polemic (v 15a), serve to close the prophet's satirical-polemical cycle that opens with "Ah, Assyria, the rod of my anger, the staff of my fury," and that ends with "Shall the axe vaunt itself over him who hews with it . . . , as if a rod should wield him who lifts it, or as if a staff should lift him who is not wood!" A similar polemical use of a rhetorical question in which is embedded a sapiential metaphor appears in another of Isaiah's Woe prophecies which apparently constitutes an autonomous unit:

> Woe to those who hide deep from the Lord their counsel,
> whose deeds are in the dark,
> and who say, "Who sees us? Who knows us?"
> You turn things upside down!
> Shall the potter be regarded as the clay;
> that the thing made should say of its maker,
> "He did not make me"; or the thing formed say of him who made it,
> "He has no understanding"? (29: 15–16)

In this Woe prophecy the prophet also cites the words of those against whom he directs his critical barbs.[17] The historiosophic lesson is common to both, namely, that it is ludicrous to pretend that it is within the power of human wisdom to alter events determined by their creator in advance. This

---

17 Childs, (n. 6) 43; Whedbee, *op. cit.* (n. 1) 73–74.

lesson constitutes an important element in Isaiah's historiosophic thinking. At times it is reflected in visions of an eschatological nature, such as "The haughty looks of man shall be brought low, and the pride of men shall be humbled; and the Lord alone will be exalted in that day" (2: 11, 17); at times it is reflected in an actual political polemic, as in the Woe prophecies directed against a political leadership that believes itself clever enough to bypass God's intent (25: 1–3; 31: 1–3). Common to them is the satirical use of antithesis and contrast between the object (human being) and the subject (God), in order to prove the folly of humankind's arrogant ambition to change the order of things as determined in the divine plan, especially with respect to political occurrences.

3) Use of allusion for the purpose of antithesis

Antithesis and reversal in the polemical confrontation in this unit are achieved by means of the two-way use of stylistic expressions and alliteration between them. We noted earlier the alliterative link between the opening epithet "rod of my anger and staff of my fury" (v 5) and the metaphorical-rhetorical question that concludes the polemic: "As if a rod should wield him who lifts it, or as if a staff should lift him who is not wood" (v 15). A similar association is also intimated between the metaphor "the arrogant boasting of the king of Assyria (פרי גדל לבב מלך אשור)" (v 12b) and its reversal in the rhetorical question "Shall the saw magnify itself (יתגדל) against him who wields it?" (v 15). Similarly, the figure "his haughty pride" (תפארת רום עיניו, v 12) and its reversal in the metaphorical-rhetorical question "Shall the axe vaunt itself (היתפאר) . . . him who lifts it (מרימו) . . . ?" (v 15).

Antithesis is apparently also achieved through associative intimation between the expression that the prophet uses in this polemic and an expression he has used for another purpose. The boastful words of the king of Assyria include the sole appearance of the unique expression "כאביר" in "like a bull I have brought down those who sat on thrones" (v 13). Some believe that this is to elicit the attributive "אביר ישראל"—which refers to God in Isaiah 1: 24. By way of associative intimation for the purpose of antithesis, several commentators appose the pride of the king of Assyria—"and I removed the boundaries of peoples" (Isa 10: 13) to "he fixed the bounds of the people" (Deut 32: 8).[18]

To these two contrasts should be joined another, which is connected to the metaphor used by the king of Assyria in his boast: "My hand has found

---

[18] J.F.A. Sawyer, *Isaiah I* (Edinburgh, 1984) 284–287.

like a nest the wealth of the peoples; and as men gather eggs that have been forsaken, so I have gathered all the earth; and there was none that moved a wing, or opened the mouth, or chirped" (v 14). Through contradictory association, this metaphor is reminiscent of Isaiah's metaphor in the description of God's protection of his city: "Like birds hovering, so the Lord of hosts will protect Jerusalem; he will protect and deliver it, he will spare and rescue it" (31: 5).

D. The political barb—at whom is it aimed? And what is its historical context?

The prophetic polemic is directed against Assyria, as explicitly stated in the prophecy itself (vv 5, 12). As distinct from what is usual in the prologue to prophecies, which might be secondary (e.g., 14: 4), the mention of "Assyria" in this one constitutes a kind of personification: "But he does not so intend and his mind does not so think" (v 7). However, it is reasonable to suppose that the intention was in fact with respect to the king of Assyria, as stated in verse 12, and that the title "king" was deleted from the opening line, either for the purpose of simplification and inclusion in it of various kings of Assyria, as a collective unit, or on account of the prosody. In any event, the political satire is directed against historical rulers (not against abstract prototypes), whether a particular king (Sennacherib) or other kings who preceded him in their conquests in the region.

The conquests included in the first boastful speech extend through the reigns of three kings of Assyria: Tiglath-pileser (Pul in 2 Kgs 15: 19), who also assumed the title "king of Babylon" (745–726 BCE), and who first introduced the method of deportation as imperial policy towards insurgent nations. During his rule were captured Arpad (740), Calno (738), and Damascus (732), and they became Assyrian dominions. He was succeeded by the king Shalmanasar V (726–722), who beseiged Samaria for three years and died before taking the city. After him came Sargon II (721–705), conqueror of Samaria, as well as Hamath (720) and Carchemish (717), among others.[19] The order of conquests that appears in Isaiah (10: 9) is not identical with this chronological order. Among the places appearing in this list of conquests of the kings of Assyria only two are named explicitly in the speech of Rabshakeh: Hamath and Arpad (Isa 37: 10–13). However, the mention of these conquests in the speech was for polemical purposes, with

19 Sawyer, *ibid.*, 111; and see *ANET* 2, 284–287.

the purpose of calling to mind the lessons of the past for application to the confrontation of the present, while the actual historical context of the prophecy was apparently the impending threat to Jerusalem by the expedition of Sennacherib (701). The message reflected in God's words (v 6: "Against a godless nation I send him"; and cf. 9: 16), and especially in Assyria's boast (v 11: "Shall I not do to Jerusalem . . . as I have done to Samaria?"; v 10: "As my hand has reached to the kingdoms of the idols whose graven images . . . of Jerusalem and Samaria"), from which it may be inferred that Jerusalem had already been captured, is, on the grounds of syntax and content, deemed secondary.[20]

In terms of its historical context this prophecy concerning the king of Assyria joins others uttered by Isaiah in the period of this grave crisis in the history of Judea, when the Assyrian menace to the kingdom and its capital became palpable. Perhaps, it just precedes that prophecy addressed to Sennacherib in 37: 22–32, and it seems to me to be later than the taunt "fable" in chapter 14.

Again, it transpires that political satire served as a keen weapon in the hands of the weak in war against a tyrant despot more powerful than he. It inspired hope in the heart of the feeble, especially when harnessed by the prophet to his theo-political philosophy of history, whereby the God of Israel alone was the planner of historical events, and even Assyria was nothing other than a temporary tool in his hands to carry out his will. Therefore, Assyria in the future would be condemned for its excessive abuse of the mission against Jerusalem, the chosen city.

2. The sequence of Woe prophecies of Habakkuk (2: 6–20)

There is a structural and formal similarity between Habakkuk's Woe prophecies and those of Isaiah. Their use for the purpose of political satire is likewise common to both, and separates them from the other prophets of the scripture. Yet in the interval of time between them, changes occurred in the international political arena; and in the century separating these two prophets, the main protagonists of world history were replaced, the Chaldeans having supplanted the Assyrians. While the politically satirical Woe prophecies of Isaiah grew up in the shadow of world hegemony of Assyria, and Judea's confrontation with it over its independence, those of Habakkuk grew up in the shadow of the world power of Babylon and the decline of

[20] Childs (n. 6) 42.

Judea. To this, and perhaps on account of this, it must be added that Habakkuk's Woe prophecies are devoid of the political censure that was directed inwards, that is, against the ruling circles of Judea, such as we found in the Woe prophecies of Isaiah (30: 1; 31: 1), to say nothing of Isaiah's series of satirical Woe prophecies aimed at the Judean ruling circles whose essence is social and ethical reproof (5: 8–25; 10: 1–4).

The prologue to the sequence of Woe prophecies of Habakkuk indicates that they constitute משל, מליצה and חידות that the nations take up against "him" (v 6), a pronoun whose antecedent is the nation depicted in the preceding verses, identified by commentators, from the explicit statement in 1: 6, as the Chaldeans. The prophet, or the author who added the prologue to the series of Woe prophecies, took pains to define the features of these prophecies in literary terms known to us elsewhere in the Bible: משל, namely a taunt poem (cf. Isa 14: 4; Mic 2: 4);[21] מליצה, apparently from לצון, "laughter" (cf. Prov 1: 6);[22] and חידות, "riddles," apparently obscure fables that have to be explained (cf. Prov 1: 6; Ps 49: 5).[23]

Whether the three terms are synonyms for a single type of satirical poetry, or whether they represent different types, they possess a common formal link in that here each opens with the elegiac word "Woe" in the polemical and satirical sense. Kaufmann rightly argued, therefore, that "in Habakkuk's oracle there is something akin to the currency of the poetry of the 'fabulists' (מושלים)."[24] The structure of the sequence of these Woe prophecies, like that of Isaiah's Woe prophecies (5: 8ff.), attests to common roots with the ancient fable poetry, if we include in it the series of Balaam's "fables" (Num 23: 7, 18; 24: 3, 15, 21, 23, 28); and to a certain extent the epigrams on the tribes (Gen 49; Deut 33).[25]

There are even grounds for assuming that a literary tie existed between Habakkuk's series of Woe prophecies and the wisdom literature. The three prefatory terms are also found in the prologue to Proverbs: "To understand a proverb (משל) and a figure (מליצה), the words of the wise and their riddles (חידתם)" (1: 6). Even if these generic terms became means for satire in the prophecy of Habakkuk, their ancestry and birth are seemingly in the

---

. 21 W.H. Ward, Habakkuk (ICC, 1911) "a taunting proverb"; *BDB* 539, "Satire, mocking poem."

22 Pesher Habakkuk scroll from Qumran reads "מליצי" instead of "מליצה."

23 Cf. Ezek. 17: 2; Ps 78: 2, and see also *BDB* 295.

24 Y. Kaufmann, *Toldoth ha-Emuna ha-Israelith III*, 363.

25 Following J. Lindblom's article, "The Political Background of the Shiloh Oracle," *SVT* 1 (1953) 78–87.

wisdom poetry, as may be realized from their use in the Bible (Ps 49: 5; 78: 2; Job 27: 1; 29: 1).

The connection to the wisdom literature is important especially for an understanding of this sequence of Woe prophecies, whose universal, and to some extent, anthropocentric elements (these being the chief features of the wisdom literature) are reflected in it.

A. The sequence

Its five-part structure is determined by the opening word "Woe" followed by an attribute in the form of an active participle in the singular (vv 6, 9, 12, 15, 19). Only in the first of these does the definite article appear with the participle. Some commentators tend to regard this entire sequence with its different attributes and its personal characteristics as a succession of taunt and doom prophecies directed against the Chaldeans. This view is based on the prophecy that precedes the sequence, in which the rise of the Chaldeans is depicted, and on the similarity between it and the terms characterizing them in this Woe series:

1: 6: For, lo, I am rousing the Chaldeans . . . who march through the breadth of the earth, to seize habitations not their own (לא-לו)
(cf. 2, 6: Woe to him who heaps up what is not his own—לא-לו);

9: They all come for violence (חמס); terror of them goes before them, they gather captives like sand
(cf. 2: 8: For the blood of omen and violence (חמס)) to the earth);

10: At kings they scoff, and of rulers they make sport
(cf. 2: 6: Shall not all these);

2: 5: He gathers for himself all the nations, and collects as his own (ויקבץ אליו) all peoples (כל העמים)
(cf. 2: 8, 10: By cutting off many peoples [קצות עמים רבים]).

The prophet makes it emerge from the mouths of all the peoples that the Chaldeans have swallowed gathered unto them (2: 5), as well as the mouths of the kings and rulers of those peoples at whom the Chaldeans scoffed (1: 10) the taunting and derisive words ridiculing the fall of that ruling nation (2: 6a). However, various signs raise doubts as to whether these taunt poems were directed against a single nation from the outset, and whether the series was from the first constructed as a single poetic unit. Two lines of the third poem (vv 13 and 14) are parallel in content and style to those appearing in the prophecies of other prophets, for example, "Peoples labor only for fire, and nations weary themselves for nought" (v 13), as compared to Jer 51: 58; and "For the earth will be filled with the knowledge of the glory of the Lord as the waters cover the sea" (v 14), as compared to Isaiah 11: 9. In content and form, the second of these lines diverges from Habakkuk's poem and appears in a more credible context in the prophecy of a prophet who predated him. So it is doubtful whether these two lines were not inserted into the series by a later author. The polemic against idolatry that concludes the fourth poem (v 18) and serves as the subject of the main polemic of the fifth stanza (vv 19–22) is exceptional in its content and religious satirical message, as the four preceding Woe poems in the sequence are morally and politically satirical in nature.[26] Its polemic against idolatry is like those in the prophecies of Deutero-Isaiah (44: 6ff.; 45: 5ff.). Moreover, the closing of the fifth poem, and of the entire sequence, with the declaration "And the Lord is in his holy temple; let all the earth keep silence before him" (v 20), is similar in content and style to that in the prophecy of Zechariah 2: 17, whose post-exilic setting is clearly evident.

The implication is that not all the Woe prophecies in the sequence were written from the outset by Habakkuk as parts of a single poem, but apparently were created under changing circumstances. There is even doubt whether from the start they were aimed at one nation, or one ruler. It is not impossible that the second Woe prophecy was against Edom, as intimated by its metaphor, "to set his net on high, to be safe from the reach of harm," which is similar to that depicting Edom in taunt elegy of Obadiah (vv 3–4; and see also Jer 49: 47). Furthermore, the fourth Woe prophecy, which contains signs linking it to the narrative of Noah's drunkenness and nakedness (Gen 9: 20–29), was not initially directed against the Chaldeans. In his commentary to the Noah narrative, Cassuto pointed out the connection between the tale of Noah's drunkenness and Habakkuk's prophecy, and in his opinion the prophecy was directed against Babylon, which is mentioned in the Table of Nations (Gen 10: 10), as the origin of the kingdom of Nimrod son of Cush son of Ham (who revealed his father's nakedness).[27] Yet with the same degree of imagination, one may explain it as being against Moab or Ammon, who were born through the conceiving of Lot's daughters by their father after they had made him drunk with wine (Gen 19: 30–38).[28]

---

26 K. Elliger, *Habakkuk* (ATD 6, 1967) 43.

27 U. Cassuto, *The Book of Genesis* (Jerusalem, 1974) 104 (Hebrew).

28 Z. Weisman, "Ethnology, Etiology, Genealogy, and Historiography in the Tale of Lot and His Daughters (Genesis 19: 30–38)" (Heb.), in *Sha'arei Talmon," "Studies in the Bible,*

So it is reasonable to assume that Habakkuk drew the sarcastic motifs he used in his political Woe prophecies from a deposit of early ethnological folklore which was not short of satirical tendencies against different nations, and that he turned them against the Chaldeans. If he in fact did so, and foresaw their downfall, he did not state it explicitly in a prophecy of doom, but preferred to apply satirical artistic means for this purpose. The first of these is disguise, one of the most important of the satirist's tools. Through its use he is freed from the need to mention his "victim's" name. He may conceal his direct target, and he may leave the work of identifying it to his audience. To enable the latter to do so the satirist is careful to drop clues. Here, as in other Woe poems, this is accomplished by the use of attributes whereby the traits and political-ethical profile of the object of his scorn take shape. Some examples are: "who heaps up what is not his own . . . and loads himself with pledges" (v 6); "who gets evil gain for his house, to set his nest on high, to be safe from the reach of harm" (v 9); "who builds a town with blood and founds a city on iniquity" (v 12).

These attributes are of a personal nature, but still they may be interpreted as the personification of a nation.[29] They allow a direct argument with the object of the derision, since they are followed by a polemic with the object of the prophecy in direct speech and in second person (vv 7, 10, 16–17). This direct polemic is absent in the third and fifth poems (whose lack of uniformity and incongruity were discussed above), which leads us to suspect that they were added to the original poems as dilations.

The anthropocentric quality of the poems is connected to their secular nature, and apart from the two divergent poems in which God is mentioned by name (vv 13, 20), God is not described as active in the quarrel between the nations and is not mentioned in the taunt poem itself. The phrase "the cup in the Lord's right hand," woven into the fourth poem (v 16), is different in content and meter from the poem as a whole and leads to the conjecture that it was added under the influence of the central image in the cup prophecy of Jeremiah (25: 15ff.), in which the king of Sheshach (Babylon) drinks the cup of wine of wrath from God's hand after all the kings on the face of the earth (*ibid.*, v. 26).[30]

Qumran, and the Ancient Near East (eds. M. Fishbane and E. Tov) (Winona Lake, Indiana, 1992), 43–52.

[29] Otherwise Watts who interprets this Woe prophecy on a personal level: see J.D.W. Watts, *Joel, Obadiah, Nahum, Habakkuk and Zephaniah* (Cambridge, 1975), 139.

[30] Elliger, *op. cit.* (n. 26), 47, but see also the phrase: "For in the hand of the Lord there is a cup" (Ps 75: 9).

Like the two exceptional dilations noted above, this phrase also reflects a theological trend, whose purpose is to expand the satirical elegies and re-fashion them as parts of a comprehensive meta-historical and eschatological vision, concerning judgment "of the nations at the hand of the Lord," the vanity of idolatry, and universal recognition of the glory of the Lord (vv 13–14, 18–20). Similar eschatological themes appear in Habakkuk's prayer (chap 3), which concludes the sequence of his prophecies.[31] If the dilations in the sequence of Woe prophecies were made in connection with this prayer, by the prophet himself, or by an author who edited the collection of his prophecies, we cannot determine. Even if the theological dilations are to be ascribed to Habakkuk himself, this does not undermine the distinctions between the political taunt poem as the core of his work and his theological exposition as an addition to it. In this case there are grounds for the belief that Habakkuk used political (and probably more ancient) taunt poems for the needs of his historiosophic or historio-theological message. In addition to those we have noted, a range of formal strategies characterizes these nuclear taunt poems as political satire.

B. The use of wordplay for the purpose of ridicule

The obvious example is verse 8: "Because you have plundered many nations all the remnant of the peoples shall plunder you." In its structure, the wordplay between its opening hemistich שלות (from שלל plunder) and its closing hemistich ישלוך, and its satirical symmetry on the principle of an eye for an eye, it is similar to the "Woe" prophecy of Isaiah 33: 1. Habakkuk's particular use of verbs from the root שלל is unique, but the combination שלל לשלל is a characteristic expression in Isaiah's prophecies against Assyria (Isa 8: 1, 3; 10: 6).

There is a touch of ridicule in the use of alliteration and the pun לא-לו in the opening line of the first Woe poem and in its continuation "and loads himself with pledges." As already stated, it is meant as a description characterizing the Chaldeans in the opening prophecy: "Who march through the breadth of the earth, to seize habitations not their own (לא-לו)" (1: 6).

C. Derision expressed in the ambivalent use of phrases
with double entendre

This is how one should understand the special combination מספח חמתך ("the joining of your wrath"), which appears in direct speech and undoubt-

---

31 J.S. Licht, "Habakkuk," *EB* III, 9 (Hebrew).

edly as a reproof חמתך may be interpreted in two ways in this context: "Your anger (cf. Est 1: 12), and "your wine" (poisoned wine: cf. Jer 25: 15), and it is possible that the prophet intended both of these in his irony: the anger of the Chaldeans is the poisoned wine they give all the nations to drink. In both, the malice and the humiliation that the "Chaldeans" pour down on the defeated peoples are prominent. Also, in the curse that follows the reproof an expression appears that may be interpreted in two ways: as ערל, in the sense of ערלה ("foreskin"), meaning "Your uncircumcised member will be exposed as you exposed the nakedness of others" (according to Kimḥi); or by transposition of letters as הרעל, in which case the word derives from רעל: "your cup will be poisoned."[32]

D. Sarcasm through use of the absurd

Sarcasm through the absurd characterizes the fifth Woe poem. Its essence is a polemic of theological nature, a continuation of that in v 18 and expressed in a sapiential rhetorical question: "Woe to him who says to a wooden thing, 'Awake': Will he order a dumb stone, 'Arise'?" (On this rhetorical-sapiential and "Proverbs-type" usage, see above on Isaiah's Woe prophecy against Assyria, 10: 5–15.) The two components of the hendiadys "stone" and "wood" also appear in the second Woe prophecy in this sequence: "For the stone will cry out from the wall, and the beam from the woodwork will respond" (v 11); and this perhaps may be regarded as a kind of contrastive paronomasia, to drive home the absurd in the behavior of the despot who "builds a town with blood and founds a city on iniquity" (v 12); he does not heed the sound of the stone crying out from the wall or the beam from the woodwork that answers it, yet he places his trust in idols of wood and stone (vv 18–19).

Conclusion

Beside the continuing use of this polemical prophetic genre "Woe to . . ." for purposes of political satire, one may discern changes that occurred between the time of the politically satirical Woe prophecies of Isaiah and those of Habakkuk. Essentially these are: a) the weakening of the national pathos connected with actual political confrontations between Judea and the superpowers (Assyria and Babylon), and its transformation into a

---

[32] Y. Avishur, his commentary to *Habakkuk* in *The Book of the Twelve Prophets II* (ed. Z. Weisman) ('Olam ha-Tannak) (Tel Aviv, 1994), 94.

universal moral pathos connected with violence and injustice in the international arena among the nations generally; b) emphatic personification of
the objects of the political satire, namely, the nation, or nations, which tends
increasingly towards the anthropocentric view typical of the wisdom literature. This largely contrasts with the theocentric outlook characteristic of the
prophetic literature of which Isaiah was the classic proponent, especially in
his great Woe prophecy against Assyria (section 1 above).

"MY 'LITTLE ONE' IS THICKER THAN MY FATHER'S LOINS"

Political Satire in the Story of the Division of Davidic Kingdom (1Kgs 12: 1–19)

The account of the division of the Davidic Kingdom consists of two major strands (1Kgs 11,12:20–30 and 12:1–19), which differ in both by their literary genre and their historiosophical views.[1] They reflect divergent tendencies with regard to the remembrance of that crucial event in the history of Israel. In its equivocal and even contradictory evaluations this account reminds us of the account of a no less crucial event which preceded it in the history of Israel, namely, the establishment of the monarchy (1Sam 8–10). However, it is not at all certain that a direct and genetic continuity can be found between the two, as far as literary sources or even social and political views are concerned; in the account of the division of the kingdom the impression of the Deuteronomist is clearly recognized, whereas in the account of the establishment of the monarchy it is hardly seen. Also, the popular oral traditions upon which the historiographer built his account differ in their origins. Whereas the account of the establishment of the monarchy displays exclusive Benjamite origins, the account of the

---

1 A literary generic analysis of these chapters is found in B.O.Long's book *1Kings with an Introduction to the Historical Literature* eds. Rolf Knierim and Gene M. Tucker (The Forms of Old Testament Literature vol. 9; Grand Rapids, Michigan, 1984), 120–140. See also the most recent socio-hermeneutical analysis of these chapters in N.K.Gottwald's article "Social Class as an Analytic and Hermeneutical Category in Biblical Studies," *JBL* 112/1 (1993), 3–20.

division of the Kingdom discloses Judaean origins, even though the Ephrai-mite traditions cannot be ruled out.[2] It is noteworthy that the two Judaean accounts of the division of the kingdom (1 Kgs 11 and 12: 1–19) represent two different views concerning the reasons and incentives which brought about the political schism in Israel and the personalities who directly or in-directly assume responsibility for it.

One writer, the Deuteronomist, attributes this crisis to the religio-cultic sins of Solomon and his love of many foreign women which when he became old, "turned his heart" to follow other gods (1Kgs 11: 1–13). The other (12: 1–19) ascribes it to the failure of Rehoboam his son to reach an understanding with the assembly of Israel who appealed to him to lighten the harsh labor that his late father Solomon imposed upon them (12: 3–5). In both these divergent Judaean accounts Jeroboam the Ephrathite is men-tioned. In the first, he is mentioned as one who rebelled against Solomon and he whom the prophet Ahijah of Shiloh designated as God's appointed king over the ten tribes of Israel (1Kgs 11: 26–40). In the other, he is the only member of the delegation of the people of Israel which negotiated with King Rehoboam (1Kgs 12: 2–3a, 12). But these two references are consid-ered by several commentators as secondary and redactional supplements. (In a later and exclusively Judaean composition, the Book of Chronicles, the prophetic legend of Jeroboam's designation by Ahijah the Shilonite prophet [1Kgs. 11: 29–39], as well as Solomon's sins which caused the division of the Kingdom [11: 1–13] are both eliminated.[3]) Thus, in this account Re-hoboam alone (who was ill-advised by his young contemporaries) bears the sole responsibility for the irreparable schism in the kingdom.

These brief observations enable us to isolate the story of the division of the kingdom (which appears both in 1Kgs 12: 1–19 and in II Chr 10: 1–19) from the historiographic framework of 1Kgs 11–12 that surrounds it, so that we may deal with it separately as an autonomous literary unit in which characteristic elements of political satire can be detected.

1. A literary-generic characterization of the story

The story begins in a major key—"(and) Rehoboam went to Shechem for all Israel had come to Shechem to make him king" (12: 1)—and ends in

---

[2] Especially those which refer to the nomination of Jeroboam as king of the ten tribes (1Kgs 11: 26–40; 12: 2, 20).

[3] S. Japhet, *Emunoth we-de'oth be-sepher Dibere-ha-yamim u-mekoman be'-olam ha-mahashabah ha-mikraith* (Jerusalem, 1977), 402.

a minor one: "King Rehoboam mounted his chariot and fled to Jerusalem" (v 18); this is followed by an etiological postscript: "From that day to this Israel has been in rebellion against the house of David" (v 19). Between the triumphal entry of Rehoboam into Shechem to assume the rule over all Israel and his shameful flight to Jerusalem after being stoned by the people in Shechem, a radical political change has occurred—the Davidic king forfeited his reign over most of Israel's tribes. Clearly, from the concentric structure of the story the writer is not so much concerned about an adequate report of the event itself as with the king's arrogant and foolish behavior during the crisis, which he believes caused the division of the kingdom. According to his evaluation, the division obviously could have been avoided, had Rehoboam followed the elders' advice rather than letting himself be misled by the youngsters. Hence, the story is not a historical report per se, but a tendentious interpretation of events that had taken place—perhaps even long ago (cf. v 18). In its historio-etiological tendency, this story differs entirely from the Deuteronomistic teleological and prophetic interpretation of the division of the Davidic kingdom.

Y. Kaufmann distinguished clearly between these two stories, but went too far when he termed the story of the rift in Shechem (chap. 12) "the realistic account of the division of the kingdom," compared with the prophetic story (chap 11).[4] The mere fact that the story of the rift in Shechem lacks the theological traits that characterize the Deuteronomistic account in the Book of Kings (except for the harmonistic-teleological gloss in v 15: "For the Lord had given this turn to the affair in order that the word he had spoken by Ahijah of Shiloh to Jeroboam son of Nebat might be fulfilled") still does not make it realistic. In his historiopolitical interpretation, which differs from the Deuteronomist's, the narrator of this story (12: 1–19) expresses an anthropocentric approach which in many respects contradicts the theocentric approach that dominates the Deuteronomistic account. According to his approach, the historical circumstances which surrounded him were the outcome of the behavior and the reactions of persons who had been active in the historical events, and not a result of a divine and transcendental intervention. True, by its very nature the anthropocentric approach is more realistic than the theocentric; but this in itself is not enough to conclude that the story as it stands is realistic and reports accurately what really happened and how the events actually occurred.

As it is, the story presents an alternative causality for the event: human causality as distinct from divine causality. The anthropocentric quality of

4 Y. Kaufmann, *Toledoth ha-emunah ha-Yisraelith* vol. 4 (1964), 465–467.

the story suggests its affinity with the sphere of wisdom literature in the Bible, in which the characters as well as the plot are designed to be para-digmatic rather than historical. This affinity will be elaborated below when we deal with the creative milieu of the story.

2. Structural analysis

We have confined the boundaries of the story, which starts with the ju-bilant entry of Rehoboam into Shechem (v 1) and ends with his flight in dis-grace back to Jerusalem (v 18). While not an organic part of the story itself, verse 19 forms an etiological epilogue that seals it off from the rest of this chapter. Verses 20–21 return us to the historical complexity which was introduced in chapter 11, and deal with the political and religio-cultic devel-opments that occurred in the two separate parts of the divided kingdom in the wake of the schism. Thus, an independent and autonomous story can be discerned within the historiographical framework, except for a few his-toriographic notes which were appended by the redactor (vv 2–3, 17), and the teleological remark in verse 15 meant to harmonize it with the dominant Deuteronomistic historiosophy.[5] The story focuses on one event—the re-bellion of the assembly of Israel against Rehoboam. The central figure who is active from beginning to end is Rehoboam. The historical plot devel-ops dramatically. From the start it is evident that the meeting between Re-hoboam and the people in Shechem is going to become a tragic confronta-tion. This opens when the assembly of Israel appeals to Rehoboam on his arrival in Shechem to lighten the heavy yoke which his father laid upon them (vv 3–4). It ends with a declaration of their secession from the Davidic kingdom after their request has been rejected by Rehoboam (v 16). So far, there is no reason to deny the historical and realistic nature of the story in which some dramatic elements are involved, especially if we follow the Masoretic text that Jeroboam led the Israelite assembly in that confrontation (vv. 2–3, 12).[6]

Within the open confrontation, and in connection with it, another con-frontation is developing behind the scenes, in Rehoboam's court. This is

---

5 Ina Plein, "Erẅagungen zur Überlieferung von 1Reg.11,26–14,20 *ZAW* 78 (1966), 8–24.

6 1Kgs 12: 2–3a is missing in LXX. We agree with Montgomery, *Kings* (ICC, 1960), 248–249, as well as with other commentators that those verses were added by the redactor in order to link this story with the account of Jeroboam in chapter 11.

latent and indirect confrontation between the "elders who had been in attendance during the life of "Solomon" (v 6) and "the young men who had grown up with Rehoboam" (v 8). The confrontation between the two influential groups whom the king consulted proves decisive for the future of the kingdom. This seems to lie at the heart of the story and to convey its cardinal message.

The transition from the direct and public confrontation between the throne and the people to the private confrontation inside the court is achieved by means of the three-day interval that Rehoboam requests before giving his answer to the assembly of the people of Israel. Rehoboam consults two opposing political groups—first the "veterans," and then the "youngsters." The consultation is held separately with each group and thus consists of two symmetrical sessions, both of which open with the same question presented by the king: "What answer do you advise me to give to the people?" (vv 6, 9).

The two answers differ radically in their style and content and the king has to decide which he prefers. This kind of political decision-making diverges far from the traditional way that is prevalent in biblical historiography, in which the king's decisions are made by an enquiry addressed to God through prophets or through priestly means (Ephod, or Urim).[7] It represents an anthropocentric approach, and it reminds us of another political and critical consultation in which the king's decision-making procedure was similar.

We refer to the decision-making procedure used by Absalom, after he was appointed king by the tribes of Israel, in the battle against his father David (2 Sam 16–17). That procedure was also conducted in two stages. The first was with Ahithophel, who formerly served as David's adviser, the second with Hushai the Archite, "David's friend" who offered his service to Absalom after his father had fled from Jerusalem (16: 16–19). In this case, unlike the consultation of Rehoboam, Absalom reveals to Hushai what Ahithophel had advised him and what has been approved by the elders of Israel (17: 6). Hushai's subsequent advice is deemed better than Ahithophel's by Absalom and all his followers; it supplants Ahithophel's advice, and so brings disaster upon Absalom (17:14a).

But here too as in the story of Rehoboam Absalom's misjudgement is followed by a teleological supplement by the editor: "It was the Lord's purpose to frustrate Ahithophel's good advice and so bring disaster on Ab-

---

7 1Sam 28: 6, 23: 6–9; 2 Sam 2: 1; 1Kgs 22: 5ff.; 2Kgs 3: 11ff.

salom" (17: 14b, cf. 1Kgs 12: 15). The correspondence between the consultation procedure in these two stories is significant: in both, the advice of the
wise and experienced is rejected and that of the aggressive and the ambitious courtiers is approved. In both, the rejection of the elders' advice
brings down the young royal successor, who intended to inherit all of his
father's kingdom. However, there is a marked difference between the two
stories in regard to the portrayal of the personalities involved in the consultation. Whereas the advisers in Absalom's consultation are historical
figures, denoted by their personal names and positions, the advisers (who
confront each other indirectly) in Rehoboam's consultation are a corporate personality denoted by their collective status—"elders" and youngsters
("children").

According to Malamat, who proposed an analogy between this story
and a Sumerian parallel, these two groups depict monarchial institutions
that played a prominent role in royal decision-making, corresponding to
similar official councils in ancient Mesopotamia.[8] However, one cannot dismiss the possibility that the collective personification of the two rival corpora is meant to be more paradigmatic and typical than historical.

The literary conventions employed by the narrator of Rehoboam's
consultation, and especially the corporate personification of the political
rivals in the indirect contest, signify the transition from the historical to the
sapiential domain. And some scholars have pointed out the folkloristic conventions used in this story, which are similar to those present in the story of
Solomon's judgment in the case of the two harlots (1Kgs 3: 16–28).[9] Some
have even suggested a popular generic affinity between the two. Since we
suppose that these conventions characterize the sophisticated wisdom literature of the Court, and not so much the so-called "folktale," a close comparison between the two stories might be illuminating.

In the anecdote of Solomon's judgment, a confrontation between two
parties also takes place. The contestants are denoted by their status (or pro-
fession) as "harlots," not by their names. At first the confrontation between
the two is also indirect. They conduct no direct dialogue and the king is
called to judge between them. As was the case with the consultation procedure of Rehoboam, the arguments of the two rivals contradict each other
and the king has to decide (make judgment) between the two. True, the pro-

---

[8] A. Malamat, "Kingship and Council in Israel and Sumer: A Parallel," *BA* 28 (1965),
34–65 (English version). The Hebrew original is in *'Oz le-David* (Jerusalem, 1964), 279–290.

[9] B. Long, *1 Kings* 135.

cedure between the two contestants in this anecdote is not symmetrical, as it is in Rehoboam's consultation, and a furious dispute develops between the two women as the first is concluding her presentation and the other interrupts. Yet the principle of giving an equal opportunity to both rivals in the procedure is upheld.

There are many obvious differences between the two stories, which perhaps even outweigh the similarities we have noted. There is no need to specify them in this context; nevertheless, the similar principal traits that we have outlined are enough to conclude that there is a generic affinity between the two stories and that they have a common origin in the Court Wisdom. The story of Solomon's wise judgment seems to us more of a paradigmatic anecdote created in the milieu of courtly wisdom than a folktale. This is evident in the epilogue that concludes the anecdote: "When Israel heard the judgment which the king had given, they all stood in awe of him; for they saw that he possessed wisdom from God for administering justice" (*ibid.*, v 28).

As already stated, in Rehoboam's dual consultation two collective types of advisers denoted by their status and age contend in a kind of indirect confrontation. The "elders," who are often mentioned throughout the Bible, probably represent in our context a political body or organ.[10] The other group, the "children," rarely mentioned in the Bible, appear here as the opponents of the "elders" and probably connote a political status. As already mentioned Malamat treats them as a Council of Princes (the king's sons), which was summoned to deal with vital political issues that emerged, corresponding to the ancient Mesopotamian Royal Councils.[11] Whether we are concerned here with a legal and official institution or not, there can be no question that the "children" depict a political circle connected to the court." They seem arrogant and treat the "elders" and the people as a whole with contempt and disdain. This is evident in the language they use in phrasing Rehoboam's reply to the assembly of Israel: "My 'little one' is thicker than my father's loins" (cf.1Kgs 12: 10), a phrase Rehoboam himself declines to use when he makes his answer to the people of Israel (v 14). This phrase, which proclaims the vulgar and aggressive style of the "children's" council versus the "elders," signals the satirical tendency of the narrative.

---

10 J.L. McKenzie, "The Elders in the Old Testament," *Analecta Biblica* 10 (1959), 388–405.
11 See note 8.

3. "My little (one) is thicker than my father's loins"

The key-word of this phrase קטני was understood by most early and
modern commentators as "my little finger."[12] Among the older (medieval)
commentators Kimḥi was the only one to suggest that קטני refers to "my
little part" (האבר הקטן שבי), although he was aware of the grammatical difficulty involved in this interpretation.[13] We propose that the original meaning was indeed "my little member (or organ)," thus following Köhler and
Baumgartner in viewing the phrase euphemistically.[14]

The use of phallic images and symbols in political satire is widespread
in ancient and modern literature.[15] Scholars who dealt with this phenomenon tried to trace phallic political humor back to ancient Greek comedy
and to point to its origin in popular fertility rites and phallic processions.[16]
This general and external reference in itself is not enough to prove that the
phrase "my little one" (and so forth) indicates the employment of sexual allusion in political satire in the Bible. We must seek more specific evidence
(in the Bible) to substantiate it.

The evidence seems to be at hand once we return to the account of Absalom, who lay with his father's concubines in the sight of all Israel (2 Sam
16: 22). This act, or rite, was performed by Absalom, who followed the
advice of Ahithophel in order to offend his father David and to confirm the
resolution of his followers (v 21). In our story Rehoboam is advised by his
colleagues, "the children," to reply to the people, using a phrase which suggests some allusion to the sexual act that Absalom performed.

This vulgar expression shows contempt for "the people," which is
understood to be the target of Rehoboam's virile aggression, as well as for
his old father, who did not exercise his own virile aggression adequately.

12 Rashi, Ibn Ezra and in almost all the modern commentaries: ICC, IB, AB, OTL

13 Kimḥi, in his commentary to this verse, points out the difficulty arising from the use
of the adjective עבה in the feminine. See also *GK*, 267.

14 *The Expositor's Bible Commentary* vol.4 (1988) 115 n.10: "my little part" is usually
understood as in the Vulgate: *minimus digitus meus* ("my little finger") but since the compared
member is lesser, *KB* (p. 835) may be correct in viewing the phrase euphemistically. *KB ibid.*,
"mein Kleiner (Finger oder Penis).

15 Charles E. Schutz, *Political Humor* (Cambridge, 1977), 33: "The pervasiveness and
popularity of phallic political humor suggests a possible relationship between its vulgarity and
democracy: the *vulgus* is the *demos*."

16 *Ibid.* 34: "Comedy originated as a social institution that contained the same permissi-
bility of the sexually prohibited. Most authorities believe that the term *comedy* is derived from
the Greek *Komos*, the phallic procession that took place as a part of the fertility rites of the ancient Greeks."

It seems only reasonable that the narrator who employed this expression, which Rehoboam himself eschewed in his reply, used it as political satire aimed against the "children" who appear tough and violent in their words but prove weak and powerless in their deeds. The figurative language which they employ in responding to the people's just appeal, and which is repeated by Rehoboam when he addresses the people's assembly: "And now whereas my father did (burden) you with heavy yoke, I will add to your yokes, my father hath chastised you with whips but I will chastise you with scorpions" (v 11 and cf. v 14), adds to the "children's" characterization and reveals their political nakedness and impotence.

It is significant that the narrator utilized a metaphorical and rhythmic rhetoric for the "children's" advice, which was formulated to be spoken before the people; by contrast, the elders' advice, which is addressed to the king directly, lacks any rhetorical devices and refers to the people in indirect speech: "If thou wilt be a servant unto this people this day and wilt serve them and answer them and speak good words to them, then they will be thy servants for ever" (v 7).

Nevertheless, this prosaic and casuistic style ("if . . . then . . .") signifies their long political experience and their sensible diplomatic approach. They do not put into Rehoboam's mouth a prepared statement as the "children" do, but suggest to him what seems to be the safest course for his reign, leaving the actual phrasing of the reply to the king. The emphasis in their advice is on the phrase "good words," which should set the major key in negotiating with the people's delegation. On the basis of Assyrian sources, Weinfeld understood the phrase "good words" to be a technical term carrying legal and political connotations, namely, reforms in forced levies and taxation.[17] However, it is not at all necessary to go so far, since the literal meaning of "good words" is sufficient to convey the diplomacy that they advise—to make good promises to the people, which does not necessarily mean making specific pledges that will commit him throughout his reign. This subtle idea is indicated in the chiastic structure of their advice (following the Hebrew syntax of the sentence, it should be literally translated: "If *today* will you be a servant to this people and speak to them 'good words' . . . they will be your servants *all the days*").

The polar antagonism in both political philosophy and diplomatic style between the "elders" and the "children" only indicates the political inclina-

---

17 M.Weinfeld, Leshonenu (Hebrew) 36 (1972), 3–11, and see also his book: *Mishpat u-sedakah be-Yisrael uba-'ammim* (Jerusalem, 1985), 76–77.

tion of Rehoboam, on the one hand, and of the narrator, on the other. Hence, there seems to be no difficulty in identifying the creative milieu of this political satirist whose sarcastic criticism is aimed against the circle of the young and ambitious courtiers.

4. The "creative milieu" of the satirical narrator

In delineating the literary identity of the satirical narrator we shall apply a reverse spiral method—from the wider circle to its approximate starting point. It is quite clear from our literary analysis that the story did not originate in the "decatribal" domain, but in Judah. The dominant figure throughout the story is Rehoboam. In center stage the two rival circles of Rehoboam's court compete, the assembly of Israel remaining in the background. The reference to Jeroboam, the son of Nebat, even if it is not an addendum as most commentators presume, still does not make him a principal figure in the story.

The Judaean identity of the narrator is recognized by his historiosophic viewpoint which regards the divided kingdom of Rehoboam as the only legitimate successor of the kingdom of David, and remains remote from a north Israelite perspective of introducing the birth of the new kingdom (v 19). Ultimately, the Judaean origin of the story is best recognized by the satirical criticism of Rehoboam and his young circle of advisers who by their stiffneckedness and arrogance bear responsibility for the dissolution of the Davidic kingdom. These observations bring us closer to the inner circle of our reverse spiral, to the so-called "creative milieu." Without doubt, this story is not a product of the prophetic circles, since it presents an anthropocentric alternative to the theocentric-prophetic account of the secession of the ten tribes from the Davidic kingdom (1Kgs 11); nor is it a product of a circle of social reformers, who argue emphatically against the tyranny of the monarchial administration. It is likelier that the narrator of this account is more concerned about the political shortcomings of the Judaean political leadership in resolving that crisis than with the success of the popular revolt against the tyrannical kingdom. In his view the schism could have been avoided if Rehoboam had spoken "good words" to the congregation of the northern tribes and—if we accept Tadmor's interpretation of this phrase—if he had made some vague gestures to them.[18]

---

[18] H. Tadmor, "Traditional Institutions and the Monarchy," in *Studies in the Period of David and Solomon* ed. Tomoo Ishida (Tokyo, 1982), 252–256.

The conclusion from our discussion is that the "creative milieu" of this story is to be found in the Royal Court, and that the satirical narrator belonged to one of the rival political circles in it. It is not at all difficult to identify that political circle, since the narrator's satirical criticism leads clearly to the position that the "elders'" advice was right and could have saved the Davidic kingdom from breaking up. We shall not speculate whether he was actively involved in the affair or sided with the opposition only later. In either case it seems only reasonable that he enjoyed the knowledge and the skills of a court personage. As noted, it is not altogether clear that he himself witnessed the events which brought about the political schism. He might have recorded his reflections on the critical events one or even two generations later, but not later than the reign of King Asa, when the rift and animosity between the two divided kingdoms still prevailed (1Kgs 15: 16).

The question whether the historiographer of the Book of Kings borrowed the satirical account from the Annals of the Kings of Judah (1Kgs 14: 29), or found it elsewhere, is beyond the scope of this study.

— 8o 9 og —

ELEMENTS OF POLITICAL SATIRE
IN BIBLICAL HISTORIOGRAPHY

The address of Rabshakeh and the countermessages of
Isaiah (2 Kgs 18–19; Isa 36–37)

In its aims, rhetorical devices and satirical barbs, Rabshakeh's speech (or two speeches as some commentators hold) is distinctly political. By directing his words beyond the nation's leaders, to the ears of the people themselves on the walls of the besieged city, he sought to decide the military and political conflict between Assyria and Judea, which the Assyrian army had not yet won on the battlefield. In other words, he sought to open the gates of Jerusalem before the army of Sennacherib, without these forces being worn down in a prolonged siege. From the extensive biblical sources that describe the event this goal was not achieved, and Sennacherib was obliged to return home no better off than when he had arrived. According to the account in the epilogue, Assyria also lost 185,000 troops to a plague. Even the Assyrian annals, which vaunt his victories over Judea (the conquest of Lachish and more than 40 other cities on the Judean plain and Hezekiah's absolute surrender),[1] do not relate the conquest of Jerusalem. The city was therefore saved from the fate that had overtaken its sister city Samaria about two decades before (722 BCE).

[1] D.D. Luckenbill, *Annals of Sennacherib* "Rassam Cylinder" OIP2 (Chicago: University of Chicago Press, 1924), 29–34, 60–61; and see also the Prism of Sennacherib, trans. by L. Oppenheim in *ANET 2* (1955), 287–288. For a comparative study of the Assyrian sources and the biblical accounts, see: M. Cogan & H. Tadmor, *II Kings* (AB, 1988), Excursus: The Biblical and Assyrian Account of Sennacherib's Campaign Compared, 246ff.

The repercussions of Jerusalem's escape from almost certain destruction, which the people of Hezekiah's generation had suffered and witnessed but a score of years earlier, would without doubt not have acquired such wide and varied historical documentation were it not for the national and religious significance that had gone with it for generations and that had eternalized Jerusalem as a symbol of the kingship of David and Mount Zion as the chosen place of God, the "Holy One of Israel." In itself, this decisive historical event in the lengthy confrontation between Judea and Assyria, the world superpower that determined the destiny of nations, served the biblical historiographer as a guiding light with which to illumine the history of the First Temple. This was done through his own historiographic and theological perspective, which by then comprehended the destruction of the Temple and hoped for its restoration. This, in my opinion, was the reason why the history writer devoted so much space to the description of the event in his account of the kingdom of Judea, which also appears in two other books, Isaiah and Chronicles, and whose echoes sound in other prophecies as well as in several of the Psalms.[2] I believe also that this is why the author gives such weight to Rabshakeh's speech of incitement and denigration, while merely outlining the military operations themselves. If it was not actually the biblical author who placed the words in Rabshakeh's mouth, at least he deserves merit for meticulously preserving and documenting them so well, a labor not carried out at all in the Assyrian sources.[3] From this stems our methodology, namely, that Rabshakeh's speech is not to be isolated from the literary historical setting in which it is placed. And it should certainly not be regarded as an independent historical document. Even if this chapter is limited to the study of the elements of political satire in the speech, to probe their meaning fully it is necessary to examine it against the background of its historical and literary context and in connection with the reactions to it.

Indeed, emphasis should be placed on a point not stressed so far in scholarship on this speech—that he who committed it to writing was careful to present it together with these reactions, perhaps, even on their account. They were spoken exclusively by Isaiah. Thus, the main clash in this episode in both its versions, 2 Kings 18–19 and Isaiah 36–37, is not between Hezekiah and Sennacherib, but between Isaiah and Rabshekeh.[4] So it

---

2 Mic 1: 8–16; Isa 10: 28–32, 31: 8; Ps 46.

3 E. Ben Zvi, "Who Wrote the Speech of Rabshakeh and When?" *JBL* (1990), 79–92.

4 G. Adam Smith, *The Book of Isaiah* (London, 1928), 375.

is no accident that the later historiographic account in Chronicles entirely omits the indirect rhetorical confrontation between these two, and portrays Hezekiah, the just king of the House of David, as the leading hero.

1. Historiographic and annalistic sources

As mentioned, Sennacherib's expedition to Judea, his conquests and his taking up a position at the gates of Jerusalem gained wide reportage. The most comprehensive account appears in 2 Kgs 18: 13–19, 37, and almost identically in Isa 36: 1–37, 38. However, three verses at the beginning of the report in the Book of Kings are missing in Isaiah. According to these verses, after the king of Assyria had taken all the fortified cities of Judea (v 13), Hezekiah sent to him (at Lachish) expressions of remorse for his resistance, as well as his willingness to remit whatever he was required, so that the king of Assyria would withdraw (v 14). This in fact he did. To pay the enormous ransom, Hezekiah was obliged to strip off the precious objects that he had overlaid on the doors of the temple of God and give them to king of Assyria (vv 15–16). It is reasonable to assume, as most commentators do, that these verses are a reliable historical account, for they are by no means complimentary towards Hezekiah, who won the highest accolades from the Deuteronomistic historiographer. Moreover, they match what is included in the Sennacherib inscriptions. Yet except for the first (v 13), these verses are missing from the parallel account in Isaiah. Some explain this omission as caused by a technical slip, a haplography resulting from the eye of the copyist skipping from וישלח, which opens verse 14, to וישלח, which opens verse 17.[5] Like many others, I tend to regard this as a deliberate omission, as this part of the report is incongruent with what follows concerning the bitter struggle between Judea and Assyria over Jerusalem.

A different account from the one in these two parallel reports appears in the description of the event in Chronicles (2 Chron 32: 1, 23).[6] Here not only is the report of the surrender of Hezekiah and the payment of the heavy ransom in items removed from the temple of God deleted, but in fact the opposite picture emerges: Hezekiah displays ingenuity in face of the terrible threat hanging over Jerusalem, increases his strength and builds the wall, and readies his army for a fearless stance against the foe, encouraging his men with words of faith and reliance in God.

---

[5] B.S. Childs, *Isaiah and the Assyrian Crisis* (London, 1967), 72–73. A.S. Herbert, *Isaiah 1–39* (Cambridge, 1974), 196–197.

[6] Childs, 104–112; J.M. Myers, *II Chronicles* (AB; New York, 1965), 188ff.

Some passages of Rabshakeh's speech are indeed cited by the chronicler, without mention of the name, nor with any indication that they were spoken to the people on the wall: they appear in a message from Sennacherib through his servants (vv 9, 16). In particular, the biting comments against the Lord, the God of Israel, stand out (vv 17–19). Unlike the account in 2 Kings and Isaiah, Hezekiah does not present Isaiah with a request for his aid and intervention in the crisis, but he addresses God directly in a prayer. Isaiah is mentioned elsewhere (v 20), not as one to whom Hezekiah appealed in his distress, but as one who joined him in his prayer—what seems like an attempt at harmonization by the later redactor. The chronicler's account, like the earlier versions, ends with the collapse of the Assyrian army and the return to Sennacherib, king of Assyria "with shame of face" to his his own land, where he is struck down by the sword of his sons; this of course is the chronicler's selective style, not omitting his indication at the end that the salvation of God exalted Hezekiah in the sight of the nations, who made sure to bring gifts to God in Jerusalem and "precious things" to Hezekiah (v 23).

We have dwelt at some length on the chronicler's telescopic and selective method in his description of the facts of the event to accord with his historiographic tendencies and his doctrine of retribution. The reason is twofold—to enable us to draw conclusions through comparing what there is in common in his inventory of the factual historical core and in the earlier writing; and to highlight the most important matter that in our view distinguishes them, namely the Rabshakeh-Isaiah clash, which is missing from the chronicler's account, in the setting of the profound crisis that threatened Jerusalem.

The common core may thus be summarized in brief statements: 1. Sennacherib marched on Judea and seized the fortified cities. In 2 Chron 32: 1 he did not actually conquer them, but he was "thinking to win them for himself," which is an obviously tendentious amendment. 2. Sennacherib sent a message to the besieged Jerusalem and tried to subdue it by threats and incitement against Hezekiah and against the Lord, the God of Israel. 3. Jerusalem was saved; the Assyrian army did not enter its gates and was forced to withdraw to its own land.

This surprising development is explained by the biblical historiographers as God's intercession, followed by an account of a miracle concerning an angel of God who went out by night and struck down many in the Assyrian camp.

In all these presentations the speech of incitement appears as a major link in the military and political confrontation, which permits us to determine accurately the historical circumstances surrounding the politically satirical speech, which is our main concern. Obviously, if the expedition had ended with the absolute surrender of Hezekiah, which indeed is the story told in the Assyrian annals, and which may be the impression gained from the brief report opening this episode in 2 Kgs 18: 13–16, there would have been no point to Rabshakeh's speech at the gates of Jerusalem nor to Isaiah's reaction to it. Rabshakeh's mission is explicable only against the background of the political and military circumstances in which the fortified cities of Judea were indeed conquered, but the fortified Jerusalem did not open its gates before the king of Assyria, who apparently feared an attack against his armies by Egypt and Ethiopia if his troops became engaged in a prolonged siege, especially against a city that had prepared itself well for such an event. Rabshakeh's mission at the gates of Jerusalem was meant to win a political and military victory by means of persuasion and intimidation, making Jerusalem surrender without a fight. Indeed, it would be easy to reach such a conclusion if internal tensions, discontinuity, and inconsistencies did not exist in the description of the episode. These inconsistences emerge not only between the report of Hezekiah's submission and payment of the ransom to the Assyrian king in 2 Kgs 18: 14–16 and the entire account that follows, but also within this continuation of the account itself (2 Kgs 18: 17ff. and its parallel in Isa 36: 2ff.).

The crux of the matter is in the middle of verse 9 of 2 Kgs 19 (cf. Isa 37: 9). According to verse 9b, Sennacherib again sends messengers to Hezekiah in Jerusalem voicing threats and calumny like those spoken earlier by Rabshakeh. Hezekiah again is hardpressed and addresses a prayer to God; yet this is after he has received the divine oracle that he sought from Isaiah through his servants: 'Behold I will put a spirit in him, so that he shall hear a rumor and return to his own land; and I will cause him to fall by the sword in his own land" (v 7). According to verse 9a, the first element of this had already materialized by that time: "And when the king heard concerning Tirhaka king of Ethiopia, 'Behold, he has set out to fight against you'." The second element materializes at the end of the account of the episode, in 2 Kgs 19: 36–37 (cf. Isa 37: 37–38): "Then Sennacherib king of Assyria[7] departed, and went home, and dwelt at Nineveh. And as he was worshipping in the house of Nisroch his god, Adram-melech and Sharezer (his sons) slew him with the sword and escaped into the land of Ararat. And Esarhaddon his son reigned in his stead."

---

7 O. Kaiser, *Isaiah 13–39* (OTL; London, 1974), 367.

Scholars have rightly discerned that a different report branches off from 2 Kgs 19: 9, and they have distinguished between two reports: one is 2 Kgs 18: 17–19: 9a; which ends with the conclusion of the episode at verses 36–37, quoted above; its parallel is Isaiah 36: 2–37: 9a; 37: 38. The other is 2 Kgs 19: 9b–35; Isaiah 37: 9b–36.[8] The debate among researchers hinges on the source and nature of the two reports. Many regard them as parallel literary sources depicting the same event, each report including the speech of the Assyrian spokesman, as well as the divine message spoken by Isaiah.[9] Others see them as reports reflecting two different time phases, associated with the two expeditions of Sennacherib against Jerusalem. The first was conducted in 701 BCE on the basis of dating in the Sennacherib prism. Regarding the second, there is no direct evidence from Assyrian sources; it is linked to the war against Tirhaka, who apparently did not become king before 694 BCE, and so the expedition is assumed to have taken place in 688 BCE, viz., a number of years before Sennacherib's assassination according to Assyrian sources (681 BCE).[10] These two assumptions do not entirely rule out Isaiah's involvement in this episode: his reactions and messages appear in both these reports, although problems of chronology arise concerning the dating of the end of Isaiah's prophetic activity if the assumption of two expeditions is adopted.[11] Yet, it is noteworthy that Isaiah's activity as conveyed in the first report is more significant for our subject. This is because we believe that the principal dramatic encounter in the episode is that between Rabshakeh and Isaiah; in the second report Rabshakeh is not mentioned at all.

2. Rabshakeh's speech

Before dealing with the speech, let us present the speaker. Who is this Rabshakeh, who was sent by the king of Assyria to Jerusalem with a great

8 Kaiser, 376ff.; Childs, 76; Herbert, 196.

9 Childs, Herbert, Kaiser (n. 8); and see aso R.E. Clements, *Isaiah and the Deliverence of Jerusalem* (Sheffield, 1980), 52ff.

10 W.P. Albright, *BASOR* 130 (1953), 9; otherwise Cogan and Tadmor in their above-mentioned Commentary, 248, n. 3 relying on K.A. Kitchen, *Third Intermediate Period*, 161–172. They claim that Tirhakah was indeed crowned in 690 BCE, but by 701 he was mature enough to wage war.

11 The date of Isaiah's death is unknown. According to some chronological schemes it is to be placed as early as 698 BCE, according to others as late as 686. According to the former, the question arises if Isaiah prophesied the accession of Tirhakah; and see: Gray, *Isaiah 1–27*, (ICC; Edinburgh, 1962), LXXIIff.

army and was commissioned by him to conduct negotiations in his name with the besieged people? At first sight the impression may be gained from the version in Isaiah (36: 2) that he was the commander of the great army sent with him by Sennacherib to Jerusalem. But the version in Kings names two envoys before naming Rabshakeh, seemingly of higher rank than he: Tartan, the most senior minister in the Assyrian realm; and Rabsaris. These officials served as military commanders-in-chief. The name Rabshakeh derives from Akkadian and means chief butler. Some believe that his main activity was in the king's court, possibly as head of his bureau. It is possible to learn about his rank from the eponymous lists in which Rabshakeh appears third after the king and Tartan, or fourth in order of importance.[12] From the biblical account of him it appears that he could speak the language of the country of Judea (Judean), and that he showed close acquaintance with the political and religious changes that occurred there with the rise of Hezekiah to the throne. Some conjecture from this that he was of Israelite origin. We find in tractate Sanhedrin 60a: "Rabshakeh was a converted Israelite."

A. The "Sitz im Leben" of the speech

This is not the only case in the Bible where officials of the king are sent by him to convey diplomatic—or military—messages in critical political and military circumstances. We read of Ben-hadad, king of Syria, who sent messengers to Ahab, king of Israel, in Samaria during his siege of the city (1 Kgs 20: 1ff.). But who the messengers were, what were their titles or their names, and so on—these questions are not addressed. In different circumstances, when Rehoboam the son of Solomon tried to renew his rule over all of Israel at Shechem, he dispatched Adoram, taskmaster over the forced labor, a high-level minister, who by virtue of his function was apparently considered right for this delicate mission, to the men rebelling against his rule. Adoram paid with his life (1 Kgs 12: 18).

In both these examples the message is not accompanied by a speech; by contrast, the rhetorical and polemical elements in Rabshakeh's speech indicate that his embassy on the king's behalf is not solely in order to submit a message to the king of Judea, but also to induce the inhabitants not to support their king's policies. This is expressed in the speech by the transition

---

12 W. Manitus, Zeitschrift für Assyrologie XIV (1910), 199–209; H. Tadmor, 'Rabshakeh' *EB* 7, 323 (Hebrew).

from the formal opening of the message to Hezekiah in the name of the Assyrian king to the fierce polemic against him addressed directly to the people. It is also reflected in what is stated expressly by Rabshakeh to Eliakim, Shebnah and Joah, the representatives of Hezekiah: "Has my master sent me to speak these words to your master and to you, and not to the men sitting on the wall. . . ?" (2 Kgs 18: 27; Isa 36: 12).

A similar diplomatic and political mission in wartime, with public attempts at persuasion, is known to us from Assyrian documents. The first of Nimrud's letters written to the king of Assyria by two of his officials, Samas-bunaia and Nabu-etir, describes their mission to Babylon.[13] On the twenty-eighth they reached Babylon and took their stand before the Marduk gate; they tried to persuade the city's inhabitants not to support Ukim-zer, chief of the Chaldean tribe of Bit-Amukkani who had rebelled against Assyria and had won the support of the residents of Babylon. Again and again they returned to the locked gate and harangued them, trying to win them over, apparently in vain, by various ploys, including both threats and cajolery. The political situation, the mention of the officials' names and the dating of their mission, and the authority granted them by the king of Assyria to test their powers of persuasion, and not merely to carry a specific message on his behalf—all these closely parallel the circumstances portrayed in the biblical report of Rabshakeh's embassy. At the same time, one should not hastily conclude from this that Rabshakeh's speech, as passed on to us in writing by the biblical author, is authentic.[14] But the historical and political context of Rabshakeh's speech indicates that it contains authentic elements in terms of history and rhetoric, and that it is not a purely literary invention of the historiographer. Detailed analysis of the speech, with attention to its special structure and its particular rhetorical devices, may confirm this cautious conclusion.

B. The genre of the speech

The speech consists of two parts, each of which starts with a formal preamble characteristic of messages in the king's name: "Thus says the great king, king of Assyria" (2 Kgs 18: 19; cf. Isa 36: 4) and "Hear the word of the great king, the king of Assyria! Thus says the king . . ." (2 Kgs 18: 28–29; Isa 36: 14–15). These two openings do not necessarily indicate two

---

13 H.S. Saggs, "The Nimrud Letters," *Iraq* 17 (1955), 23–26.
14 Childs, 81ff.

different and separate speeches, one to the king's representatives (2 Kgs 18: 19–25; Isa 36: 4–10) and one to the people on the wall (2 Kgs 18: 27–35; Isa 36: 12–20). According to the narrative itself they are simply two stages in the same speech, the second developing in response to the request of Eliakim, the chief delegate of Hezekiah: "Pray, speak to your servants in the Aramaic language, for we understand it, do not speak to us in the language of Judea within the hearing of the people who are on the wall" (2 Kgs 18: 26). This means that Rabshakeh began his speech in the Judean language rather than Aramaic, the language of diplomacy. The repeated preambles in the name of the king are meant to stress the source of authority for his statements, but do not typify the speech itself in terms of its genre. Attention has rightly been drawn to its divergences from the ready-made pattern of the "messenger's speech," characterized by the preamble we have quoted, as it does not contain an ultimatum sent directly from the king to the recipient. Rabshakeh's speech, therefore, should be viewed in terms of its internal rhetorical dynamics, which demonstrate, as noted, how free he is in his choice of words and spontaneity of delivery, their main purpose—and presumably the king's also—being to obtain the surrender of Jerusalem without a battle. An ultimatum, like that of Ben-hadad to Ahab, would not further this goal. Nor would words of persuasion in themselves, however reasonable, bring about the surrender of the city. Rabshakeh's mission is characterized by a combination: a direct military threat, made tangible by the presence of the great army that accompanies him to Jerusalem (2 Kgs 18: 17), together with the attempt to soften the stance of the besieged people with propaganda on the power of the Assyrian king in contrast to the errors and weakness of Hezekiah, king of Judea. In modern political jargon this is known as "psychological warfare."[15]

C. The preamble or caption

It is not surprising, then, that he opens his speech with a declaration: "Thus says the great king, the king of Assyria," which is meant to present not only the source of his authority but the power and confidence that stems

---

[15] Adam Smith (n. 4) went too far in the value and weight which he attached to Rabshakeh's oratory and diplomatic skills: "He had indeed the army behind him, but the work to be done was not the rough work of soldiers. All was to be managed by him, the civilian and orator. This fellow, with his two languages and clever address, was to step out in front of the army and finish the whole business" (p. 360).

from the title "the great king."[16] This is the starting point from which he tries to shake the self-confidence of Hezekiah, who has dared to rebel against the king of Assyria, and the reliance of the people of Judea on their king. It has already been remarked that the underlying word in this passage of the speech is בטח, "to be confident," which appears seven times in the speech. The question that begins the message and that is presented in the second person to Hezekiah directly, without the royal address, is: "On what do you rest this confidence of yours?" It has the ring of arrogant and scornful irony on the part of the "great king" toward the vassal who has dared to rebel against him and who is not even worthy of being addressed by his royal title.[17] This tone is explained immediately afterwards: "Do you think that mere words are strategy and power for war?" This is a sapiential elliptical sentence, whose barb is directed against one who has dared to rise up against the "great king" without possessing the military might to triumph in war.

So much for the caption, or the preamble, which serves as the leitmotiv throughout the speech. The transition from it to the body of the speech is the word "now," as is usual in other official documents and letters of a political slant that we know (e.g., 2 Kgs 5:6, 10:2; Ezra 4:11, 17; 7:2). Yet even after the word "now" a question is posed, whose details complement the question in the preamble: "Now, on whom do you rely, that you have rebelled against me?" This question too, like the first, is merely contrived, for Rabshakeh (the king's spokesman) is well aware of the answer. He at once replies himself, using a metaphor whose images clearly point to the land of the Nile (the reed),[18] and which also opens with the bridging word "now"— "Now, you are relying on that staff of a broken reed." This is a double image, consisting of two epithets, one in the construct, "staff of reed" (cf. Ezek 29: 6), the other using an adjective, "broken reed" (cf. Isa 42: 3). But to dispel all doubt as to its target, the land is named: Hezekiah is relying "on Egypt." Only then is the second part of the metaphor, the object of comparison, stated, and directed at Hezekiah: the broken reed "will pierce

16 This title appears also in the preamble to his second speech (v 28). The title itself, in Akkadian *Sarru rabu,* is ascribed to each of the Assyrian kings from Samshi-Adad I on. It appears in Hebrew on an ivory which was found in Nimrud's excavations (*Iraq* 24, 1962, 45–49). Yet, there are no grounds to deny the psychological effect that Rabshakeh worked in his speech.

17 The omission is glaring considering the preamble to Sennacherib's official message to Hezekiah in 2 Kgs 19:10, where the title "The King of Judah" appears.

18 Ex 2:3; Isa. 18:2; 35:7; Job 8:11 and see also *BDB,* 167.

the hand of any man who leans on it." The sapiential formulation of the metaphor, generalized and neutral, apt for different people in like circumstances ("any man who leans on it"), is explained in a political sense by the orator himself: "Such is Pharaoh king of Egypt to all who rely on him." Not by chance does the speaker replace the usual biblical form of . . . בטח ב ("trust in . . .") by בטחים עליו ("rely on"), for the subject is a "staff of broken reed" that one leans on. This usage is repeated in the continuation of the polemic, when Rabshakeh repeats this argument: "when you rely on Egypt" (v 24).

The negative connotation of בטח על ("rely on") may be gathered from the rare use of this form in the Bible (e.g., Isa 31: 1; Jer 28: 21; Hab 2: 8; Ps. 49: 4). By contrast, immediately following his politically satirical argument against the illusion of confidence in Egypt, Rabshakeh shifts to a religious argument against the illusion of trust in God. In the latter, he applies the verb בטח with a different preposition, אל ("to"): "But if you say to me, 'We give our trust to the Lord our God . . .'" (v 22).[19] We realize, therefore, that the key word (in our context this term is preferable to "guiding word" because it refers to the orator and not to the reader seeking signs in the text to guide him in understanding what is written!) in the first part of Rabshakeh's speech is בטח, and he uses it adroitly, with the appropriate prepositions, in various forms to suit his arguments. The word serves as a focus for the satirical note running through his polemic. Thus, from the preamble his speech bears a distinctly polemical character. It opens with a question (v 19) and it ends with a rhetorical question (v 25). Its polemical quality is expressed in its content and style, as well as in its structure and form.

D. *Structure and form*

The Archimedean point of the speech is its foreword, or "overture": "What is this confidence that you rely on?" From this point the oration develops, built on two central arguments that are not given in succession but are intertwined in spiral fashion. This attests to the dynamics of the speech, retaining the spontaneity of improvised delivery. The question in the preamble is complemented, as noted, by another: "On whom do you rely, that you have rebelled against me?" (v 20). The first question, in its caption-like

---

19 Cf. Ps. 4:6; 31: 7; 86:2; Prov. 3:5. Twice this usage appears in negative connotation: Jud 20:32; Jer 7:4.

and elliptical formulation, may perhaps also be understood as referring to his trust in God; he deals with this later. The second question obviously refers to reliance on Egypt, in that it is followed by the argument ridiculing and scorning trust in that country (v 21). The second argument develops against trusting in God, harking back to the question in the preamble. Rab-shakeh duels verbally with Hezekiah, quoting, as it were, the latter's words or thoughts ("But if you say . . .")[20] so as to demolish them. What is the point of trust in God when Hezekiah himself has removed God's high places and altars, and restricted his domain to Jerusalem alone? (We shall return to the ideological and political meaning of this argument below.)

As for the dynamics of the speech, we observe a spiral form that continues on, as in verses 23–24 in which Rabshakeh returns to his first argument about reliance on Egypt and its chariots, but from a different direction. He dismisses it, ridiculing Hezekiah's paucity of troops and his inability to deploy chariots and horsemen. He then goes back once more to the second argument, concerning religion and ritual, in order to explode that position by the second approach: it is precisely that same God in whom you trust who guided me to come up against this place to destroy it (v 25). These acrobatics from the one argument to the other seem to some critical commentators like confusion and disruption of the natural and proper order of a speech of this type (what *type?!*), and altogether a medley of authentic elements and later additions.[21]

Yet for the associational dynamics of spontaneous speech, is it essential for the arguments and points to appear in succession, and not in the way we have suggested calling "spiral"? This way may be described thus: there are two questions, the second complementing the first (couple 1), followed by two arguments contesting the antagonist's premises, but in chiastic order, the first argument coming immediately after the second question and the second argument apparently returning to the first question (couple 2). Then follows the rebuttal of the premises in their original order by means of two rhetorical questions that revert to the opening questions, but chiastically, in the opposite order (couple 3). The development may be presented schematically:

$$A \; B \; B1 \; A1 \; B2 \; A2,$$

that is, two chiasmata that cross at the central couple B1 A1. The first, between couples 1 and 2, is the questions and arguments A B B1 A1; the

---

20 Following the reading of Isa 36:7, which seems to me preferable.

21 E.J. Kissane, *The Book of Isaiah* (Dublin, 1960), 394–395; Kaiser, *Isaiah*, 380–381; Wildberger, *Jesaja* 28–39 (*BKAT*, 1982), 1387.

second, between couples 1 and 3, is the opening questions and their connected rhetorical questions A B B2 A2. This order of argumentation, which seems so exceptional to commentators, is not unique to this speech alone (cf. Gen 31: 26–30; Eccl 2: 24–26). This structure characterizes the first part of Rabshakeh's speech, but does not exist in this form in the second part, to which we now turn.

3. The second speech (or the second part of Rabshakeh's speech)

Rabshakeh's speech is interrupted by the reaction of Hezekiah's ministers. This follows Rabshakeh's rhetorical question, "Now, is it without the Lord that I have come up against this place to destroy it?" (v 25). Many of the critical commentators maintain that it is impossible for such a theological claim to be made by a representative of the king of Assyria, and that it was none other than the author who placed this theo-political claim in Rabshakeh's mouth.[22] Admittedly, the claim reflects a religious idea matching Isaiah's prophetic outlook that is stated in several of his prophecies on Assyria as the rod of God's anger and sent by him to punish his people for their sins. Examples are 5: 26–30 (by conjecture: Assyria is not expressly named here); 7: 18–20; and especially 10: 5–16.[23] It does not accord with the idol-worshiping outlook of Sennacherib and his spokesman. However, one should not entirely reject the possibility that here Rabshakeh is actually quoting the Isaiaic view, to which he does not personally subscribe, for the purpose of convincing the men of Judea; previously he had applied the argument regarding the removal of God's high places and altars by Hezekiah with the same goal of inciting the men of Judea against him. It cannot be overlooked that this view, if indeed it was quoted for the purpose of the polemic, is not repeated and does not develop in the continuation of the speech in the second stage, but actually contradicts Rabshakeh's stinging and derisory comments regarding God's ability to deliver Jerusalem from him (vv 33–34). This factor may even reinforce the view that the statement in verse 25 is a later addition.

Whether Rabshakeh's speech was halted by the interjection of Hezekiah's ministers at this point or earlier, considering that this rhetorical

---

22 Childs, 84; Kaiser, 380.

23 Tsevat finds evidence here of a divine message which Sennacherib received from the Lord to punish Hezekiah for breaking the treaty with Assyria; see M. Tsevat, "The Neo-Assyrian and Neo-Babylonian Vassal Oaths and the Prophet Ezekiel," *JBL* 78 (1959), 199–204.

question might have been added later, he does not proceed from it. He skill-fully grasps the opportunity arising from the ministers' interruption to address the people directly. Rabshakeh passes from debating directly with Hezekiah, so to speak, with the aim of undermining the latter's confidence in the delivery of Jerusalem, to disparagement and incitement against him. The target of his words, which he now addresses, in the name of the great king, in the plural—"the men sitting on the wall," who have been most harmed by the siege. This part of the speech is no longer laced with rhetori-cal questions, but with quasi-apodictic negative statements warning the people not to obey their king: "Do not let Hezekiah deceive you . . . Do not let Hezekiah make you rely on the Lord by saying . . . Do not listen to Hezekiah" (three negative imperatives, opening with the word אל, "do not," vv 29–31).

This categorical form of speech is then substituted by positive state-ments, in which Rabshakeh, on behalf of the Assyrian king, calls on the people to submit to his will and to enjoy the many benefits he will present to them, whether in their land or in his: "Make your peace with me and come out with me; then every one of you will eat of his own vine, and every one of his own fig tree, and every one of you will drink the water of his own cis-tern . . ." (vv 32b–32a). These too are in the apodictic style, but in the positive sense. Then he reverts to the opening of this section of his speech (namely verse 29) with his fourth sentence beginning with אל: "And do not listen to Hezekiah when he misleads you by saying, The Lord will deliver us" (v 32). This time he disputes Hezekiah's assertion that God will save the city by means of three rhetorical questions that conclude his speech: "Has any of the gods of the nations ever delivered his land out of the hand of the king of Assyria? Where are the gods of Hamath and Arpad. . . . ? Have they delivered Samaria out of my hand? Who among all the gods of the countries have delivered their countries out of my hand, that the Lord should deliver Jerusalem out of my hand?" (vv 33–35). Nine times the verb הצל ("deliver") appears in this short passage of the speech, and there is no doubt that this word is the key word and leitmotiv.[24] As with the rhetoric of the first section of the speech, he adeptly develops it in its second section in a circular struc-ture, albeit less spirally.

The circular structure is built on the pattern of "three and four," but not in an ascending graded form. Three sentences open with אל ("do not") and are interrupted by the quotation of the political message from the king of

24 R. Weiss, *Mishut ba-Mikra* (Jerusalem, 1976), 26 (Hebrew).

Assyria to the besieged people (vv 31b–32a). The fourth sentence that begins with ואל ("And do not") (v 32b) reiterates the third "do not" sentence (v 31a) and closes the circle that opened with the first two "do not" sentences.

In this part of the speech two arguments are also intertwined, one political and one religious-ideological. Rabshakeh opens his speech with the first: "Do not let Hezekiah deceive you for he will not be able to deliver you out of my hand" (v 29), and he moves on immediately to the second: "and do not let Hezekiah make you rely on the Lord by saying, The Lord will surely deliver us and this city will not be given to the hand of the king of Assyria" (v 30). As a positive alternative to the two "do not" (אל) arguments, Rabshakeh cites the Assyrian king's proposal, assuring them, in return for their submission, personal benefits to "everyone" (איש) from his possessions (גפנו תאנתו בורו) and prosperity to all of them after their deportation to his land (vv 31b–32a). Finally, he returns to the arguments at the beginning of this section of his speech, when he takes issue primarily with the assumption that God will deliver his city (vv 33–35).

We find, then, that the second part of the speech, like the first, consists of three couples, the middle one focusing on the concrete political message. Here the message is seemingly positive—"Make your peace with me an come out with me" (i.e., surrender) and win peace and land, while in the first part the political message is negative: Do not rebel against me because your strength and the aid of Egypt are not enough to save you from my hand. However, in the second part of the speech Egypt is not mentioned at all. The political barb thrust against the tendency to seek help from Egypt in the first part has disappeared. It is replaced by a theo-political barb, directed against the tendency to seek help from God. It appears starkly in the polemical rhetorical questions (the final component of the speech), belittling God's power to save Jerusalem and comparing him to the gods of other nations who have failed to save their peoples. But it also appears camouflaged in the positively formulated middle section: "Make your peace with me and come out with me; then every one of you will eat of his own vine and every one of his own fig tree . . ." (v 31). That is, he who is able to assure the ideal that all await, namely, dwelling in safety, each under his vine and each under his fig tree, and which, according to the historiographer of Kings, had been fully realized in the time of Solomon (1 Kgs 5: 5), is no other than the great king, the king of Assyria.

The contrary, which is not expressly stated, is nevertheless clear: it is not God, in whom you believe. This irony also suffuses his subsequent promise made in the name of the king of Assyria: "until I come and take you away to a land like your own land, a land of grain and wine, a land of bread and vineyards, a land of olive trees and honey." It is a kind of grotesque parody[25] of the divine promises often repeated in the Torah regarding the yield of the Promised Land, such as the repeated combination of the three kinds of produce: "A land of grain, wine and oil";[26] or even the unique phrase "a land of olive oil and honey."[27] This occurs at a time when the promises of the Lord, the God of Israel, have not withstood the test of history and are expected to collapse in light of the array of the Assyrian army at the gates of his chosen city. The parody is so ironic and so tragic that it arouses the suspicion that whoever made use of speech for such obvious patterns of the Deuteronomistic biblical historiography is not Rabshakeh but an Israelite satirist from the Deuteronomistic school who disguised his criticism, and perhaps even his heresy, by placing these words in the mouth of Rabshakeh, the representative of the Assyrian empire.[28] Is it perhaps on this account that the Sages called Rabshakeh "an Israelite convert"?

Despite the structural and formal differences between the two parts of the speech we have described, and despite the clearly Deuteronomistic tinge of the second part, we still hold that the two speeches constitute two stages of a single oration. This is especially so when we consider not only the thematic and circumstantial continuity reflected in them, but also their characteristic polemical rhetorical dynamics; their satirical devices deserve close scrutiny.

4. The satirical means in Rabshakeh's speech

The satirical tendencies in Rabshakeh's speech that we have noted are reflected in the arguments, the polemical style and the use of epithets and appellations. Some means are overt and some are disguised.

1. In the arguments, they are reflected especially in the central parts of the two sections of the speech in which the major political and ideological

25 On the employment of parody and grotesque in political satire, see M.D. Fletcher, *Contemporary Political Satire* (London, 1987), 3ff.

26 Deut 7:13, 11:14, 12:17, 14:23, 28:51 and also Hos 2:10; Jer 31:11, so that it is fully justified to regard this triple combination as a Deuteronomistic phrase.

27 The same phrase appears in Deut 8:8; on the other hand the following phrase, "a land of bread and vineyards," appears only in Rabshakeh's speech (2 Kgs. 18:32 = Isa 36: 17).

28 On the usage of disguise as a satirical device, see I. Freedlander, *be-Mistarey ha-Satira* (Ramat-Gan, 1984), 145 (Hebrew).

contrasts in terms of content are focused. In the first section this is apparent in the belittling of Hezekiah, who has dared to rebel against the king of Assyria with "mere words" while relying on Egypt's promises, which in fact are empty, and on chariots and horses, which he cannot field with his own troops. In the second section the satirical means exist in the concealed irony inherent in the promises made by the king of Assyria to the besieged people of Jerusalem, which are similar in content and style (and are therefore parodic) to those given to Israel by their God, in whom they believe. The latter promises have not been realized historically but are in danger of being finally rendered null and void with the conquest of Jerusalem, God's own chosen city and the last political stronghold of the faithful.

In these two examples there is ironic contrast between reliance on verbal undertakings and trust in powerful and skilled force. This contrast is given succint elliptical expression at the beginning of the speech: "Do you think that mere words are strategy and power for war?" This kind of irony is encountered elsewhere in similar circumstances of military confrontation; there is keen political irony in the words of Zebul to Ga'al the son of 'Ebed, who rebelled against Abimelech and challenged him: "Then Zebul said to him, Where is your mouth now, you who said, 'Who is Abimelech, that we should serve him?' And are not these the men whom you despised? Go out now and fight with them" (Jud 9: 38). To the taunt and boasting of Ben-hadad, king of Aram, who threatens Samaria, the king of Israel replies, "Let not him that girds on his armor boast himself as he that puts it off" (1 Kgs 20: 11). In Rabshakeh's speech the political confrontation expands into a meta-political and theo-political confrontation—the king of Assyria against the God of Israel.

2. The satirical trends are reflected in the form of the argumentation, especially the stream of rhetorical questions that go unanswered by the party under attack, while the polemicist himself debates the premises of the opponent, whom he pretends to quote, and refutes them one by one, without the opponent having stated them. He plays the part of both sides in the political polemic, the clear advantage obviously being on the side that he represents. This mode of polemical argument is especially characteristic of the first section of the speech. In the second section only once does he trouble to cite the words of Hezekiah in direct speech (2 Kgs 18: 30).

3. Rabshakeh often resorts to epithets and appellations for the purpose of scorning and ridiculing the weakness and unreliablity of the opponent, in contrast to his own strength and self-reliance. In the second part of his speech he never refers to Hezekiah as "king," while the king of Assyria

is called by his full title, "the great king." This device stands out in light of the fact that in the letter that Sennacherib has sent to Hezekiah he addresses him by the title "king of Judea" (2 Kgs 19: 10). Furthermore, when he occasionally mentions God explicitly, he does not add any attributes to this name, not even the connection to his people or his land, such as "God of Israel," as he does when he enumerates the gods of the nations: "the gods of Hamath and Arpad" (2 Kgs 18: 34). Pharaoh admittedly appears with the title "king of Egypt," but only after he has been given the satirical image of "a broken reed of a staff" (18: 21). The purpose is apparently to prevent any misunderstanding regarding the target of his critical barbs. The note of political satire is especially biting when it is camouflaged in polite diplomatic language, as in 18: 24, when after showing Hezekiah to be powerless, he makes his suggestion of a wager (v 24): "How then can you repulse a single captain among the least of my master's servants when you rely on Egypt for chariots and horsemen?" The diplomatic language he employs regarding one whom he has just called "my master" only doubles the contempt and the irony. On the one hand, dubbing himself "one of the lowly servants of my master" (not, to be sure, out of self-abasement) only emphasizes the gap between the power and majesty of his master, the king of Assyria, whom he, Rabshakeh, represents as but one of his lowly servants, and Hezekiah, who has not even the capacity to commit two thousand horsemen to battle. Rashi discerned the barb here in his explanation: "How will you confront a single one of my master's servants, when every lowly one among them is commander of two thousand men, and you cannot muster two thousand?" Ehrlich added: "Rabshakeh speaks of the least of the lowly servants of his master, from which one may make all the greater inference regarding his master, the great king, himself."[29] On the other hand, he snipes indirectly at Egypt, for how is it possible to respond (empty-handed) to the least of the lowly servants of Sennacherib whose power is probably greater than Egypt, and to rely on the latter for chariots and horsemen? (v 24b).

The qualities of Rabshakeh's speech as an oration of political satire are especially salient when it is compared with the message that Sennacherib has sent to Hezekiah through his messengers from Libnah (2 Kgs 19: 9–14). The message briefly repeats one main argument that is present in the second section of Rabshakeh's speech, referring to Hezekiah's delusion that Jerusalem will be delivered by virtue of his trust in God. However, the opening words of Rabshakeh's speech to the people accuse Hezekiah of misleading

---

29 Ehrlich, *Mikra ki-Pshuto* II (New York, 1969), 375.

the people: "Do not let Hezekiah deceive you . . . and do not let Hezekiah make you to rely on the Lord by saying, The Lord will surely deliver us and this city will not be given into the hand of the king of Assyria" (2 Kgs 18: 29–30). Sennacherib, on the other hand, places blame for the deceit on God (or perhaps on the prophet Isaiah): "Do not let your God on whom you rely deceive you by promising that Jerusalem will not be given into the hand of the king of Assyria" (19: 10). He too concludes his direct message to Hezekiah with the reasoning offered at the close of Rabshakeh's speech to the people on the wall, when he lists the countries he has conquered without their gods being able to save them. The point is that neither does Hezekiah stand any chance of being saved by his God. Yet Sennacherib does not end with a rhetorical question whose barb is directed against God, as does Rabshakeh: "Who among all the gods of the countries have ever delivered their countries out of my hand, that the Lord should deliver Jerusalem out of my hand?" (18: 35).

The use of this rhetorical interrogative "Who?" in the syntactic structure of the sentence expresses scorn and denigration in that it is directed at the identity of the subject, while the resolving conjunction "that" is applied to his words or deeds. The nature of this satirical "who" may be gathered from similar reactions in early biblical historiography, such as Pharaoh's response to Moses' demand to let the Children of Israel go forth out of Egypt: "Who is the Lord that I should heed his voice and let Israel go?" (Ex 5: 2).

A further example involving circumstances of military and political confrontation is the scorn in the words of Ga'al the son of 'Ebed, who rises against Abimelech and incites the men of Shechem: "Who is Abimelech, and who is Shechem that we should serve him?!" (Jud 9: 28). Still more evident is the contempt in the reply of Nabal the Carmelite to David's servants when they ask him, on David's behalf, for suitable compensation for their behavior towards his shepherds and his servants: "Who is David? Who is the son of Jesse? There are many servants nowadays who are breaking away from their masters!" (1 Sam 25: 10).

The major element in the second section of Rabshakeh's speech, comprising the promises made by the king of Assyria to the besieged people, does not appear in the message, for Sennacherib sends his letter to the king Hezekiah, and does not deliver a speech of propaganda before the people. Naturally, it lacks that parody through which Rabshakeh, adopting the Deuteronomist's style of promise-making, alludes to the goodness of the land and intimates that it is within his power to bring about what the Lord, the God of Israel, has not fulfilled of his promises. The essence of the first part of Rabshakeh's speech is omitted entirely from the personal royal letter, except perhaps for the hypothetical citation of Hezekiah's statement, "But if you say to me, We rely on the Lord our God . . ." (18: 22), which serves as a starting point for Sennacherib's message. Missing, of course, are all the satirical elements glinting through Rabshakeh's polemic with Hezekiah over reliance on help from Egypt and his barbs about his ritual reform.

A comparison between the two versions of the Assyrians' diplomatic offensive against Hezekiah, confined to Jerusalem "like a bird in a cage,"[30] illustrates the principal difference between formal negotiations, through a letter or a brief communique, and the dynamics of a verbal discussion centered on political rhetoric. The latter's purpose is psychological warfare and for this it employs the weapons of satire, as in such a situation nothing compels them to strike at the foe.[31] This difference explains the role and place of Rabshakeh in the episode of the Assyrian siege of Jerusalem. On the other hand, it also explains the pivotal place of the prophet Isaiah in this fateful encounter. For it is Isaiah, not Hezekiah the king, who responds in words to the threats of Rabshakeh. It is he who does not fear them. True, according to the narrative in the second report of the event, regarded by critical commentators, as we have noted, as version B of the same event (or even as source B), the prophetic message delivered is that Jerusalem will be saved from the hand of the Assyrian king through Hezekiah's prayer to God (2 Kgs 19: 15–20).

But Hezekiah's prayer was addressed to God and was not a direct response to Sennacherib's words, certainly not on the actual political level regarding the surrender of the city. By contrast, after Isaiah has conveyed to Hezekiah God's acceptance of his prayer, he goes on with biting words of scorn hurled directly against Sennacherib, in the second person (vv 21–28), ending in a prophecy on the return of Sennacherib to his own land without having implemented his threats against Jerusalem (vv 32–33). Thus, even in the second version Isaiah plays an active role in this political confrontation.

This conclusion is not acceptable to several scholars, who hold that Isaiah did not take an active part in the crisis and is no more than a "shadow" of the real Isaiah;[32] the words attributed to him are not his own, but

---

30 From the Prism of Sennacherib, *ANET,* 287–288.

31 On the magic power of satirist in the battle, see Robert C.E. Elliott, "The Satirist and Society," in *Satire: Modern Essays in Criticism* (ed. Ronald Paulson, Englewood Cliffs, 1971), 208ff.

32 Sheldon H. Blank, *Prophetic Faith in Isaiah* (New York, 1958), 8.

are those of someone who wanted to grant his rehabilitation—after his prophecies on the ruin that Assyria would bring upon Judea did not materialize—through ascribing to him a prophecy foreseeing the delivery of Jerusalem.[33] However, regarding the role and function of the king and the prophet in this episode, these scholars somehow overlook a serious problem: if a later rehabilitation of Isaiah was accomplished by his disciples and admirers, how is it that this finds expression precisely in the Book of Kings (from which the episode was apparently copied in Isaiah), which is a historiography of the kings of Judea and in which, moreover, Hezekiah wins enormous esteem, unmatched by the other kings of Judea?[34]

The various reports of this event (known as source A and sources B1 and B2) in fact show Hezekiah, God's adherent, as he who surrenders to Sennacherib (2 Kgs 18: 14—source A), fears the threats of Rabshakeh and sends his ministers and his priests to Isaiah covered with sackcloth (19: 1–4—source B1), and turns to God with a very late version of a prayer which is put into his mouth (19: 15–19—source B2). Moreover, the positive evaluation of his kingship (18: 5–8) contains no hint that he saved Jerusalem from Sennacherib through his heroism. Hence, if a later rehabilitation is reflected in the reports of the delivery of Jerusalem from Sennacherib's siege it should also apply to the king, who failed in his reliance on Egypt. Furthermore, if a theologization of the delivery is made, as is undoubtedly evident in the account, it should pertain to the characterization of the joint role of the two Judean protagonists of the episode, and our definition of the relationship remains intact: the king is helpless, the prophet is steadfast, in face of the enemy in this confrontation. The relationship is completely different in the account in 2 Chronicles 32: there Hezekiah is the active and inspiriting factor, while Isaiah is only mentioned in the background.

5. The reactions of Isaiah to the Assyrian threats to Jerusalem

Isaiah's two reactions to the Assyrian threats, one at 2 Kgs 19: 6–7 (report B1) the other at 19: 20–34 (report B2), are addressed to Hezekiah. The first is after Hezekiah sent a deputation of ministers and priests to him with a request: "Therefore, lift up your prayer for the remnant that is left" (19: 4); the second is after Hezekiah has prayed to God and Isaiah is sent to him with God's response (19: 20). In the first reaction a short, encouraging

---

33 Blank, 10–11, and also Clements (n. 9), 91.
34 See 2 Kgs. 18: 5–8.

message appears, in reaction to Rabshakeh's threats: "Thus says the Lord: Do not be afraid because of the words that you have heard, with which the servants of the king of Assyria have reviled me. Behold, I will put a spirit in him, so that he shall hear a rumor and return to his own land; and I will cause him to fall by the sword in his own land" (19: 6–7). The second reaction opens with a poem of contempt and scorn against Sennacherib (vv 21–31), followed by a brief oracle in God's name: "Therefore thus says the Lord concerning the king of Assyria, He shall not come into this city or shoot an arrow there, or come before it with a shield or cast up a siege mound against it. By the way that he came, by the same he shall return, and he shall not come into this city, says the Lord" (vv 32–33). This is followed by the positive closing, substantiating God's intervention: "For I will defend this city to save it, for my own sake and for the sake of my servant David" (v 34). This reasoning and the derisory poem preceding the second message are deemed additions by the critical commentators.[35] As for the messages themselves, there is no convincing reason not to ascribe them to Isaiah, for both refer directly to Assyria's threats against Jerusalem.

(1) The connection of the messages to military and political situation

Both messages are apt for the military and political situation described, since they refer directly to the Assyrian threat to attack Jerusalem, and they do not presage a military victory over Assyria or foresee such a miraculous salvation as that portrayed in consequence of second prophetic message: "And that night the angel of the Lord went forth and slew a hundred and eighty-five thousand" (19: 35). Nor is the conclusion of the first prophetic message—"and I will cause him to fall by the sword in his own land" (19: 7), which relates to the fate of the king of Assyria—a sort of prophecy after the event.[36] The connection between it and what is told at the end of the entire episode—"And as he was worshiping in the house of Nisroch his God, Adram-melech and Sharezer, his sons, slew him with the sword" (19: 37)—is slight: prophecies ending with a vision of the death to a sinner, without detailing how and where, are not uncommon in the Bible. An obvious example is the prophecy of Amos, "Jeroboam will die by the sword" (Amos 7: 11), which was not realized at all (cf. 2 Kgs 14: 29). Such oracles are in the nature of a curse, and in certain cases they do indeed come to pass, as it is not rare for a king to die by the sword in his own land.

---

35 See Childs, 103.

36 Kaiser, in his above-mentioned Commentary on Isaiah 37:7, regards it a "vaticinium ex eventia."

(2) Their connection to his theo-political outlook

Both messages accord with Isaiah's political positions, albeit not with the positions of those scholars who attribute a pro-Assyrian orientation to Isaiah by virtue of his prophecies against the treaty with Egypt (chaps 30, 31).[37] Even though we find in Isaiah's prophecies the motif, "Assyria is the rod of God's anger," not in a single one of them before the king and people does he preach surrender to Assyria, as Jeremiah preaches surrender to the king of Babylon: "Bring your necks under the yoke of the king Babylon and serve him" (Jer 27: 12). Admittedly, Isaiah comes out openly and strongly against Hezekiah and his court's policy of making a pact with Egypt and relying on the latter's aid in chariots and horses, but his prophecies contain no criticism of Hezekiah's insurrection against the Assyrian yoke. On the contrary, in various prophecies he attacks the despotism and hubris of the kings of Assyria, directing sharp satirical barbs against them. Furthermore, in this episode he limits himself simply to the threat against Jerusalem, not countering Rabshakeh's arguments about reliance on Egypt, for on this they are not divided. Nor does he react to the arguments directed against Hezekiah, as he himself is not among the supporters of his policy. Still, it is only natural that at this time of national emergency Isaiah will take a stance against those who threaten Jerusalem, will cooperate with the king, and will encourage him to adopt a firm posture without referring to the dispute between them.

(3) Their connection to his ways of expression

A thematic and stylistic examination of Isaiah's two messages indicates the evident connection between them and other prophecies he has uttered that are unequivocally his.

Message A (2 Kgs 19: 6–7 = Isa 37: 6–7) is similar in form and style to the one that Isaiah was commanded to convey in the name of God to Ahaz, when Rezin, the king of Aram, and Pakah son of Ramaliah, the king of Israel, went up against Jerusalem to wage war on the city (Isa 7: 1ff.). It begins with the encouragement of Ahaz in his stance against them: "Take heed, be quiet, do not fear and do not let your heart be faint" (v 4). To those threatening him he applies a double satirical epithet of scorn and derision: "these two smoldering stumps of firebrands . . ." (ibid.). His polemic con-

---

37 Jesper Hogenhaven, "The Prophet Isaiah and Judaean Foreign Policy under Ahaz and Hesekiah," *JNES* 49 (1990), 351–54, went too far in this direction.

tinues with his citing the scheme of the two kings—"Let us go up against
Judea and terrify it, and let us conquer it for ourselves . . ." (7: 6)—in order
to frustrate it, and it closes with a categorical declaration in the name of
God, "It shall not stand, and it shall not come to pass" (7: 7), together with
an exposition of the causation of the disaster expected to fall on those two
kingdoms, Aram and Ephraim (vv 9–10).

This is the structure of Isaiah's first message to Hezekiah in response to
Rabshakeh's threats. He begins with a statement in the name of God, meant
to strengthen his spirit and his stance in face of Assyria's threats against
Jerusalem: "Do not be afraid because of the words that you have heard"
(Isa 37: 6). A statement in a similar style also appears in another polemical
prophecy against Assyria, perhaps referring to the same event: "Therefore
thus says the Lord of hosts, O my people who dwell in Zion, do not be
afraid of the Assyrians when they smite with the rod and lift up their staff
against you as the Egyptians did" (Isa 10: 24). From this expression of encouragement he shifts to a polemical note, applying a stinging attribute to
Rabshakeh and the messengers of the Assyrian king: "The servants of the
king of Assyria have reviled me" (37: 6). The title "the great king, the king
of Assyria," which resounded again and again in Rabshakeh's words, has
shrunk here to "the king of Assyria." To Rabshakeh, who did not conceal
the military and political power he disposed of even in his sarcastic self-
abnegation—"How then can you repulse a single captain among the least
of my master's servants, when you rely on Egypt for chariots and for horsemen?" (Isa 36: 9)—and to the accompanying ministers, he applies a con-
temptuous epithet: "the servants (נערי) of the king of Assyria." Although
the imprecations they utter are not quoted, they are intimated. The ending of
the prophecy in its lapidary style and paratactic graded structure—"Behold,
I will put a spirit in him, so that he shall hear a rumor, and return to his own
land; and I will make him fall by the sword in his own land" (Isa 37: 7)—
predicts the unexpected frustration of the Assyrian king's goal of conquer-
ing Jerusalem. And his sudden return to his country hints at its cause, and
foretells his death by the sword.

In its component parts this prophecy is thus similar to that of Isaiah
to Ahaz, albeit not in content and style. The ironic element in it is perhaps
the most prominent. The "spirit" and the "rumor" instantaneously turn Sennacherib's threats against Jerusalem into "mere words," and he no longer
possesses the "strategy and power for war." He himself, who sent his servants to revile the Holy One of Israel, falls by the sword in his own land—
not by force and not by an army but by "spirit." This idea appears in other

prophecies of Isaiah, especially the one censuring the supporters of the treaty with Egypt: "those who go down to Egypt for help and rely on horses and trust chariots because they are many . . . The Egyptians are men and not God; and their horses are flesh, and not spirit" (Isa 31: 1–3 *passim*).[38]

Many attempts have been made by scholars to give an actual circumstantial political explanation to this prophecy. Some expound the "rumor" that Sennacherib heard as having to do with the advance of the army of Egypt and Ethiopia, in accordance with what is related subsequently in verse 9: "Now the king heard concerning Tirhakah king of Ethiopia, He has set out to fight against you."[39] Some explain it as having to do with the ferment against Sennacherib in his own country, word of which reached him at Lachish. This view is influenced by the epilogue on his being killed by his sons' swords (2 Kgs 19: 36–37). Whether or not the rumor was indeed connected with some political circumstance, according to Isaiah its source is the spirit that God puts into the king of Assyria.

Message B (2 Kgs 19: 32–34 = Isa 37: 33–35). This, like the first message, is also directly connected to the Assyrian king's threat to Jerusalem, and his return to his own land by the way in which he came, but without reference to the circumstances that are to bring about this revolutionary change or to Sennacherib's impending death in his own land. It is doubtful whether this should be seen as the continuation of the first message.[40] At any rate, Isaiah's style is imprinted in it. I believe it is not entirely impossible that although the two messages do not depend directly on each other they complement each other. The first, addressed to Hezekiah, is meant to boost his spirits in withstanding the threat, and it hints at a revolutionary change that will occur in the crisis; the second, which is addressed directly to the king of Assyria, even though it is in the third person, states decisively that he will not attack the city, that Jerusalem will be saved from the siege. The prophet expresses this by means of four short negative sentences opening with "He shall not" in an ascending spiral graded sequence, followed by an assertive positive sentence. The prophecy closes chiastically, the last sentence returning to the first "he shall not" in opposite order:

Therefore, thus says the Lord concerning the king of Assyria: (a) He shall not come into this city, (b) and shall not shoot an arrow there, (c) and shall

---

38 See also Isa 19: 14; 29: 10.
39 J.A. Montgomery, *The Book of Kings* (ICC; Edinburgh, 1960), 491, 515.
40 Kaiser, 376.

not come before it with a shield, (d) and shall not cast up a siege mound against it. (a1) By the way that he came, by the same he shall return and he shall not come into the city says the Lord (Isa 37: 33–34)

After the four negatives, the assertive sentence, which is stated in the positive, is also chiastic in terms of its internal alliteration: בה/בא. Only in one other place in the Bible does a sentence similar in structure and style appear, and it too is linked with a divine message (command) of the man of God, but in the negative: "So he did not return by the way he came (בה/בא) (1 Kgs 13: 10). It appears as the fulfillment of a divine command to the man of God that precedes it, which contains three negatives: "You shall neither eat bread, nor drink water, nor return by the way that you came" (13: 9). This parallel does not prove that Isaiah's message is in fact authentic, but it approximates the probability that in both cases we have a special structure of an oracle arising out of a prophetic milieu.[41] It is noteworthy that the structure of oracles in the apodictic style opening with the negative words לא ולא are found almost exclusively in the prophetic literature, principally in Isaiah,[42] which constitutes probable proof that the message is Isaiac.

Isaiah's second message, with the satirically polemic element echoing through it, has similar structure and form to those in Rabshakeh's speech to the people. Rabshakeh's four apodictic negative sentences open with אל ("Do not") (2 Kgs 18: 29 = Isa 36: 14–15) and also contain two polemical arguments using לא—"for he will not be able to deliver you out of my hand" (2 Kgs 18: 29) and "and this city will not be given into the hand of the king of Assyria." Against these there are the four "noes" of Isaiah's second message, whose essence is that the city and its dwellers will be delivered from the hand of the Assyrian king and he will be forced to return from it to his own land without harming it with his weapons of war. Moreover, that same great king, who assured the besieged people of Jerusalem—"Come out with me . . . I will come and take you away to a land like your own land . . . that you will not die" (18: 31–32)—will return to his own land "by the way that he came." The paradox and irony of a symmetrical reverse whose outcome is the diametrical opposite of the intention is, as we have stated in earlier chapters, a means of scorn and ridicule in satire generally and in political satire in particular.

41 On the prophetic milieu of this story see: A. Rofé, *The Prophetical Stories* (Jerusalem, 1986), 145 (Hebrew).
42 Isa 5:6, 11:3, 17:8, 22:11, 30:1, 31:1, 2, 32: 5; Jer 4:28, 7:24, 11:8, 17:23, 44:5; Hos 11:9; Mic 6:15.

ELEMENTS OF POLITICAL SATIRE
IN MEGILLAT ESTHER

Two factors combine to indicate that Megillat Esther is a composition including political satire: the literary principle of antithesis (ונהפוך),[1] which constitutes its main axis; and its connection with a popular mass festival of merrymaking and frivolity.[2] We note that such a connection is apparently the background to the growth of satire as a genre in Rome in the first century CE.[3] Scholarship has raised various questions regarding the connection between the Purim festival, whose origins are purportedly related in the Megillah, and the narrative itself (see below). However, a connection between them exists, whether the story constituted the historical foundation for the development of the festival, or whether it was taken to provide grounds for a festival which had long existed and whose origins were blurred. It is impossible to decide in a scholarly debate what came first, the festival or the tale. Nor can there be conclusive resolution of the question, provoked by those positing mythological roots for the composition—as to whether the myth that was adapted to the story predated the customs and habits from which the Purim festival evolved or the opposite.[4]

It may be that the Megillah and the festival whose origins it relates were preceded by various mythological deposits; yet, they were implanted

---

[1] H. Striedel, "Untersuchungen zur Syntax und Stilistik der hebräischen Buches Esther," *ZAW* 55 (1937) ". . . die ganze Erzählung ist eine grosses mahpok," 91–92.

[2] L.B. Paton, *The Book of Esther* (ICC, Edinburgh, [1908] 1951), 92–93; and C.A. Moore, *Esther* (AB 7B; Garden City, NY, 1971) LI.

[3] See above Chapter One, and the select bibliography there.

[4] Paton, *Esther*, 89–91.

in and adapted to a story whose main characters are of Jewish descent and whose basic theme is the peril of Jewish extermination and its being averted from the Jews' miraculous salvation. In this process itself there lies a kind of disguised satire against the pagan world with its great changeability and extreme contrasts. Certainly, this quasi-historical narrative evinces sharp ridicule of the world power that boasts of combining within itself many nations and states under the scepter of a capricious king, who is no more than the object of trivial personal harassment. If the assumption regarding the elaboration of a myth into a quasi-historical account is true, it did not occur in the way familiar to us in the biblical literature, whose principle is the historicization of pagan epics and myths and the placing of God at their center.

The linkage of the story of Esther and Mordecai with a festival notable for its frivolity and almost pagan license, in complete opposition to the other Jewish festivals, was apparently a vital need for the Jewish diaspora in its grim historical struggle for existence in a world replete with misfortune, in which the miracle and the paradox became almost commonplace. Only this fundamental, existential need for survival in an alien world might explain the fact that a festival and a miracle story of this kind expanded beyond their historical and geographical location in the Persian empire and turned into a hallowed tradition upheld yearly at its appointed time throughout the Jewish dispersion.

In studying Megillat Esther, account must be taken of the methodological difficulties stemming from its complex and non-uniform nature, particularly due to the relationship between the story in chapters 1–8 and the epilogue in chapters 9–10. It is in any case necessary for anyone in search of elements of political satire in the Megillah to decide which composition is meant—that known as the "pre-Masorah," before it was connected to the Purim custom, or the "proto-Masorah" (early Masorah); they are not identical.[5] In addition, there is the Masorah version as we have it, which is the basis for our discussion.

In this confusion, one would consider it necessary to look for what is common in the composition in all stages of its evolution. But the definition of the literary nature of what there is in common, namely, the basic narrative, without accumulated additions, is also disputed in modern scholarship. This dispute turns on the question of whether the composition may be defined as a historical novella, even among scholars who are divided over its

---

5 See D.J.A. Clines, *The Esther Scroll* (Sheffield, 1984); M. Fox, *The Redaction of the Book of Esther* (SBL Monograph Series 40, Atlanta, 1991), disagrees with some of his major conclusions regarding the composition and the redaction of the book.

nature. Those in doubt as to its historical reliability stress the novella component, while those who disagree emphasize the historical definition. One of the features of a historical novella is that it is replete with the characteristics of political satire.

1. The multiple facets and interpretations of Megillat Esther

Megillat Esther differs from other compositions in the Bible, and is also unique in the Jewish and pseudo-epigraphic Apocrypha, in that it is a multi-faceted work. On this account, too, it has acquired varied interpretations subsumed under the heading of historical novella. Three main directions have developed in modern scholarship:

(1) A mythological interpretation, which searches for the mythological roots of the story chiefly in Babylonian myth, and explains the names of the protagonists, Mordecai and Esther, as the incarnation of names of Babylonian gods (Marduk, Ashtar), or of Elamite gods (Vashti, Haman, Zeresh).[6] Hence, there are those who interpret the festival as the evolution of the Babylonian New Year festival.[7] Others, relying on Greek sources (Berossus, Starbo), identify it with the Persian festival celebrated by drinking and jollity, which in their view was the source from which the Jews of Persia copied the Purim festival which they historicized in Megillat Esther.[8]

(2) A folkoristic and ethnographic interpretation, which links the tale and the festival to motifs of popular wisdom prevalent in the east, especially Persia, from which the writer of the narrative fashioned the story of the festival.[9]

(3) A "sapiential" interpretation, which analyzes the story in the Megillah according to evident elements of Wisdom literature that typify the "court wisdom" genre in the Bible and the Apocrypha and regards it as the historicization of a wisdom tale.[10]

Without denying the worth of the interpretations we have listed, there seems to be room for considering Megillat Esther as political satire.[11] Below

---

[6] Paton, *Esther,* 90–94; S. Hartom, "Esther," *EM* 1, 486–492 (Hebrew).

[7] See *puḥru* and *Zaqmuk,* Paton, 92–93.

[8] See *Sakaea,* ibid., 93–94.

[9] See E. Bickermann, *Four Strange Books of the Bible* (New York, 1967), 171–240; and S.D. Goitein, 'Iyyunim ba-Mikra (Tel Aviv, 1958), 59–71 (Hebrew).

[10] S. Talmon, "'Wisdom' in the Book of Esther," *VT* 13 (1963), 419–455.

[11] Some hints in this direction I have found in: S. Abramsky's article "Return to the Kingdom of Saul in the Books of Esther and Chronicles," *Millet, Everyman's University Studies,*

an attempt is made to interpret the entire composition in all its different levels as one characterized by elements of political satire, which single it out from other biblical and post-biblical writings. These elements, whether overt or covert, are reflected in the structure of the Megillah, the shaping of the plot and its chief characters, particularly the sapiential political messages intimated in it.

2. The reversal-parallelistic structure of Megillat Esther and its various cycles

In itself, structure does not attest to the literary nature of a work, certainly not to its character as political satire. This applies still more to a composition that is not homogeneous and to which additions have been attached (9: 20—10: 3).[12] But a consideration of the structure of the Megillah is essential as it reflects reversal, which is the leading representative of the politically satirical tendency of the composition. Reversal is the core of the Megillah in the view of the author himself (9: 1); and this dictates its structuring in a form that will lead up to the reversal and in a way that its effect will be plainly visible. Its results will be seen as the complete opposite of the events that preceded it. Such a design requires a kind of counter-parallelism, one thing opposed to another, not only as regards the "pur" (lot), which plays a central part in the etiological-etymological legend of the name Purim (3: 7; and cf. 9: 15), but also as regards its other components— plot, characters and setting.

The "miraculous" reversal that occurs in Megillat Esther is not ex machina,[13] namely, the intervention of an external and unexpected supernatural factor that effectuates the miracle, but is the result of confrontations, albeit indirect, among the protagonists of the story who display initiative, planning and sophistication. Here the nature of the "miracle" is different from that encountered elsewhere. It does not bring about "welfare and sal-

---

vol. I (Tel Aviv, 1983) 39–63 and his book *Koheleth* (Ramat Gan, 1989), 48, and n. 120 on p. 191 (Hebrew). L.A. Snijders, "Ester, enwiize Satire" *NedTTs* 44 (1990), 109–120.

12 Clines (n. 5) 50–63; however, Fox considers the additions as the essence of the book: "The Purim etiology (and not the exciting narrative or its ideology) is the essence of MT-Esther. Rather than call it an 'addition' to the book of Esther, we should think of the rest of the book as a prelude to it." See his book (n. 5), 125.

13 J.A. Loader, "Esther as a Novel with Different Levels of Meaning" *ZAW* 90 (1978), 417–421: "Now the same *deus ex machina* pattern so typical of the Old Testament, is also found in the Esther novel—but without the *deus,*" 419.

vation," but causes a complete revolution in the status and circumstances of the characters. It operates on a principle akin to measure for measure: Haman is hanged on the tree he prepared for Mordecai; Mordecai inherits his office, his regal attire and his authority; the Jews, who were condemned to suffer riots and destruction on the thirteenth day of Adar, run riot among their enemies and destroy them on that very day. The counter-parallel that is the essential feature of the Megillah does not develop linearly in the sense that it runs throughout the entire work, traversing it lengthwise. Even those who maintain that the story was assembled from two parallel narrative sources, the "Story of Esther" and the "Story of Mordecai,"[14] believe that there is a kind of parallelism throughout the plot. But nor is this reversed. The counter-parallelism is between what is told from the beginning until the revolutionary change, and what is told from that point until the end. Three cycles are discernible, constructed one within the other and at times touching:[15]

A. The External cycle

The external cycle is "chronistic" in nature; it reports and its style is official. It is the frame that encompasses the Masora version of Megillat Esther from beginning to end. It opens with "Ahasuerus king of Persia and Media who reigns from India to Ethiopia over one hundred and twenty-seven provinces" and describes the great feast that he held (1: 1–8). It concludes the story with Ahasuerus, whose "every act of power and might . . . are written in the Book of the Chronicles of the kings of Persia and Media" (10: 1–2).[16] In between there occur the events marking the mighty reversal that the last author of the account saw fit to illumine principally by means of the counter-parallel, the same materials of content and language serving a contrary purpose. As distinct from the feast held by King Ahasuerus "for all his princes and servants . . . and for all the people present in Susa" at the start of the narrative (1: 3–8), its end tells of the two-day festival feast that the Jews celebrated in all the provinces of the kingdom, the Purim festival

14 H. Cazelles, "Note sur la composition du rouleau d'Esther," in *Lex tua veritas, Festschrift fur Hubert Junker* (ed. H. Gross and F. Musner; Trier, 1961) 17–29.

15 These three cycles somewhat correspond to the three "compositions" defined by Clines: Masora, proto-Masora and pre-Masora. See his above-mentioned book, chapters 5 and 8 and the summary on p. 139.

16 V 3, which concludes the Megilla with acclaim for Mordecai, is by the Jewish historiographer to whom we ascribe cycle 2.

designated by the seal of the king as an annual appointed season (9: 30–31; and see 9: 22). The feast that opens the Megilla (1: 3), the occasion for which is not explained, is the root of all the events related in the story, while the occasion for the feast recounted at the end is the reversal in these events (9: 21–32).

Some have detected the "satirical tone" in the description of the prolonged and frequent feasts of the king at the beginning of the story (the word משתה appears twenty times in the tale),[17] but they have not noted that it also continues at the chronistic end of the narration. A note of political satire appears in the brief report concerning King Ahasuerus, who has laid tribute on the land and the islands of the sea (10: 1), juxtaposed to the acclaim that concludes the account of his rule: "and all the acts of his power and might. . . ." (v 2). Is the imposition of the tribute perhaps all that "his power and his might . . ." amount to? Is it possible that in fact everything told in the story of his drunkenness and his lust for women, his capriciousness and his manipulation by courtiers, has produced this ironic acclaim?

Echoes of the reversal itself resound in the chronistic conclusion about Mordecai, "whom the king advanced (גדלו)" (2: 10), its wording being identical with that in the description of the rise of Haman at the beginning of the story: "After these things King Ahasuerus promoted (גדל) Haman" (3: 1).

B. The cycle of Jewish historiography

At the center of the cycle of "Jewish historiography" (as distinct from biblical Israelite historiography, which concerns the history of Israel in its land) is the fate of the Jews dispersed through all nations. In this sense the subject is historiography, or rather exilic quasi-historiography,[18] and many others have addressed this matter. This cycle opens with Mordecai presented as "a Jewish man . . . who had been carried away from Jerusalem in the captivity with Jeconiah king of Judea" (2: 5), and concludes at the end of the composition with words of praise for Mordecai for his greatness and his support for his Jewish brethren (10: 3).

But in nature and essence the cycle has already ended in chapter 9. The cycle of Jewish historiography has an etiological tendency aimed at explaining and establishing Purim as the festival of all Jews, wherever they may be. This tendency is particularly conspicuous in chapter 9, which tells

17 Goitein, 59.
18 See Talmon, 433.

that Mordecai (and Esther, by virtue of her royal prerogative) sends letters to all the Jews in all the provinces of King Ahasuerus, enjoining them "that they should keep" the days of Purim (9: 20ff.). Whether chapter 9 is integral to the story or whether it (entirely or partially) is an addition by a later author, its intention is to connect the celebration of Purim to the events recounted in the tale. It uses the principle of reversal (9: 1), whereby Mordecai is Haman's successor in his high office in the king's court, in authority and deed (chap 3); but he acts contrary to him with respect to the Jews of the kingdom. He, like Haman, sends letters under the king's seal, and fear of him also falls on all the nations "and all the princes of the provinces helped the Jews for the fear of Mordecai had fallen on them" (9: 3–4). He gives the Jews license to take revenge on all their enemies, to smite them with the sword, slaughtering and destroying them, and doing as they wished with those who hated them (9: 5). He too bases himself on the lot that Haman has cast, and in accordance with it converts that selfsame day—the thirteenth of Adar, when Haman intended to destroy the Jews—into a day when the Jews slay their enemies; Mordecai and Esther perpetuate the pur in an annual festival called Purim. The parallel between Haman's initiative and scheming in chapter 3 and its reversal at the initiative of Mordecai and Esther in chapter 9 is almost perfect. At first sight it might be defined as tragi-comic, but a leaning towards political satire may be discerned in it, the arrows being directed this time chiefly at the mobs, the haters of the Jews, who are the main object of the reversal at the pinnacle of power. Those very ones who bowed down and did obeisance before Haman and were ready to execute his foul plot and annihilate the Jews suddenly turn into the "helpers of the Jews" for fear of Mordecai. Not only do they cause them no harm, they are killed in their masses by the Jews who do with them as they please (9: 5–16).

The concealed ridiculing of the mob overcome by fear of the successor to the ruler and the decree sealed by the king's ring is somewhat reminiscent of the anecdote of Koheleth, in which "all the living that move about under the sun" rejoice with every king in turn who succeeds his predecessor (4: 15,16). But nor should one disregard the self-irony towards the Jews, who behave as the gentiles behave when given the opportunity through a royal decree "to destroy, to slay, and to annihilate any armed force of any people of any province that might attack them with their children and women and to plunder their goods" (8: 11), of which only the last part, the plunder, was not carried out.

Yet perhaps this self-criticism is what elicited the note of apologia repteated three times by the Jewish "historiographer": "But they laid no

hand on the plunder." Daube noticed the link between the repeated remark
on the Jews' renunciation of plunder (9: 10, 15, 16) and the odd report of
the tribute imposed by King Ahasuerus on the land and the islands of the
sea (10: 1). He explained this as an expression of a realistic approach by the
Jews and their representative Mordecai, intended to influence the king to
exchange his policy of plunder and looting, which had filled the king's cof-
fers, for one of taxation.[19]

C. The inner cycle of the plot

The inner cycle opens with Haman's advancement to greatness in the
royal court (3: 1) and closes with the death of Haman and the rise of Esther
and Mordecai to greatness and decisive influence in the king's court (8: 17).
The stars of this court intrigue, rich in comic and satirical features, are the
three characters mentioned, as well as King Ahasuerus, who constitutes a
main axis in the plot, though not its principal hero. In its course, more characters appear in secondary roles. Many commentators on the Megillah
regard this plot as a court novella in the spirit of the Persian period, a kind
of "mirror of Persian court life," centered on banquets, women, manipulation, jostling for position at the top, and the like.[20]

However, from start to finish, the plot is combined with the theme of
the fate of the Jews, and it turns on the peril of extermination to which
Haman condemns them at the very start of the action, and the release and
salvation that befalls them after his downfall with the rise of influence at
court of Queen Esther and Mordecai the Jew (8: 7–17). The private plot and
the political events are bound up with each other, and efforts to separate
them and regard only the private court plot as the original story have not
met with success.

The fate of the Jews serves as a main subject in the power struggle
and it depends on the arbitrariness of a fickle king but chiefly of the string-
pullers who manage to manipulate him and draw him to their side. This
cycle too (which many see as the basic story, before being made into the
etiology of the Purim festival) is based on the principle of counter-parallel
éven more markedly than the two outer cycles. The reversal occurs following the insomnia of King Ahasuerus (6: 1), when he decides to reward

---

19 D. Daube, "The Last Chapters of Esther," *JQR* 37 (1946–47) 139–147.

20 Goitein, 62, compares it with the competition held among the three attendants of
Darius in the apocryphal book of Ezra, chaps 3–4.

Mordecai who has saved him from the conspiracy of Bigthana and Teresh to assassinate him (6: 2–5).

From this turning point events move along rapidly to the beginning of the cycle, almost in the opposite order. Haman, in a burning rage because Mordecai did not bow down before him, is ordered at the king's command to set Mordecai on a horse, and to call out before him in the city square, "Thus shall be done to the man whom the king delights to honor" (vv 11–12). Queen Esther, who seemingly favored him by twice inviting him to banquet with the king, turns against him (7: 5–6); and the king who has promoted him and raised him above all others, sentences him to be hanged on the very tree that he has prepared for the hanging of Mordecai (vv 9–10).

The reversal in Haman's personal fortune affects the reversal in royal policy on the Jews. The decree he issued with the king's seal to annihilate the Jews on the thirteenth of Adar is replaced by a decree to take vengeance against the oppressors of the Jews on that same day (8: 3–14). The sack-cloth donned by Mordecai on hearing Haman's sentence is replaced by royal apparel (8: 15), instead of the mourning and weeping and lamenting that beset the Jews with the news of Haman's decree (4: 3) they experience light and gladness and joy and honor (8: 15); many of the nations of the land who had been preparing to destroy the Jews hastily convert to Judaism for fear of the Jews (8: 17).

There is little doubt, therefore, that the principle of "reversal" is not the invention of redactors and elaborators who added the chronistic and historiographic elements to the story but it inheres in the tale itself. The satirical tendency in the two large cycles in which the hand of a writer and redactor is evident has grown out of the innermost cycle of the narrative.

3. Shaping of the plot and the characters

The characters of the story move in the wide spectrum between a historical account that has been "dramatized" and a fictional account that has been "historicized."[21] On the one hand, each of them has a name and a function,[22] and some characters even have historical names.[23] On the other hand,

---

21 Talmon, 419–424.

22 Goitein, 62.

23 The name Ahasuerus also appears in Ezra 4: 6; Daniel 9:1 and in Aramaic papyri. The name Mordecai is common in Babylonian documents from the Persian epoch.

their individual make-up is schematic and simplistic, and lacks the psychological depth of drama. It mainly highlights one particular trait that signifies
one character over against another, as in puppet theater. Nevertheless, the
characters behave as if driven by their own natural forces and are not activated by any extraneous factor. The leading characters take the initiative,
plan, and even show restraint when necessary (5: 10).[24] The plot is marked
by the conflicts among them, in which greed, envy, suspicion, loyalty, pride
and passivity play a major part. The characters are not moved by any supernatural or divine cause. Even the "pur" (lot, fate) which fulfills so fundamental a role in the story is not supernatural but at most non-natural. It
is cast before Haman (3: 7). In this respect, the characters represent an extreme form of the anthropocentric tendency typical of the wisdom literature
of the Bible and the ancient Near East, which attests to the creative milieu
of the work, and no less to its political and cultural environment: an eastern
world power, a bureaucratic apparatus composed of members of various na-
tionalities, and a court ambiance of characteristic feasting and intrigue.

Yet, as a wisdom work, it lacks the optimistic didactic motive that
informs pragmatic wisdom writings that pretend to serve as a kind of guide
to success in life. Its comic, almost grotesque nature prevents its definition
as pessimistic. However, the important role of fate in the plot points to a
fatalistic element; and if fate is erratic, it certainly has a paradoxical element. Indeed, the more intense the heroes' activity the more paradoxical the
outcome.

(1) King Ahasuerus is the only character who appears throughout the
Megilla from beginning to end. He is undoubtedly its central character. It is
he who seems to determine the destinies of persons and nations; it is in his
power to put to death or to reprieve, to choose and to dismiss. He dismisses
Vashti and chooses Esther. He puts Haman to death and raises Mordecai to
greatness. His seal is impressed on Haman's decree of annihilation of the
Jews, which is replaced by a decree written by Mordecai and Esther enjoining the Jews to strike at those who rise against them. People fear him and
hide from his anger. Modern commentators link this to the nature of the
despotic regime, against which Koheleth has justly warned: "I keep the
king's command . . . Go from his presence, do not delay when the matter is
unpleasant, for he does whatever he pleases. For the word of the king is
supreme, and who may say to him, What are you doing?!" (Ecc 8: 2–5). But
while the king is the main character he is not the main hero of the plot.

24 Goitein, 62–63.

Although he holds the power to decide destinies, this is only the appearance of things. He does not take any initiative, he does not plan or act, and does not move the plot forward; he merely reacts to the initiative of others; and he himself is moved by his greed and by the effect others work upon him. He is the object, not the subject. The only initiative attributed to him in the entire story, and only in the exterior framework, is the great feast that he holds for all his princes and servants and all the people of Susa at the beginning (1: 3), and the tribute he imposes on the land and the islands of the sea at the end (10: 1). This royal portrait is a target for political satire. But more than satire against the despotic monarchial regime, it contains a note of "lenient" satire towards the king who is able to retain power despite his weakness, and to keep his throne despite the external shocks and upheavals in his kingdom that occur not at his initiative. He himself, drunk or not, is drawn in his decision making in the wake of initiative of his courtiers.

Such is the case with Vashti, such is the case with the reward to Mordecai and the punishment of Haman, and such is the case with the lot of the Jews in his kingdom. He who sent letters to all the provinces of his kingdom, at the suggestion of his servant Memucan, "that every man be master in his house" (Esth 1: 21–22) proves not to be master in his own. Vashti disobeys the king's command, and Esther comes to the palace despite the prohibition. His political decisions, which contradict each other, are taken at the initiative of his servants and courtiers.

The turning point that brings about a miraculous reversal is connected to the insomnia that attacks Ahasuerus at night. The Sages sensed the connection between this and the invitation to Haman to attend Esther's banquet. Others interpreted it as rumblings of jealousy that rose within him and disturbed his sleep.[25] Indeed, the reversal itself occurs after the second feast, when he sees Haman falling onto Esther's bed and he shouts out, "Will he even assault the queen in my presence, in my own house?" (7: 8). While emotions of suspicion and jealousy are human weaknesses, it is not appropriate for an all-powerful monarch who rules from India to Ethiopia to succumb to them and on their account to reverse his decisions affecting the fate of his subjects. Is this perhaps the fine distinction between comedy and political satire?

(2) The other central character, Queen Esther, is the one who brings about the extreme reversal in the king's attitude to Haman and hence in the

---

[25] J. Magonet, "The Liberal and the Lady: Esther Revisited," *Judaism* 29 (1980), 167–176.

fate of the Jews in his realm. Her entry into the plot takes place after the crisis with Vashti. Esther and her uncle Mordecai the Jew open the "Jewish historiographic cycle." Their presence in the plot, from the beginning to the end and as the representatives of the Jews at court in the epilogues that close this cycle, signifies this tendency. Yet not only in the historiographic design of the story does Esther play a major role, but also in the design of the internal plot. At first she is a passive and obedient character, her sole advantage being that she finds favor in the eyes of all who see her on account of her beauty. In the continuation of the plot and towards the climax she reveals deeper qualities: daring, initiative and feminine wiles, all of which make it possible for her to frustrate Haman's scheming and to entice the king to do as she wishes. Because of her deeds, she becomes the main heroine of the tale.

The change in her personality occurs after she learns from Mordecai of the condemnation of the Jews to extermination. While at first she refuses to intervene directly with the king, as Mordecai has instructed her (4: 5–11), later in the indirect debate with Mordecai she is won over by his reasoning: "And who knows whether you have not come to the kingdom for such a time as this?" (4: 14). When she sees her queenship as a mission of a Jewish nature, she radically alters her behavior. Now it is she who commands Mordecai: "Go, gather all the Jews . . ." and he obeys (vv 16–17). From a meek and obedient queen in the palace of the king of Persia, she becomes a fighter on an errand of national salvation, the keenest weapons in her struggle being her female attributes.

Not by chance has a parallel been drawn between Esther and Judith. Both are Jewish women under the aegis of gentile rulers, who effect a "miracle" of national salvation. But the "miracle" runs according to a coolly calculated plan in which the women exploit their advantages—physical beauty, cunning and a quick tongue.[26] Did Megillat Esther serve as a prototype for the author of the Book of Judith, and was the latter work, imbued with a religious outlook, intended to "sublineate the qualities" of Megillat Esther?[27] This problem does not concern the present discussion. The two works are differentiated by the complete absence of a religious motive in Megillat Esther and the spirit of political satire that it contains. Esther, without being called to the king, invites him to banquet with her and arouses his desire for her with the aim of moving his heart to the benefit of her people.

---

[26] Y.M. Grintz, *The Book of Judith* (Jerusalem, 1957), 53 (Hebrew).
[27] Grintz, 55.

Already at the first banquet she succeeds in creating the "triangle" necessary to awaken jealousy (this is the only time in the story that three of its principal protagonists are present together). Yet she asks nothing of the king at the first banquet, postponing her request until the second banquet, on the following day.

The second invitation arouses curiosity in the king, and pleasure and conceit in Haman. There are those who deduce from the change in the wording of the first invitation—"Let the King and Haman come to a dinner I have prepared for the King"—to that of the second invitation—"Let the King and Haman come to the dinner which I will prepare for them"— that her purpose here is to provoke the king's jealousy of Haman. This was the cause of the insomnia that beset the king that night. (6: 1).[28] The king's curiosity is substituted by suspicion. In this way Esther has prepared the psychological ground for a confrontation between Ahasuerus and Haman, and hence the latter's eventual fall. The confrontation is realized at the second banquet, in the scene where the king in his fury finds Haman falling on the bed on which lies Esther (7: 8). In her clever and calculated plan to bring about Haman's downfall, and to win the king's affection, she applied well-known "sapiential" formulas. She nourished Haman's pride ("pride comes before a fall") and stimulated the king's curiosity and his desire for her, precisely when she withheld her request from him, and so insured his obligation in advance (5: 8).

In the grotesque-dramatic design of the "triangle," each of its members is open to satirical criticism. Esther, the successor of Vashti, at first representing the opposite of Vashti in her obedience and modesty (because when she was called to go to the king "she asked for nothing" [2: 15]), changes as a result of her actions not only into the harbinger of national salvation, but into a source of authority and dominance (9: 29–32). Ahasuerus, who commands all the people of his kingdom "to be every man master in his house," is master of his wife (Ibn Ezra's interpretation), and suddenly turns into one who obeys his wife the queen and fulfills her wishes in conducting matters of state. And Haman, the successful chief minister, one with initiative and arrogance, but who also is capable of self-restraint (5: 10), becomes giddy with the gesture of warmth and respect shown to him by Esther, and he falls into the trap she has prepared for him.

Whether the author intentionally aimed his satirical barbs at Esther, or whether a priori he did not mean to do so, he left an opening a posteriori for

28 Magonet, 173.

the author who completed the story to further exploit the reversal which she brought about in it, and which had taken place in her, by adding to her petition to overturn Haman's condemnation of the Jews the petition to add an extra day after the thirteenth of Adar when the Jews might continue the killing of their haters and the petition to hang the ten sons of Haman from the tree (9: 13). For us he left signs that can only be interpreted as elements of political satire.

(3) The place of Haman in the order of the discussion does not determine his rank and importance among the chief characters of Megillat Esther. He is undoubtedly the main character in the plot, even though his entrance is later than that of Ahasuerus, Mordecai and Esther; and he departs before they do. It is he who sets in motion the historical drama related by the story and he who is its main protagonist. His entry into the field of the plot—even in the formal chronistic style—is impressive compared with the others. It displays him as one who has risen to sudden greatness in the royal court. While in the sentence introducing him, he is still described as the object—"King Ahasuerus promoted Haman . . . and advanced him and set his seat above all the princes that were with him" (3: 1), immediately afterwards, through the conjunctive (or perhaps conversive?) waw (וכל, "and all")—he is nevertheless presented as the subject: "all the king's servants who were at the king's gate bowed down and did obeisance to Haman" (3: 2). The exception is Mordecai, who has been introduced earlier, sitting at the king's gate (2: 19, 21), who alone (ומרדכי)—"but Mordecai" (with contrastive waw)—does not bow down or do obeisance to him (3: 2). Here begins the central conflict on which the plot of Megillat Esther turns. It grows sharper with the interference of the king's servants, who, on the one hand, warn Mordecai that in refusing to bow down before Haman he is disobeying the king's command, and on the other, inform Haman that Mordecai has told them that he is a Jew (vv 3, 4).

Thus, the private enmity and conflict become national. Haman decides to take revenge on all of Mordecai's people. His personal motive, his wish to take revenge on Mordecai for the affront to his dignity, he conceals in political and ideological guise. He explains his request to destroy the Jews by reasons of state: "Their laws are different from those of every other people and they do not keep the king's laws" (v 8). Various scholars have indeed taken pains to find personal motives in Mordecai's refusal to bow down and do obeisance to Haman, linking this with his envy of Haman's elevated rank.[29] But it is clear from the narrative that Haman himself under-

[29] Bickermann (n. 9), 179.

stood the deed differently. He interpreted Mordecai's behavior as stemming from his being a Jew, and saw this as testimony to the rebelliousness of that scattered and dispersed people, loyal to their own laws, and whose loyalty to the kingdom was dubious, "so that it is not for the king's profit to tolerate them" (3: 8). He plans the extermination of the Jews as a far-reaching state operation: letters are sent "just as Haman commanded to the king's satraps and to the governors over all the provinces" (3: 12). A day is appointed for the extermination, and on that day all the peoples of the kingdom are ordered "to annihilate all Jews, young and old, women and children" (v 13). The courtiers go in haste "and the king and Haman sat down to drink" (3: 15). The narrator, who in the description confines himself to technical details and formal style in the manner of the king's scribes, rounds off the scene with this satirical and bitter comment on the cynical behavior of the king and Haman. Then, and perhaps as a counterweight, appears the terse and (for commentators) confusing sentence "but the city of Susa was perplexed."[30] Was this an attempt to signify that the citizens of the capital were bewildered by this satanic plan? In any event, there is no sign of an active response on their part against the decree.

Clearly, then, Haman's entrance into the story opens the main plot with two aspects, the personal and the historical. He and his plan to destroy the Jews are united inextricably. He initiates the plan, and the plan represents him and his personality as "the enemy of the Jews." The plan materializes with him, and with him it will collapse. If the author envisaged some sort of model of extermination of the Jews, he could have found no type more fitting than Haman to represent it. He has the initiative, the power and the authority; he is a planner on an imperial scale and a thorough organizer, astute and cynical, and, above all, wicked. Haman, in contrast to Ahasuerus, has a strong and pronounced personality. This design of his character is necessary for the narrator in order to effect through him the great reversal that serves as the pivot of the entire story. Precisely the gifted and successful one, the master planner, fails, and with him his plan. Not because he erred in elaborating any of its details, and not because he was suddenly punished from on high for his evil, but because he was caught in the meshes of a woman. The fall of Haman occurs through a twofold reversal: the first is on the occasion of his setting Mordecai, "the man whom the king delights to honor," on a horse, and his marching before him in the city thoroughfare.

---

[30] Moore, 44, relates it to the entire population of Susa; however, Paton, 211, rightly commented: "That the people of Susa would feel any great grief over the destruction of the Jews is improbable. The author here ascribes his own emotion to them."

Thus, he is humiliated before his foe, who did not bow down before him. The second is when he falls onto the bed with Esther upon it, and the king commands that he be hanged on the tree that he had prepared for Mordecai.

The principle of inversion acts principally in connection with Haman, especially in connection with the conflict between him and Mordecai. Haman the Agagite, whom the king elevates and whose chair the king sets above all the princes, falls in a twofold and final manner, and his "elevation" finds its ironic contrast in his being hanged from a tall tree in sight of all. The description of Haman's humiliation and downfall is colored by malicious joy. In this respect he is the only one among the protagonists of the Megillah who arouses in us feelings of hatred and malicious delight at his misfortune. Not for nothing is he the main hero of the Purim festivities, being a focus of scorn and ridicule. He serves as a symbol for simple faith and a vindication of the popular optimistic view that the end of an evildoer is hanging. It is doubtful that this optimism is the result of the moral educational leaning of the author, wishing to prove that justice and just deserts prevail in our world. Despite the comic and grotesque elements that accompany the fall of Haman, it is doubtful that the tale radiates optimism;[31] after all, the "Hamans" of the world have not disappeared with his demise.

(4) With Mordecai, the Jewish historiographic cycle opens and closes. He is present in the story almost from beginning to end. He is a central character in the development of the events connected with the "lots" (Purim). It is not at all by chance that the festival is also known as "Mordecai's Day" (2 Mac 15: 31). However, in attempting to depict his personal profile from what is described in the story itself, it proves difficult to draw any lines that might portray his special personality in contrast to others. He appears as a representational figure, a sort of personification of the Jews in the Persian kingdom. He has no personal ambition, no personal emotions and drives, and there is hardly any hint about his private life, apart from his being Esther's guardian. He is characterized as one whose life is dedicated to the struggle for the survival and well-being of the Jews.

At first sight, and from the inversionary nature of the tale, Mordecai is the opposite of Haman. Haman is evil, Mordecai righteous. But this is a stereotypical definition, affected by the aspect of the national conflict between them. And it is difficult to ascertain from it the personal qualities of Mordecai compared to his enemy. Commentators seeking to define his per-

---

31 In this respect we differ from A. Brenner's view that the message of the story is basically optimistic, see her article in *Beit Mikra* 25 (1980), 267.

sonality through counter-parallelism with those of his foe Haman, in keeping with the "wisdom" principles that characterize rivalry and opposition between court ministers, invented personal traits and motivations to suit their models.[32] They assumed that these traits and motivations, which they believed existed in the "wisdom" or "folklorist" precursor to Megillat Esther, were blurred and "Judaized" in the process of its elaboration and recension as Jewish historiography.[33] According to this "sapiential" interpretation, in Mordecai, too, there are careerist drives as in his enemy Haman. And like Haman, Mordecai craved greatness in the king's court. He too, like Haman, is of royal stock (Mordecai the son of Kish, a Benjaminite, as against Haman the Agagite). Both apply devious measures in their struggle for primacy at court, and the means adopted by Mordecai during his climb to power are no different, morally, from those of his rival.[34] Mordecai's triumph in the clash between them is the fruit of his considered moves in court wisdom: discovery of the conspiracy of Bigthana and Teresh to harm the king and ensuring its documentation in writing, and the precautions he took.

Haman fails because he does not think to act with care. In his ostentation, and drunk with success, he exposes his weaknesses, while Mordecai successfully conceals his aims and acts behind the scenes. It is of course possible to compose a synthetic literary character by comparison to the partially parallel motifs that appear in the Jewish "wisdom" literature of the Persian or Hellenistic period (Aḥiqar, Daniel). But such a jigsaw puzzle is more the fruit of commentators' imaginations than of the narrator himself. In the tale before us, Mordecai is neither a prince nor a courtier. He does indeed sit "at the king's gate," observant of what occurs there out of concern for the welfare of his adopted daughter Esther (2: 1; 3: 3), but he occupies no position of power or judgment.[35] His refusal to bow down and do obeisance to Haman is not explained there as motivated by envy of Haman, but by the fact of his being a Jew.[36] His refusal to bow down to

---

32 Talmon, 433.

33 Bickermann, 181.

34 Brenner, 277.

35 Paton rightly noted in his commentary to the Book of Esther (n. 2), 188: "This shows him to have been a man of leisure, but not necessarily a royal official. His reason for sitting here may have been solely his desire to pick up news concerning Esther" (2: 5, 11).

36 This motif with its religious implications is prominent in the Midrash of Megillat Esther; Ehrlich in his commentary rejects the religious interpretation and substitutes it with a national-ethnological one: "Die Verweigerung der Proskynese hat mit der Religion Mordachais

Haman is a principle for which he is willing to imperil himself. It was not at his initiative that Esther "was taken" into the king's palace (2: 8). It is true that on his instructions Esther did not reveal her Jewish origins after being taken there (2: 10), but there is no hint in the story that Mordecai also initiated the move from the start, foreseeing how matters would turn out.

The diametrical change that occurs following the king's insomnia is not the direct result of any meticulous planning by him to achieve decisive influence at court as the chief minister, but a by-product of Esther's involvement in the frustration of Haman's scheme to destroy the Jews. True, the intervention is at Mordecai's behest. From the moment Esther acquiesces to his urging her to plead before the king, and undertakes the risk and initiative of overturning Haman's decree, Mordecai's activity comes almost to a standstill; previously he had cried out, and alerted the Jews to react with fasting and lamenting at the decree that had been published in the king's name (4: 1–3).

From the descriptions of Mordecai's deeds a typical character emerges of a father devoted to and anxious about his daughter, and of a father devoted to and anxious about his people. On account of his concern for Esther's welfare he walks daily in front of the courtyard of the harem (2: 11). This was probably unusual behavior and fraught with danger.[37] After her coronation in Vashti's place, he sits at the king's gate (2: 21), not as an official of the king, for Esther has still not revealed to Ahasuerus "her birthplace and her people" (v 19), but to observe and hear what is taking place in the king's court, be it out of concern for Esther or, as it transpires later, out of concern for the fate of the Jews. In these circumstances, he also discovers the conspiracy of Bigthana and Teresh and Haman's plan to exterminate the Jews.

In this manner the hero of the tale takes shape before us as the father of Esther and as the father of the Jews. Just as he is not Esther's biological father, but her adoptive father, who assumed this role by his own volition, neither is he the legal and official leader of the Jews of Susa. All that he does for their salvation and welfare is by his own initiative and choice. Only when he becomes chief of the ministers instead of Haman does he

---

nicht zu tun; Sie war eine Eingebung des Jüdischen Nationalgefühls. Der Jude konnte es nicht über sich gweinnen sich vor dem Amalekiter dessen Volk von alters her der Erzfeind seiner Volkes war, so sehr zu demutigen." B. Ehrlich *Ranglossen zur Hebräischen Bibel,* 7 (Hildesheim, 1968) 115.

37 Paton, 188.

become "great among the Jews and popular with the multitude of his brethren" (10: 3).

Without doubt, Mordecai embodies the positive, in contrast to the negative, hero. His initiative and his ingenuity are revealed when danger threatens his daughter or his people, and he actively defends himself against Haman's plot; by contrast, Haman's initiative and acumen are intended to magnify his fame and to ensure his high status, and to this end he is ready to injure others, even an entire nation. But the reversal on which the story hinges also effects a change in him. This has two stages: the same Mordecai sitting at the king's gate and still in his sackcloth and ashes (4: 1) is all at once garbed in royal attire by him who wished to hang him from a tree. He is set on a horse on which the king has ridden, and is led through the open places of the city, Haman marching before him declaring, "Thus shall it be done to the man whom the king delights to honor." Mordecai himself does not react, not by word and not by gesture, as if the entire grotesque scene does not touch him at all. Mordecai the Jew, he who reacts and calls the alarm, suddenly becomes a kind of tool in the hand of the king, who in his grace bestows on him honor, that which Haman sought for himself.

After this grotesque scene, which serves as an intermezzo in the development of the plot, Mordecai is no longer the same man of anxiety and suspicion who acts and activates others. He takes for granted all the wealth and glory bestowed on him by the king: in royal robes . . . with a great golden crown, and all the political authority, which Haman previously enjoyed in his position as chief of the princes, to seal decrees with the king's ring, and so on. He exploits his high station, together with Esther for the benefit of the Jews, and at the same time fear of him falls on all the nations: "and all the princes of the provinces and the satraps and the governors and the royal officials helped the Jews for the fear of Mordecai had fallen on them" (9: 3). "For Mordecai was great in the king's house and his fame spread throughout all the provinces; for the man Mordecai grew more and more powerful" (9: 4). Suddenly the description "Jew" is dropped and the title "the man" appears alone. Did the redactor wish to end the story with words of praise for Mordecai the Jew—"Next in rank to King Ahasuerus and great among the Jews and popular with the multitude of his brethren, for he sought the welfare of his people and spoke peace to all his people" (10: 3)—in order to amend the impression that Mordecai had inherited not only Haman's high status in the royal court, but also something of his domineering ways? Is the praise for Mordecai not diluted with a touch of satire?

4. The sapiential-political messages in Megillat Esther

The etiological tendency of the authors of Megillat Esther is transparent: to explain the origin of the Purim festival, its appointed time and the ways it is celebrated, and its connection to the days of feasting and rejoicing held by the Jews of Susa after being saved from extermination at the hands of their enemies. As this is not a festival prescribed by the Torah and since it is different in form from all the other Jewish festivals in the Bible, justification for its existence is adduced from the letters sent by Mordecai "to all the Jews who were in the provinces of King Ahasuerus, both near and far, enjoining them to keep the fourteenth day of the month Adar and also the fifteenth day of the same, year by year" (9: 20–21). Further justification is provided by the letter dispatched by Esther (9: 29). Thus, official authority, represented by Esther and Mordecai by virtue of their high official status in the court of the king of Persia and Media, has substituted for the absent religious authority in the story. In this sense Purim is different even from the Hanukah festival, which also is not ordained by the Torah, but is celebrated on the occasion of the purification of the Temple and the renewal of the Temple service. Moreover, in letters sent by the Jews of Eretz Israel to the Jews of Alexandria, which open the Book of Hasmoneans (2: 1–2, 18), they wrote that they resolved to celebrate the Hanukah festival after having purified the Temple; and they determined its length as eight days in remembrance of the Sukkot festival which they were forced to desecrate owing to their being persecuted by their enemies. Therefore, at first they called that festival Sukkot, and celebrated it by taking up the four kinds of plants (10: 6–7).[38]

The etiological tendency of the Megillah embodies a national message: this is not only the festival of the Jews of Susa who were saved from destruction, but the festival of all the Jews who "ordained and took it upon themselves and their descendants and all who joined them that without fail they would keep these two days according to what was written and at the time appointed every year" (9: 27). This national message also contains a general implication for Israel and the nations, especially since Megillat Esther was included among the holy scriptures. It was to this that R. She-

---

[38] Bickermann explains the possibility of initiating festivals that are not based on the Torah on the basis of the universal and monothesistic nature of the Jewish religion, according to which the worship of God is not confined to one place. See his above-mentioned book, 204–205.

muel bar Yehuda apparently alluded: "Esther sent to the sages: Appoint me for the generations; they replied to her: You kindle jealousy against us by the nations. She replied in return: I am already written in the chronicles of the kings of Media and Persia" (Megilla 7a). The jealousy kindled by Esther among the nations against Israel is the central message, which changes Megillat Esther from a story of an amusing political incident into political satire of import for generations, accompanying the Jews as a recurrent experience in their relations with the nations and the kingdoms where they are. The reason this festival is to be celebrated and is called Purim, even if added subsequently by a later redactor,[39] is paradigmatic: "For Haman the Agagite, the son of Hammedatha, the enemy of all the Jews, had plotted against the Jews to destroy them . . . his wicked plot which he had devised against the Jews should come upon his own head" (9: 24–25). Here use is made of a "reversal" as a model of what may be expected in every generation for all enemies of the Jews wherever they may be: their plot is overturned and they are subject to derision and contempt.

The perfect ("symmetrical") reversal in itself is still not evidence of the politically satirical nature of the story. It constitutes a principle in works of different kinds, primarily comedy and tragi-comedy. It serves as a means for political satire in that in its own paradoxical way it exposes the inner contradictions and the feebleness of the political system in all its various components: the king, the court, decision-making on affairs of state, writing of records, the absolute autonomous power of a decree sealed by the king's ring. Those who have discerned the satirical aspect of Megillat Esther refer to these elements. One commentator even likened the political satire in the story, showing up the density of those in power, to that of the story of the poor man of Nippur, centuries earlier.[40] But even if there is something in this comparison—and it is noteworthy that controversy exists over the satirical nature of the Akkadian story of the poor man of Nippur[41]—it applies only superficially to Megillat Esther. The satire in the latter goes much further in its politically sapiential messages and is more colorful in its artistic devices.

Reversal, which is the central theme of the main plot of the story, is not only external. It is not constructed on the principle of disguise, as in

39 Clines, 50–63, deals with this aspect substantially.

40 S. Abramsky, *Malkkuth Saul we-Malkkuth David* (Jerusalem, 1977), 386; and see J.S. Cooper, "Structure, Humor, Satire in the Poor Man of Nippur," *JCS* 27 31/4 (1979) 189–215.

41 H. Jason, "'The Poor Man of Nippur' an Ethnopoetic Analysis," *JCS*, 31/4 (1979), 189–215.

comedy, namely role reversal,[42] exchange of personal identity by means of costume, and so on, but it is an essential internal principle: the plot is turned upside down, the destinies of the protagonists are reversed, the king over-turns his decrees and replaces the leadership of his realm. But the per-sonality of the protagonists also changes with the development of the plot. The reversal is reflected especially in the behavior of Esther and the king. But it also occurs even in that of Mordecai and Haman (see above).

An external reversal takes place not only in the condition of the Jews who have been saved from the directive ordering their extermination, but also in their behavior towards those who hate them. A reversal of this sort is not of the "comedy of errors" kind, at the end of which everything returns happily to normal. It is laced with irony and a large measure of doubt about the stability of the order of things, about the validity of absolute values, and about innate qualities. Its anthropocentric message on the personal level is that a person, or at least a person's behavior, is likely to change almost from end to end with circumstances. There is no absolute good in contrast to ab-solute bad, there is no absolute truth in contrast to falsehood; at the counsel of the righteous Mordecai, Esther concealed her identity from Ahasuerus and the royal court, and the man Mordecai, who did not rise and did not tremble before Haman (5: 10), imposed his fear on all the princes of the provinces and the satraps and the governors and the royal officials (9: 5).

Its sapiential and moral message on the universal political level is more skeptical and satirical. The fate of people and nations is determined by the whims of a king who attends to matters of state between one feast and the next. Yet the keen arrows of satirical criticism are not aimed primarily at the king but more at the string-pullers, and no less at the internal contradic-tions that characterize this cosmopolitan world power, steered successively by two ministers between whom, through their origins and pedigree, an infinite enmity exists. It is highly doubtful that the political satire was in-tended aimed at Achaemenid empire, and there is some point to the surmise that it was perhaps actually aimed at the Hellenistic empire and was only disguised in Persian dress.[43] Not by chance, therefore, does the author of the addenda to the Greek translation of Megillat Esther distinguish between the Persian Ahasuerus and the Macedonian Haman.[44] But irrespective of whether its origins are in the Achaemenid empire, or whether it was com-

---

[42] See Cooper, "Structure. . . ," *ibid.*

[43] Paton, 60–63; R. Pfeiffer, *Introduction to the Old Testament* (New York, 1948), 740–742; Bickermann, 204ff.

[44] See Esther 8: 12k.

posed only after Alexander the Great's conquest of the east and his attempt to establish a world power from India to Ethiopia, its messages characterize it as political satire suitable for its own age and for generations to come.

There is no satire without a tendency, and there is no tendency without practical motives. Regarding political satire, the motives principally concern affairs of state. Yet this is not to say that the motives are bound to be dressed up in the garb of an actual political program, not even in its utopian opposite. On the contrary, insofar as this is satire, it is the Hellenistic elements that count. The tendency of the author of the story is not to correct or overturn the order in the Achaemenid or Seleucian empire, or to decide among the political elements active in it, but to expose, in the most amusing way possible, its nakedness, in the manner of "The King's New Clothes." He does this by descriptive means of drunken feasting and women, accompanied by driving urges: hatred, envy, fury. Whoever defines the heroes of Megillat Esther by "abstract" qualities of wisdom versus folly, cunning versus innocence, and perseverance versus impulse, introduces into it concepts from other works of widsom literature. These rational, or theological, concepts are left out of Megillat Esther, apparently deliberately.

"Reversal" cannot be completely isolated from another factor that appears in the background of the story, albeit not actively and overtly, like the three others we have described (the power of the king, of wine and of women).[45] The reference is to "the force of destiny." The "pur" (namely the lot) opens the cycle of events in the Megillah (3: 7) and serves as a focus for the etymological etiology in the frame of its Jewish historiographic cycle (9: 16). It marks the significance of the timing of the reversal, but not its reasons and its causes. The "pur" itself represents meanings diametrically opposed to each other: the day meant by destiny to be the day of violence against the Jews turns into the day of violence against the non-Jews. The day of misfortune for the Jews turns into the day of their gladness and rejoicing at the distress of those who hate them. The conception reflected in the single Purim-like reversal, whether rooted in Babylonian mythological perceptions or influenced by the conception of time (Zaman Zurvan) as the uniter of opposites in the Persian Zurvan religion,[46] represents the nihilistic historiosophic outlook of the author, that fate, which

---

45 Goitein, 64.

46 The tendency now is to consider Zurvanism a religio-philosophical trend which evolved within the Persian Zoroastrian religion and not an alternative and independent religion. G. Gnoli, "Zurvanism", *The Encyclopedia of Religion*, 15 (ed. Mircea Eliade), 595–597; R.C. Zaehner, *Zurvan: A Zoroastrian Dilemma* (Oxford, 1955).

rules history, is not entirely fortuitous and chaotic, and is certainly not simply disposable. It is likely, or liable, to turn again, like a wheel. Hence, the practical sapiential message in the epilogue is ambivalent. The day of "welfare and salvation" and "relief from their enemies" is to be celebrated with feasting and gladness year after year at the appointed time, because it is not final. The relief is for a day or two, and the annual wheel of time rolls on, and more "reversals," for good and for evil, may be expected.

The historical dress of Megillat Esther and the emphasis on historiographic documentation and writing, especially in the external chronistic cycle of the story, are no more than illusion. They serve as a disguise for a perception that essentially denies history and derides its heroes. The heroes of Megillat Esther, rather than being makers of history, are subject to contrary forces that play with them and to the human drives and weaknesses that move them.

The counter-parallelism that characterizes the story in structure, plot and style probably has a direct or oblique connection with the Persian dualist perception,[47] and it also has some tie with the Jewish wisdom literature of the Hellenistic period:

> (In the presence of evil) good and in the presence of life, death. In the presence of a good man an evil man, in the presence of light, darkness. See all the works of God, all utterly different, one compared with (the other) (Sir 33, 16–18)[48]

but the Jewish author has made shift towards "monism." He has confounded opposites to create a kind of unity of contrasts. They do not appear separately and parallel, one against the other, throughout the entire story, but intersect and clash at the junctures of the great reversal that takes place in it. They reflect the irony and even the satire of the writer; conscious of the fact that more than history is split along its length between two forces of light and darkness, it unites opposites dialectically. They conflict with each other, alter each other and to a large extent even convert each other as a result of the confrontation between them.

The links to ideological and religious tendencies alluded to and whose nature is plainly sapiential indicate the wide erudition of the author and his

---

47 J.R. Russel, "Zoroastrian Elements in the Book of Esther," *Irano-Judaica* II (Jerusalem, 1990), 34–40; R.C. Zaehner, "Zoroastrian Survivals in Iranian Folklore II, *Iran,* xxx (1992), 65; M. Boyce, "Ahura Mazda," *Encyclopaedia Iranica* 1 (London, 1985), 684–687.

48 Cf. *The Book of Ben Sira* (The Academy of Hebrew Language, Jerusalem, 1973), 34.

origin within the circles of "sages." Only one familiar with court proce-
dures and the leadership of the state, and the spiritual and cultural currents
at work in his age, would be able to compose a work which at face value is
popular and theatrical but in fact disguises his satirical outlook on matters
of religion and state.

BIBLIOGRAPHIC ABBREVIATIONS

AB	Anchor Bible
AfO	*Archiv für Orientforschung*
ANET	*Ancient Near Eastern Texts Relating to the Old Testament*, J. B. Pritchard (ed.), Princeton 1955
ARM	Archives royales de Mari, Paris
ATD	Das Alte Testament Deutsch
AThANT	*Abhandlungen zur Theologie des Alten und Neuen Testaments*
BA	*Biblical Archaeologist*
BASOR	*Bulletin of the American Schools of Oriental Research*
BDB	Brown-Driver-Briggs, *A Hebrew and English Lexicon of the Old Testament*, Oxford 1906
BIES	*Bulletin of the Israel Exploration Society*, Jerusalem (Hebrew)
BKAT	Biblischer Kommentar Altes Testament
BZAW	*Beihefte zur Zeitschrift für die alttestamentliche Wissenschaft*
CBQ	*Catholic Biblical Quarterly*
EB	*Encyclopaedia Biblica*
EH	*Encyclopaedia Hebraica*
EJ	*Encyclopaedia Judaica*
ERE	*Encyclopaedia of Religion and Ethics*
GK	*Gesenius' Hebrew Grammar*, ed. E. Kautsch, Oxford 1910
HAT	Handbuch zum Alten Testament
HKAT	Handkommentar zum Alten Testament
IB	*Interpreter's Bible*
ICC	International Critical Commentary
IDB	*The Interpreter's Dictionary of the Bible 1–4*, New York-Nashville 1962
JAOS	*Journal of the American Oriental Society*

JBL	*Journal of Biblical Literature*
JCS	*Journal of Cuneiform Studies*
JNES	*Journal of Near Eastern Studies*
JQR	*Jewish Quarterly Review*
JSS	*Journal of Semitic Studies*
KAT	Kommentar zum Alten Testament
KBL	L. Koehler & W. Baumgartner, *Lexicon in Veteris Testamenti libros,* Leiden 1958
NedTTs	*Nederlands theologisch tijdschrift*
OIP	Oriental Institute Publications
OTL	Old Testament Library
OTS	*Oudtestamentische Studien*
SBL	Society of Biblical Litereture
SVT	*Supplement to VT*
VT	*Vetus Tetamentum*
WBC	Word Biblical Commentary, Texas 1987
WMANT	Wissenschaftliche Monographien zum Alten und Neuen Testament
ZAW	*Zeitschrift für die alttestamentliche Wissenschaft*

INDEX OF BIBLICAL REFERENCES

INDEX OF AUTHORS

	DATE DUE		